George R.R. Martin and the Fantasy Form

"Young deftly explains the sophisticated literary techniques underpinning *Game of Thrones/A Song of Ice and Fire*, showing George R.R. Martin to be a master craftsman of the fantasy epic. *George R.R. Martin and the Fantasy Form* is a pioneering work of Martin criticism."

—Kris Swank, Signum University and Pima Community College

"Dr. Young's treatment of Martin's *A Song of Ice and Fire* through the perspectives of most of the important theories of fantasy of the past thirty years makes it a critical book for the student of Martin and, indeed, for the student of fantasy literature."

—Susan Johnston, Department of English, University of Regina

Using the frameworks of literary theory relevant to modern fantasy, Dr. Joseph Young undertakes a compelling examination of George R.R. Martin's *A Song of Ice and Fire* and his employment of the structural demands and thematic aptitudes of his chosen genre. Examining Martin's approaches to his obligations and licenses as a fantasist, Young persuasively argues that the power of *A Song of Ice and Fire* derives not from Martin's abandonment of genre convention, as is sometimes asserted, but from his ability to employ those conventions in ways that further, rather than constrain, his authorial program.

Written in clear and accessible prose, *George R.R. Martin and the Fantasy Form* is a timely work which encourages a reassessment of Martin and his approach to his most famous novels. This is an important work for both students and critics of Martin's work and argues for a reading of *A Song of Ice and Fire* as a wide-ranging example of what modern fantasy can accomplish when employed with an eye to its capabilities and purpose.

Joseph Rex Young lives and works in Dunedin, New Zealand, where he pursues his research interests in Gothic literature, neo-Romanticism, and the intellectual history and structure of the modern fantasy narrative. He has taught at universities in Bosnia and Herzegovina, Germany and New Zealand. This is his first monograph.

Routledge Studies in Contemporary Literature

23 **Women on the Move**
Body, Memory and Femininity in Present-Day Transnational Diasporic Writing
Edited by Silvia Pellicer-Ortín and Julia Tofantšuk

24 **Gender and Short Fiction**
Women's Tales in Contemporary Britain
Edited by Jorge Sacido-Romero and Laura Mª Lojo-Rodríguez

25 **Prequels, Coquels and Sequels in Contemporary Anglophone Fiction**
Edited by Armelle Parey

26 **From the Delivered to the Dispatched**
Masculinity in Modern American Fiction (1969–1977)
Harriet Stilley

27 **Theorizing Ethnicity and Nationality in the Chick Lit Genre**
Edited by Erin Hurt

28 **Extreme States**
The Evolution of American Transgressive Fiction 1960–2000
Coco D'Hont

29 **Transmodern Perspectives on Contemporary Literatures in English**
Edited by Jessica Aliaga-Lavrijsen and José María Yebra-Pertusa

30 **Origin and Ellipsis in the Writing of Hilary Mantel**
An Elliptical Dialogue with the Thinking of Jacques Derrida
Eileen Pollard

31 **Haruki Murakami**
Storytelling and Productive Distance
Chikako Nihei

For more information about this series, please visit: https://www.routledge.com

George R.R. Martin and the Fantasy Form

Joseph Rex Young

NEW YORK AND LONDON

First published 2019
by Routledge
605 Third Avenue, New York, NY 10017

and by Routledge
2 Park Square, Milton Park, Abingdon, Oxon, OX14 4RN

First issued in paperback 2021

Routledge is an imprint of the Taylor & Francis Group, an informa business

Publisher's Note
The publisher has gone to great lengths to ensure the quality of this reprint but points out that some imperfections in the original copies may be apparent.

Library of Congress Cataloguing-in-Publication Data
CIP data has been applied for.

ISBN 13: 978-1-03-209348-2 (pbk)
ISBN 13: 978-1-138-50216-1 (hbk)

Typeset in Sabon
by codeMantra

Contents

Acknowledgements

When preparing the proposal for this book, I compiled a list of likely publishers to whom I could submit it. Routledge was a late addition to that list, since research into modern fantasy constitutes only an incidental part of their publishing program, but I included them on the basis that the worst they could do was say no. The proposal landed on the desk of Jennifer Abbott, who said something considerably more intimidating, for which I offer her and her colleagues my thanks.

Over the twelve months I have worked on this project various people have been forthcoming with their time and effort in the battle to make any of it make any sense. They have variously offered advice, commentary on draft material and straightforward moral support. To the following people, therefore, I offer my thanks:

Doug Anderson, Bryan Attebery, Josie Carter, John Clute, Nicky Conroy, Michael Cop, Janet Croft, Nicola Cummins, D933, Leslie Donovan, Verlyn Flieger, Colin Gibson, David Howard, Kit Hume, Craig Johnson, Susan Johnston, Rebecca Kloess, Karen McLean, Farah Mendlesohn, Lynda and Phillip Morrison, Dana Moss, Christoph Reinfandt, Andrew Robins, Paul Tankard and Peter Winnington.

Also deserving of thanks are the contributors to and curators of *A Wiki of Ice and Fire*, the online encyclopaedia of Martin's invented world. Their tireless cataloguing of every chapter synopsis, tertiary character and cultural foible in that world has saved me countless hours of page-flipping, as well as a few amusingly dreadful howlers.

This book is dedicated to Bill Gray, who was unable to help with it directly, but whose advice and support on previous projects – in light of which I was able to build the credibility to get this one off the ground – has far overrun that which our professional relationship seems to warrant.

Parts of Chapter 1 initially appeared in *Epiphany* and *The Journal of the Fantastic in the Arts*; while a shorter version of Chapter 2 appeared in *Mythlore*. I thank the editors of these journals for their permission to reuse that material here.

And to Martin, I would not presume to suggest he write swiftly. Some commentators have done so, and keen as I am to find out what happens next I obviously wish him steady progress. But conversely, I would observe that he is in the rare and enviable position of being a creative person who has become best known and most rewarded for his "one from the heart", his passion project, the thing he did for his own satisfaction. I am not a creative person, but years of essays and dissertations have taught me the pleasure of watching the power of logic and emotion run through a composition. Martin deserves that pleasure. It only comes from hard graft, however, and the only reliable harbinger of its arrival is the suspicion that the project is about to fall into pieces. As such, and insofar as I have any business offering advice to someone who has published many more books than me, I suggest only what I tell myself: If it's easy, you're doing it wrong.

Abbreviations

Throughout this book the five entries in Martin's *A Song of Ice and Fire* (extant as of 2018) are referred to by their opening noun, as follows:

A Game of Thrones – Game
A Clash of Kings – Clash
A Storm of Swords – Storm
A Feast for Crows – Feast
A Dance with Dragons – Dance

All page numbers refer to the 2011 British Commonwealth paperback editions of these novels. This edition breaks *A Storm of Swords* into two separate volumes – *Steel and Snow* and *Blood and Gold*. References to *Steel and Snow* are given as *Storm* 1.x; those to *Blood and Gold* as 2.x. The edition in question has preserved *A Dance with Dragons* as a single volume, which was not published until 2012.

Introduction

"I study fantasy literature," I say. "At the moment I'm looking at George R.R. Martin."

My new friend smiles. "The *Game of Thrones* guy?"

"That's him. He's..."

"In *Game of Thrones* lots of people die."

"That's true," I admit, "although it's less true of the books. There are about forty characters who were killed in the show but are still alive in the books."

"I saw a bumper sticker about this," they reply. "It said *Guns Don't Kill People; George R.R. Martin Kills People.*"

"That's funny," I allow, "but there's more to it than that. For example, in *A Dance with Dragons* Princess Shireen..."

This time I am interrupted. "Princess Shireen is dead. In *Game of Thrones* everybody dies."

I decide to persevere. "There's more to Martin than that. He's colouring inside the lines of his genre very cleverly. For example, the way the story is developing..."

"*Game of Thrones* will end because everyone will be dead."

"Steady on. There's a lot of ambiguity about where things are going. If you look at how he presents magic, it begs the question..."

At this stage, my interlocutor leans forward. "Joe," they say, carefully and quietly, as if explaining a hard truth to a child, "This is *Game of Thrones*. Everybody dies, and the only question is whether Martin will ever finish the story. Which he won't, because he'll die first. That's why I don't read them." Then, satisfied with their incisively original, closely informed analysis of the topic, they change the subject.

I have had this conversation, in its essentials, on numerous occasions since my scholarly activity turned to Martin in 2015. The success of *Game of Thrones* has been tremendous, demonstrating that the hearty receptions of earlier screen adaptations of the novels of J.R.R. Tolkien and J.K. Rowling were not aberrations; the general public will, it seems, happily watch well-resourced, carefully written renditions of modern fantasy. They will also read such material. Martin's books are now mainstays of the commercial book trade, packaged, repackaged and proudly displayed in storefronts around the world. Under pressure from online retailers, brick-and-mortar bookstores will hardly grant shelf space to product that does not move. The existence of slip-cased collector's editions of Martin's novels – destined to be out of date the moment his sixth volume is published – demonstrates the story's popularity, as does that of *The Wit and Wisdom of Tyrion Lannister*, the perfect gift, it seems, for the Martin fan who already has all the books. Yet this popularity has come at a price. Martin's world is ripe for caricature, a point exacerbated by screenwriters accelerating the already brisk rate of character mortality in the books. Martin has thus become akin to Keith Richards, Michael Jackson, Yoko Ono, Margaret Thatcher or Bill Clinton – a public figure that people enjoy talking about, but about whom it is paradoxically very difficult to have a conversation, because such discussions are so apt to devolve into recitations of a handful of already shop-worn jokes at his expense.

Academic criticism has advanced the discussion of Martin, but only up to a point. At this writing, for example, Valerie Frankel has produced six books on Martin's work. In *Women in Game of Thrones; Power, Conformity and Resistance*, she puts noteworthy qualifications on the prominence of the show's female characters, observing that the tale is feminist and anti-feminist by turns (184). Her focus on the show is sensible – *Game of Thrones* undeniably warrants critical attention – as are her informed references to the books, but that focus curtails her assessment of Martin's techniques and accomplishments as a writer. Her other books tend to extend this pattern. In *Winter is Coming; Symbols and Hidden Meanings in* Game of Thrones, she warns briefly of "mild book five spoilers" (61) before speculating at length on the possible identity of the "warrior with the burning sword" that the thaumaturge Melisandre prophesises in episode 2.1. She lists a number of exciting possibilities, but offers little discourse on how or why Martin is using the trope of "the chosen one", or the effect it has on the reader. The "spoiler alert", furthermore, shows that her intended readers are those who have not, in fact, read Martin's books. Similarly, Carolyne Larrington's book *Winter is Coming* provides a wide-ranging catalogue of likely historical inspirations for Martin's world. Larrington's breadth of knowledge is impressive and her discussions of, for example, the likely medieval inspiration for the crannogmen of the Neck (66–68) demonstrate the depth of Martin's historical reference. Her analysis of how such borrowings contribute to the literary effects Martin achieves, however, tends to be slight. Furthermore Larrington, like Frankel, includes sidebars warning readers of upcoming passages that may "spoil" the plot of the books. Although such work is credible on its own terms, literary criticism aimed at people who have not actually read the subject texts is of obviously limited use to those who have. Frankel's and Larrington's books do more to demonstrate the resonance of Martin's work than to explain it. Academic work that meaningfully pursues the latter aim is still in its early stages.

Attempts to place Martin within the modern fantasy genre tend to position him as a justified and courageous transgressor of long-established rules. This, for example, from his occasional collaborators Emilio Garcia and Linda Antonsson:

> Previous works of epic fantasy tended to operate with a straightforward moral compass where the antagonist was some variety of evil "Dark Lord" and the protagonists were defined by their opposition to this evil character based on their obvious moral goodness. In contrast, Martin's series has been written with no dark lord to speak of, instead focusing the narrative on the dynastic conflicts that rend the Seven Kingdoms apart beneath the shadow of a looming catastrophe. (x)

Garcia and Antonsson applaud Martin for introducing moral complexity into fantasy, and for turning genre conventions on their heads. They do not provide any examples of the texts they generalise about here, but they are presumably referring to practitioners of genre fantasy (Grant 396), the commercial genre that has sprung up since the 1960s (Williamson 186) to satiate public appetites for tales much like those they describe. Such literature is typically indebted to the work of J.R.R. Tolkien (Clute and Grant 341) and direct comparisons between Martin and Tolkien have thus been frequent. Matt Staggs, for example, a contributor to *Beyond the Wall: Exploring George R.R. Martin's* A Song of Ice and Fire, commends Martin's work thusly:

> Martin's saga is often compared to J.R.R. Tolkien's *The Lord of the Rings*, but with all due respect to Professor Tolkien and his wonderful work, the psychological complexity just isn't there. With the exception of Boromir, Aragorn and company are "good" in a way rarely encountered outside of fiction. The One Ring corrupts good men. It is clearly a supernatural evil in a word where people (and elves, dwarves and hobbits) are essentially good. Martin doesn't introduce and external form of evil because it isn't required. (149)

I address Staggs's construction – Tolkien is straightforward, Martin complex – in Chapter 1, although I note it here as an example of the reflexive comparison between the two authors by critics seeking to explain what makes Martin's work stand out from typical fantasies. The use of Tolkien as an exemplar of fantasy is understandable, given the abiding popularity of his novels. It is problematic, however, because Tolkien was a hugely idiosyncratic writer whose inspirations, motives and methodologies bear little resemblance to those of the authors of genre fantasy, much of which consists of narrative iterations of pre-existing intellectual properties. Games Workshop's *Warhammer 40,000* tabletop wargame, for example, is currently the setting for over fifty *series* of novels. The most fecund of these, *Horus Heresy*, currently runs to forty-nine books by a cadre of authors working assiduously to ensure that this tale of the apocalyptic war against the Primarch of the Black Legion expands by three to four volumes per year. The villain Horus is the sort of Dark Lord Garcia and Antonsson discuss. His treachery against his heroic brothers, engendered by the dark gods of Chaos, closely parallels the operation of Tolkien's Ring as Staggs estimates it. These books are cracking reads. But it is surely questionable to press *The Lord of the Rings* – a deeply personal experiment in linguistics, medievalism and moral philosophy, gestated over a dozen years of an academic career in which the writing of novels was a largely incidental concern – into service as an exemplar of such attempts to monetise public tastes. Critics who present Tolkien as typical and Martin as atypical of fantasy also ignore Martin's professional background. He got his start writing for science fiction magazines, edited numerous volumes of the *Wild Cards* super-hero series (inspired, much like *Horus Heresy*, by a game, according to his own journalism on the matter) and began *A Song of Ice and Fire* after spending much of the 1980s as a screenwriter. As such he fits the profile of a typical genre fantasist – the sort of person who might write a *Horus Heresy* novel – far more closely than Tolkien. Attempts to differentiate him from the pack have led to frequent assertions that he has somehow overturned the fundamental rules of fantasy. Put simply, I regard this as a critical misstep. What struck me on a first reading of *A Song of Ice and Fire* was not that Martin was abandoning fantasy formulae, but that he was following them to such good effect.

Make-believe, after all, has rules. The act of crystallising one's imaginings into a package of prose and passing that package to a reader obligates an author to do certain things. If that package includes things the reader has never seen before and never will – jabberwocks, Martians, hobbits, dragons, shadowbinders from Asshai – then the author has a further set of obligations to bear in mind. First, such literary artefacts must be explained. Second, the author asks the reader to trust them to deploy such narrative elements in a way that provides some recompense for the effort involved in imagining them. How an author approaches and discharges those obligations is crucial to the effectiveness of a fantasy narrative. As fantasy has struggled towards literary respectability in the last half-century, a body of critical theory has emerged to systematise the study of such authorial decisions. By accident or design, many of the critics who have examined Martin to date have overlooked these critical tools. I hope to remedy this problem. When teaching these theories, I liken them to the mazes that scientists are popularly supposed to use to test the intelligence of laboratory mice. Having just upbraided critics for erroneously holding Tolkien to be typical of his literary genre, I should admit that I do not know how often scientists really do this, but the cliché is surely familiar. By observing a mouse's behaviour in a maze, a scientist can learn a lot about the animal. I aim to let *A Song of Ice and Fire* loose inside some of the theories relevant to modern fantasy to show that Martin, rather than abandoning or subverting the conventions of his genre, is actually using them particularly well.

As a preliminary to this discussion, Chapter 1 interrogates the commonplace that Martin is "the American Tolkien". This comparison predates Lev Grossman's iteration of it in *Time Magazine*, although his use of the term is interesting. Grossman qualified his point, contending, like Staggs, that Martin differs from Tolkien, and other fantasy authors, via his presentation of morally ambiguous characters. Using comparisons with the works of J.K. Rowling, Mervyn Peake and Tolkien himself, I will demonstrate that Martin is actually continuing a long tradition of moral experimentation in modern fantasy. Such experimentation is, in fact, a central strength of the genre. Having established this point, I will go on to use Frye's theory of modes to demonstrate a distinct contrast between Martin and Tolkien. Where Tolkien, a medievalist by training, resonantly recapitulated Frye's high mimetic mode, Martin delights in the ironic mode, routinely discussing the lavatorial activities of his characters in ways that undermine their self-bestowed dignity. In this sense, therefore, these two authors are in fact working at complete cross purposes. The British author who Martin most closely resembles, I maintain, is Terry Pratchett, a writer abidingly concerned with depicting ironic modalities. I will demonstrate further nuances that these two literary cynics have in common, including a shared regard for the abstract concepts that they accuse high mimetic authors of overselling, and a habit of suspending their irony to celebrate those ideas when the occasion genuinely arises.

Chapter 2 approaches one of Martin's more striking themes – his frank depiction of human sexuality. I contend that neither the sex nor the sexual violence in Martin's tale are as gratuitous as they may appear. The violence is there to further Martin's critiques of the claims of exceptionalism and moral authority on the part of his invented aristocracy. His sexual discourse nuances that critique, providing variously positive or negative impressions of characters such as Tywin and Tyrion Lannister, Theon Greyjoy and Catelyn Stark. These nuances involve the reader in his creative processes. Martin cannot do this by qualifying the violence of his world, since that would be the sort of compositional overdetermination that phenomenological critics like Wolfgang Iser caution against. The sex in Westeros, in Iser's terms, "shades off" from the fully formulated game of thrones, a device with which Martin can delegate a proportion of the characterisation in the story to the reader and thus make characters like Cersei Lannister, Sandor Clegane and Khal Drogo all the more vivid. This discussion raises a subsidiary point about Martin's medievalism, which closely parallels that of the Gothic authors of the late 1700s. Such novelists emphasised their portrayal of the barbarities of history by visiting them upon characters with discernibly modern mores. The contrast between the brutal sexual mores of characters like Gregor Clegane and Ramsay Bolton and the more relatable sex lives of Daenerys Targaryen and Robb Stark show Martin doing exactly the same thing, furthering the impact of the story as a critical, interrogative text.

Chapter 3 begins the genre-specific examination of Martin's work. *A Song of Ice and Fire* takes place in a world palpably diminished – morally, institutionally and magically – from its perceived past. This links Martin to an existing, pervasive theme in modern fantasy, expressed in works ranging from Jack Vance's 1950 story collection *The Dying Earth* through to the televisual fantasies of the twenty-first century: John Clute's concept of thinning, "the passing away of a higher and more intense reality" (942). Farah Mendlesohn's theories on fantasy exposition serve to demonstrate how Martin builds this impression. Martin constructs most of his world via what Mendlesohn calls "immersion," ironically presenting oddities as normal. The strengths of this method of exposition are numerous, as can be demonstrated via a comparison of Martin's Arya Stark and another immersive focaliser, Lyra Belacqua of Philip Pullman's *His Dark Materials* trilogy. Chief among these effects is the interrogative position in which it places the reader. The focalisation of Daenerys Targaryen shows how this method tends to promote thinned worlds by calling certainties into question and challenging the notion of inherent meaning, forcing readers to question the assumptions and ideals of the characters. The chapter concludes with an examination of the focalisation of Sansa Stark, often cited as Martin's most idealistic character, whose focalisation actually serves to focus reader attention on the thinned nature of Westeros.

Chapter 4 continues the Mendlesohnian theme by examining in detail two of Martin's subplots that clearly follow different patterns. Bran Stark is undertaking a Mendlesohnian portal-quest, entering into a new state of being and relying on a succession of guides to explain it to him. Jon Snow, meanwhile, is suffering what Mendlesohn calls an intrusion, his story moving via an escalating intuition of something dreadfully amiss with his universe. Both of these methods of explaining the invented fantasy world lean heavily towards an orientalised view of the supernatural as a static, unyielding narrative presence serving largely as a test of moral, physical and intellectual fibre for the hero. Though this seems to create a clash with the overall scepticism of the immersive narratives offered by the other focalisers, I argue that it furthers that scepticism, forcing readers to observe the absences of moral literacy focalised by Sansa Stark in full, certain, incontrovertible knowledge of the tests this invented society is about to face. Martin's particular blend of expository methodologies, I suggest, produces a textbook example of Tolkien's concept of formalised Recovery, the use of fantasy to reveal something about humanity.

Chapter 5 examines Martin's work with reference to Tzvetan Todorov's ideas about fantasy as a genre of hesitation between magical and rational explanations for oddities within the narrative. Although many scholars of modern fantasy see these ideas as unhelpful, I feel Martin's narrative constitutes something of a special case for Todorovian analysis. Examples of putative supernatural phenomena in his story occupy points along Todorov's taxonomy from the patently magical to the unnervingly mundane. This, I contend, helps along Martin's medievalism. In a text so frequently involved with the uncanny (that which is intended to unnerve the reader), Martin uses Todorovian hesitation, per Tobin Siebers's critique of the fantastic, to direct reader opprobrium against certain characters at certain times. Aeron Greyjoy and Cersei Lannister are examined as examples of this in action. Meanwhile, Melisandre of Asshai provides a clear example of what Todorov cites as the central purpose of the literary supernatural, to dissolve "median disequilibria" and allow narratives to continue past self-imposed blockages without compromising the themes and characterisations that caused them. Melisandre's shadow demons clearly accomplish this during the War of Five Kings. The point can be expanded to the tale as a whole, with the onset of Westeros's imponderable winter – and its monstrous exemplars the Others – lending narrative shape to the game of thrones by providing otherwise absent context for the evils that the characters inflict upon each other. As with Mendlesohnian analysis, a Todorovian critique of Martin's story eventually leads back to Tolkienian Recovery.

Chapter 6 analyses Martin's work in relation to David Sandner's analysis of fantasy literature in terms of the resolution of "the anxiety of the sublime moment". Between them, Martin's characters demonstrate all four of Sandner's codified reactions to the literary supernatural, as demonstrated via comparisons to other examples of those reactions in the fantasy tradition. Samwell Tarly closely apes the heroes of Bram Stoker's *Dracula* in attempting to "possess" the supernatural; Stannis Baratheon (among others) mirrors J.R.R. Tolkien's Saruman in trying to "domesticate" it; Davos Seaworth suffers "fragmentation" akin to that of H.P. Lovecraft's focalisers, and Daenerys Targaryen undertakes a "dispossession" that merits comparison to that displayed by J.K. Rowling's Harry Potter. Examination of these examples will demonstrate once again that Martin's world is less innovative than it is constructively wide-ranging in its orthodoxy. Daenerys's relationship with her dragons demonstrates this point further by launching another of John Clute's central leitmotifs of fantasy, the notion of a movement from thinning to formalised healing, which shows Martin engaged in the essentially Romantic "high argument" of modern fantasy, the aestheticisation of religious experience. The resulting re-engagement with the world provides yet another impetus for Tolkienian Recovery.

My conclusion is that Martin's contribution to fantasy is not a fundamental innovation of the genre but a wide-ranging example of what can be achieved with it. Martin has not actually circumvented or broken any of the commonplaces of fantasy. Rather, he has utilised the patterns and requirements of his chosen genre as tools, instead of as crutches or restrictions as is sometimes the case with genre fantasy. In something of the manner of a skilled poet using the structural features of a sonnet or limerick to direct the emotional impact of their poem, Martin employs the basic patterns of the modern fantasy novel in ways that foreground the human questions and critiques he makes.

This study will remain focused on Martin's novels rather than their screen adaptation. As a scholar and aficionado of fantasy, I am only too pleased that the contemporary "golden age of television drama" features an example of the genre alongside its staple crime stories and historical studies. I certainly refer to *Game of Thrones* as it becomes relevant. But my objective here is to examine how Martin evokes and uses fantasy via the written word, not the moving image. This is what I am trained in, and where I feel I have the most useful things to say. Comparison of the audio-visual game of thrones to the prose iteration also carries the danger of devolving into a discussion of what the producers of the show got "wrong" or "right" – scant justification for a book, since my opinions on that are no worthier of attention than those of any other fan. Those looking for fan engagement with *Game of Thrones* – much of it commendably insightful – need only search YouTube. I aim to provide a scholarly, theory-led assessment of *A Song of Ice and Fire*.

One of the advantages of this approach is that it requires no spoiler alerts. My aim is not to preserve the narrative tension of these novels, but to account for it. I wish to explain why people actually care about Martin's characters, how he gives life to these bundles of description and dialogue and makes that life precious to his readers, and why their world and the challenges it faces seem so vivid and resonant to so many people. This happens, I contend, because *A Song of Ice and Fire* is a shrewdly assembled example of the modern fantasy form. My goal here is to explain how Martin uses the shapes, imperatives, capabilities and proclivities of fantasy to create something compelling enough to get people anxious about having their enjoyment of it spoiled.

1 The American Pratchett? – Muck and Modality

It is a commonplace of both popular and academic criticism of Martin to cite the death of Eddard Stark as the point at which the game of thrones became a distinctive, original contribution to fantasy. Brian Cowlishaw observes Stark's execution as something that "should" not have happened, a "shocking" contravention of reader expectation with which Martin alerts his readership that they should not count on any previous experience to help them predict the course of his narrative (66). The execution is now looked upon as a programmatic example of Martin's lack of hesitation about killing off significant characters. It contradicts what the reader thinks they know about "storytelling generally," Cowlishaw states, ushering in a period of chaos and uncertainty. If a putative protagonist can die, it seems, nobody is safe.

One of the things overlooked about Stark's death, however, is how unusual it is within Martin's story. Eddard dies, almost literally, on-stage, in front of a crowd, in a manner carefully arranged by characters and author alike for maximum dramatic effect. King Joffrey clearly mounted the steps of the Sept of Baelor intending to flex his autocratic muscles and make a public example of Stark. For Martin as well, this is a major piece of theatre, the climax of sixteen chapters of narrative tension since Stark was arrested and 59 since he received word that Jon Arryn met with foul play. Most of the deaths presented by Martin are much more banal. Mycah, Arya Stark's plebeian playmate, dies almost by accident. He is pointlessly killed by Sandor Clegane, largely as a consequence of living in a society that trains its ruling class to kill whether or not they possess the moral literacy to exercise that skill responsibly (*Game* 153). Clegane later suffers a flesh wound which becomes infected; Arya unceremoniously leaves him for dead (*Storm* 2.463–2.464). Other deaths are stupid. Ser Vardis Egan trusts his armour overmuch, allowing Bronn to tire and outmanoeuvre him (*Game* 424–427); Rolley breaks his neck climbing into Craster's attic (*Storm* 2.458); the Mountain's Men kill Lommy Greenhands to avoid the work of carrying him (*Clash* 278). Death in Westeros is an occasion of perplexing bathos more often than the theatrics – diegetic and heterodiegetic – of Stark's execution. "Killed by a pig," croaks Robert Baratheon: "Ought to laugh, but it hurts too much" (*Game* 488).

Martin often specifically thwarts attempts by the Westerosi to dramatise the passing of their fellows. Hoster Tully, for example, dies in bed after a long illness. Catelyn Stark means to take comfort from the dignity and traditionalism of her father's funeral. Tully's body, resplendently armed and armoured, will be set adrift in a boat on the Green Fork of the Trident by an honour guard of great lords. The boat will be set ablaze with a burning arrow fired by Edmure, Tully's heir, and sink, uniting him bodily to the waters surrounding his ancestral home. Thus, the Tullys observe their defining connection to the lands they received from Aegon the Conqueror. Sadly, Edmure drowned his sorrows the night before and is still "tight." He misses three times before swearing angrily and thrusting the bow at his uncle, who manages the shot just before the boat passes out of range (*Storm* 1.474–1.478). The effective failure of Tully's funeral is more typical of Martin's story than the theatrics of Eddard Stark's execution. Catelyn's sense of peace is tainted; Edmure seems to take none at all.

How different this funeral is from the departure of Boromir in *The Lord of the Rings*. Arrayed much like Tully, Boromir is set adrift on the Anduin, a river of rich symbolic importance to his family, but human error is not admitted into Tolkien's report of this ritual. Aragorn and Legolas improvise songs as if they had been rehearsing for years and graciously accept Gimli's appropriate declination to join them (*The Two Towers* 543–544). Tolkien does not allow Aragorn to slip in the mud – the difficulties encountered in carrying Boromir to the river indicate his stature rather than the weakness of his mourners (541) – or Gimli to insist on singing an inappropriate song. If an arrow needed to be fired, Legolas would surely have made the shot effortlessly, with the wind rippling his hair. Boromir's funeral is exactly the sort of dignified, elegiac occasion the Tullys hoped for.

Such occasions are rare in Martin's story, however, where conceits of glamour, ritual, aristocratic pretension and even personal dignity are frustrated or spoiled. Some of these let-downs are the result of villainy but others are the result of predictable complications – mourners drink; drunks are poor shots – that these people seem to have overlooked. This theme has itself been overlooked by those who seek to compare Martin and Tolkien. Such comparisons predate *Time Magazine* reviewer Lev Grossman's 2005 "proclamation" of him as "the American Tolkien". In his 1996 review of *A Game of Thrones*, Dave Gross of *Dragon Magazine* opined that its implied sequel "promises to exceed all the epic fantasy series since...you're not going to make me say it, are you?" (59) More recently, Susan Vaught has praised Martin's invented world as being "unlike the almost allegorical worlds of J.R.R. Tolkien and his contemporaries, which are imbued with unambiguous representations of good and evil" (105). This no doubt gratifies Martin and his promoters, whose decision to include his middle initials – identical to Tolkien's – in his nom de plume, and to trumpet his books as "the greatest fantasy epic of the modern era" (*Clash* back cover blurb), are surely calculated attempts to provoke such comparisons. No interview with or blog post about Martin is complete without a query regarding how his work relates to *The Lord of the Rings*. Given the centrality of Tolkien's novel to perceptions of modern fantasy, this discussion is hardly unexpected. It is risky, however. Although he has become a *locus classicus* of modern fantasy, Tolkien is in fact a highly idiosyncratic practitioner of the form whose methodologies and output can only be cited as typical of the genre in certain broad respects (Attebery 1992 14–17). Accordingly, the overreliance on Tolkien as a stereotypical fantasist has led to some significant errors of analysis. Reviewing Martin's *A Feast for Crows*, for example, Grossman observes:

> What really distinguishes Martin, and what marks him as a major force for evolution in fantasy, is his refusal to embrace a vision of the world as a Manichaean struggle between Good and Evil. Tolkien's work has enormous imaginative force, but you have to go elsewhere for moral complexity. Martin's wars are multifaceted and ambiguous, as are the men and women who wage them and the gods who watch them and chortle, and somehow that makes them mean more. *A Feast for Crows* isn't pretty elves against gnarly orcs. It's men and women slugging it out in the muck, for money and power and lust and love.

These qualifications gesture towards the deflated glamour in Martin's writing; his characters are "slugging it out in the muck". Grossman makes this observation, however, in the course of establishing his broader point, that the conflicts of Martin's morally ambiguous characters are more interesting than Tolkien's depictions of noble heroes and evil villains. Subsequent critics, such as Staggs and Vaught, have echoed this point. In doing so, such critics have made two significant errors. They overstate the importance and innovation of Martin's morally ambiguous characters and overlook the importance of his muck to the impression he creates of those characters. Martin's characters are undoubtedly, commendably complex, though this is not as great a difference from Tolkien as the likes of Grossman, Staggs or Vaught contend. Nor is it particularly innovative within the modern fantasy genre. Three brief studies below will demonstrate that modern fantasy is in fact abidingly concerned with the ambiguities of good and evil. In presenting characters who force the reader to engage with such matters, Martin is continuing a trend rather than ploughing a furrow of his own. More innovative, particularly in a post-Tolkienian context, is the muck in which Grossman states the game of thrones is being conducted. Martin's innumerable references to dirt and ordure are not merely gestures towards realism. They are carefully targeted to fundamentally alter the reader's perception of the characters, serving as a crucial difference between his work and Tolkien's. The effect of this theme can be elucidated with reference to Northrop Frye's theory of modes. Tolkien recapitulated the rhetoric of the heroic age for the modern world, creating what Frye would define as a high-mimetic narrative in which readers are encouraged to look up to the characters. Martin, by contrast, uses filth as part a long-established technique for rendering medievalist texts modally ironic; readers look down upon his characters. His use of this mode, furthermore, closely parallels that of Terry Pratchett. His occasional decisions to *stop* using irony and employ Frye's higher modes also echo Pratchett's. If Martin must be called the American equivalent of any British fantasist, then Pratchett seems a more appropriate candidate than Tolkien.

In the first instance, Grossman's suggestion that Martin's morally ambiguous characters represent an innovation within the genre seems mistaken. Fantasists of literary ambition have long used the possibilities of the genre to raise, rather than settle, questions about the nature of good and evil. Some, such as E.R. Eddison and David Lindsay, do so very deliberately, presenting novels that exist largely to illustrate idiosyncratic meditations on moral philosophy. Other authors do so as the existence of magic in their written worlds causes them to gravitate towards the issue of whether and how such power affects the invented societies they depict. Three brief examples will serve to demonstrate that this is a central attribute of the modern fantasy genre.

Mervyn Peake's *Titus* novels, for example, propose a supernatural situation that queries the nature of human morality. The supernatural element in these books, Gormenghast Castle, is a crumbling, ageless institution that, in its preposterous size and age, bears passing comparison to Martin's Wall. The castle is home to hundreds of people but is nevertheless cavernously under-occupied. Characters walk miles between rooms and conceal themselves and each other for years at a time in labyrinths of forgotten chambers and corridors. No particularly comprehensive floor plan exists. Nobody born there has ventured out of sight of it; those few who arrive seem to lose interest in anything beyond it. This entirely self-contained society is governed by a series of inane rituals laid down by unknown scholars in time immemorial. None of these rituals make any sense, or have the slightest utilitarian value, but everyone in the castle treats them as utterly sacrosanct. Peake's novels combine intricate, verbose descriptions of this environment with intimate portraits of the dehumanising effect it has on the characters. This of the incumbent ruler, Earl Sepulchrave:

> How could he *love* this place? He was part of it. He could not imagine a world outside it; the idea of loving Gormenghast would have shocked him. To have asked him of his feelings for his hereditary

> home would be like asking a man what his feelings were towards his own hand or his own throat. (*Titus Groan* 42)

Sepulchrave sees himself as part of the castle. His fellows similarly reckon their existence almost solely in the context of their position there and engage in strikingly pointless, amoral skulduggery to protect their status in this castellated universe. Devoid of any other frame of reference, the inhabitants of Gormenghast behave and indeed exist only as this bizarre institution would have them do.

Into this world of rust, cobwebs and lunatics, however, Peake inserts Steerpike, a kitchenhand with the almost unique capacity to see the castle as the absurdity it is. Absconding from the kitchens Steerpike quickly begins to hatch plots for self-advancement that gradually bear fruit, as well they might. The other inhabitants of the castle divide their time between the plodding cyclical ritual and vicious scrabbling for meaningless pretences of power. Steerpike, by contrast, is a sensible, industrious lad capable of using his time effectively, moving up through the castle hierarchy and eventually becoming Master of Ritual, and thus one of the chief arbiters of his universe. He initially comes across as something of a hero, kicking against a repressive institution, though this view quickly becomes unsustainable. Steerpike is a picture of utilitarian rationality but not morality. He unhesitatingly causes several deaths and ruthlessly manipulates the other characters to his own ends. By the opening of Peake's second novel, when Sepulchrave's feeble-witted sisters displease him, he orders them to crawl under the carpet of their room:

> Steerpike derived as much pleasure in watching these anile and pitiful creatures, dressed in their purple finery, as they crawled beneath the carpet as he got from anything. He had led them gradually, and by easy and cunning steps, from humiliation to humiliation, until the distorted satisfaction he experienced in this way had become little short of a necessity for him. Were it not that he found this grotesque pleasure in the exercise of his power over them, it is to be doubted whether he would have gone to all the trouble involved in keeping them alive. (*Gormenghast* 404)

Steerpike begins as a seventeen-year-old boy with an independent streak and an active dislike of a bizarre, absurd institution. He ends up "an almost legendary monster" (748), a grumpkin to frighten Gormenghast's children. This trajectory stems not from any predestined capacity for evil but from his humanity, untouched by the stultifying, cretinising atmosphere of Gormenghast, and his willingness to abuse that advantage over the other characters. Out of a dissatisfaction with something the reader has also been encouraged to dislike, Steerpike uses the human characteristics his fellow inmates have been lampooned for lacking – rationalism, initiative, creativity, sensible ambition – to undertake a series of murderous, callous, dehumanising actions. Thus, the villain of the piece is also its most readily relatable character (Johnstone 8). The qualities that initially made him praiseworthy are those that make him abhorrent. This demonstrates Peake's concern for using fantasy to raise, rather than settle, moral debates. Evil in this story stems not from any external threat, but from a human mind freed of moral constraints by a supernatural situation, forcing readers to reassess precisely what they mean by humanity. This, as much as Peake's lavish prose, is what makes his work such a memorable read.

The story of a supernatural situation catalysing the native human capacity for evil also appears in J.K. Rowling's Harry Potter novels. At first glance Rowling's tale of the heroic wizard ingénue Harry and his nemesis Lord Voldemort seems to be a straightforward case of good versus evil. To begin with the two antagonists seem polar opposites. Harry's native moral courage is identified by his school's Sorting Hat while Voldemort seems abidingly heedless of the human consequences of his expanding power. But Voldemort, like Steerpike, was not born bad, at least not inescapably so. He is a convincing villain in part because Rowling has provided an explanation of how he got that way. As the series progresses, Harry's mentor Dumbledore reveals more about the Dark Lord. Voldemort was once a boy named Tom Riddle, who had much in common with Harry. Both are orphans, offspring of mixed marriages between a wizard and a non-wizard, raised in unpromising circumstances – Harry by boorish foster-parents, Tom in a "grim" (*Half-Blood Prince* 251) orphanage – before being whisked away to Hogwarts at age eleven. Both come to regard the school as their true home. From the same combination of problems and opportunities, Harry becomes a promising, upstanding wizarding citizen while Riddle becomes "the most dangerous Dark wizard of all time" (258).

Rowling has constructed Voldemort in such a way that it is possible to hazard guesses as to where he went wrong. Christopher Bell goes so far as to describe Voldemort as "wholly a creation of environmental circumstance" (45). Bell cites Riddle as a classic case of moral disengagement – a lack of investment in the moral orthodoxies of his society (43–44). He notes how Rowling's wizarding world, like our own, features a number of institutions – notably Hogwarts itself – that both encourage the pursuit of power, rank and material success as well as moderating that pursuit by encouraging moral and humanitarian behaviour. As headmaster of Hogwarts, for example, Dumbledore enjoys unparalleled respect and freedom of action in the wizard community; he also carefully teaches his students "not only to use magic, but to control it" (*Half-Blood Prince* 256) via strict moral accountability. Riddle, Bell suggests, coverts the first part of this equation – the power and respect Dumbledore enjoys – but has been excluded from the moral community

Dumbledore seems to try so hard to build. Isolated among Muggles, he also fails to form resonant friendships among wizards, something that Harry does singularly well. Thus, Tom does not have a stake in the moral regime of Hogwarts; the human relationships and lives that morality safeguards are of little concern to him. After he leaves Hogwarts, furthermore, his attempts to climb the ranks of wizard society are stymied as he is repeatedly passed over for a job at his prestigious school. A young man has joined a society that respects power and then been foiled in his attempts to gain respect within the moral orthodoxies of that society. As Bell notes (46), this kind of situation tends to produce moral dislocation in real human beings; when improperly integrated into the moral frameworks of society, people often resolve to pursue what their society values and applauds without reference to the strictures that society places on that pursuit. Although Rowling leaves the details sinisterly vague, by his twenties Riddle is already doing this:

> "You call it 'greatness,' what you have been doing, do you?" asked Dumbledore delicately.
>
> "Certainly," said Voldemort, and his eyes seemed to burn red. "I have experimented; I have pushed the boundaries of magic further, perhaps, than they have ever been pushed –"
>
> "Of some kinds of magic," Dumbledore corrected him quietly. (*Half-Blood Prince* 415)

Thus, Riddle matures from bad boy to evil wizard. He is pursuing power without concern for the human consequences of that pursuit, an undertaking that troubles the man who took responsibility for his moral education. Voldemort's unconcern for Dumbledore's lessons stems from his inability or unwillingness to form genuine relationships with those around him and thus enjoy the wages of proper engagement in a moral community. Magic, an inarguable, supernatural power, provides Rowling with a mechanism to demonstrate this moral disengagement. Magic does not turn people evil, it provides a litmus test for the extent to which people remain morally engaged, literate and responsible. As in Martin's work, evil in Rowling's world is a human thing; as in Peake's, the literary supernatural highlights moral issues rather than putting such issues to rest.

Tolkien's characters are especially interesting in this regard. Critical dismissals of his work as morally simplistic date back at least as far as Edmund Wilson's 1956 description of *The Lord of the Rings* as "juvenile trash" (314) presenting only a battle "of the Forces of Evil with the Forces of Good, the remote and alien villain with the plucky little home-grown hero" (313). This is the tradition to which critics like Grossman have made slightly more diplomatic contributions. A careful reading of *The Lord of the Rings*, however, reveals a sophisticatedly ambiguous construction of morality. The One Ring, the central vector by which evil acts in the story, might be described as an amplifier for the existing character flaws of the heroes; it is, in the words of Tom Shippey, "addictive" (119). A single use of the Ring achieves a goal and produces no apparent ill effects, so the user uses it again, and again, and so on, becoming accustomed to using its power to solve problems and increasingly heedless of (disengaged from) other concerns, including any moral convictions they may hold dear. Their ability to act increases without any accompanying expansion of their ability to grasp the consequences of those actions. Power thus swamps morality; the most noble of intentions are twisted to heedless, arrogant evil. But, as Shippey observes, "there has to be something there for it to work on" (138), some attribute or impulse for it to pervert, be it Smeagol's avarice, Galadriel's majesty or Boromir's patriotism. In a sense, therefore, wrongdoing in *The Lord of the Rings* is born from the character flaws of the individual. The Ring simply brings out the worst in its user, turning them into the most hideously amoral version of themselves possible. With this device in place, Tolkien offers chilling depictions of the ugly sides of even his prettiest Elves (*The Fellowship of the Ring* 356–476).

Conversely, Shippey observes, there are moments in which the Ring appears to be the sort of external, Manichaean evil Grossman describes, a fragment of its creator's will actively picking away at the willpower of the heroes. Shippey charts Frodo's uses of the Ring in the novel, in which, like the affliction of an addict, its power over him seems to grow with time. He "firmly"(206) resists the temptation to disappear at the *Prancing Pony*, but mysteriously and sinisterly does so anyway; confronted by the Nazghul at Weathertop he finds resistance "unbearable." (255). Donning the Ring to escape Boromir at Amon Hen, he finds himself "perfectly balanced" (523) between the power of his own will and the apparently active, external stimulus of this infernal device. Hiding from the Lord of the Nazghul at Cirith Ungol, he feels that stimulus explicitly as "the beating upon him of a great power from outside" (*Towers* 925). Finally, at Mount Doom itself, Frodo announces that "I do not choose now to do what I came to do" (*Return* 1,237) – that is, destroy the Ring. Shippey cleverly interrogates Frodo's odd turn of phrase here. He suggests that Tolkien's decision to have Frodo say "I do not choose" instead of "I choose not to" is quite deliberate, indicating that the Ring is doing the choosing (136–140). Over the course of the novel the Ring grows in influence over its bearer, eventually usurping his will.

Tolkien has been criticised for this inconsistency between depictions of evil as an internal or external force (Manlove 1975 177–178), though Shippey cites this ambiguity as a major contribution to the resonance of his work. It ensures that the question of where evil comes from remains open; characters are neither wholly responsible for their misdeeds nor able to conveniently palm it off on remote, impersonal forces. Shippey suggests that this closely mirrors the wrongdoing most readers observe in their everyday lives, which stems from a convoluted, fluid, unpredictable combination of human imperfections and apparently imponderable, unrelatable outside villainies (2002 142). The evil in Tolkien's most famous novel is neither wholly human nor wholly inhuman, an ongoing challenge to characters and readers alike in that it is impossible to conclusively define. Tolkien's work is powerful in significant part because his epic conflict between good and evil is, on examination, so eerily, realistically inconclusive in its definition of terms.

The foregoing discussions of Peake, Rowling and Tolkien distil some complex issues into a small space, the better to move discussion on to the actual subject author. Nevertheless, the fact that those complexities require such compression demonstrates, in itself, that fantasy has a long history of moral sophistication. In using the fantasy genre to present the reader with a series of moral conundrums, Martin is contributing to a long-standing tradition rather than doing anything as innovative as Grossman suggests.

Grossman's accompanying supposition, also echoed by other critics, that Martin abjures Manichaean evil is similarly questionable. Exactly such an evil appears in the prologue to his first volume as Ser Weymar Royce and his rangers encounter the Others. The appellation is significant. The ranger Will identifies these creatures as totally and definitively inhuman, as active, external, antagonistic intelligences defined by their lack of humanity. With this point entered into the narrative record. Old Nan's tales of the terrors of the Long Night and Jeor Mormont's observation that "you don't build a wall seven hundred feet high to keep savages in skins from stealing women" (*Storm* 1.451) become deeply ironic. The Others that Nan fancifully witters about are quite real; the reader knows what the ancient Wall is for and observes the game of thrones in the knowledge that these monsters are on their way. Staggs, in asserting that "Martin doesn't introduce an external source of evil in his work because it's not needed" (149), is arguing directly against the evidence. Martin has arranged his narrative to give readers a clear demonstration of the superhuman power of the inhumanly evil monsters that absolutely do exist in his invented world before even venturing on his plot. Human actions proceed against a background of supernatural activity.

This is something that Anglophone fantasists have been doing with the supernatural for as long as there has been Anglophone literature. In Tolkien's estimation, the legendary warrior-king Beowulf, who defeats two horrifying ogres before going down fighting against a marauding dragon, is operating in something akin to the literary equivalent of laboratory conditions. His struggle against such literary contrivances – things created solely *because* they do not exist outside poesy – stands "amid but above the petty wars of princes, and surpasses the dates and limits of historical periods" ("The Monsters and the Critics" 33). The monsters mean that Beowulf's story ceases to be about a medieval Scandinavian adventurer and becomes an illustration of what human abilities – courage, strength, prowess, fidelity to purpose – can accomplish in the darkest of imaginable circumstances. Elsewhere Tolkien refers to this capacity of the literary supernatural as Recovery, the recovery of a clear view of the essential qualities of real things via their juxtaposition with something that exists purely to test them ("On Fairy-Stories" 146). Such ideas are obviously applicable to Martin. Like Beowulf's strengths, the shortcomings of the Westerosi are made more apparent in the context of things Other. The tragic irony the game of thrones is that Westeros is ripping itself into pieces at a time that calls for unity against a terrible, essentially and definitively external threat. Martin continues a long tradition of using monstrosity to accentuate humanity, a tradition that many other fantasists, pertinently Tolkien, have been perpetuating for literally a millennium.

Why, then, does Martin's tale seem so different from Tolkien's, if he is pursuing an authorial strategy that Tolkien himself not only used in fiction but also identified and analysed in his non-fiction? Grossman gestures towards an answer with his observation that Martin's characters are "slugging it out in the muck". That muck is often strictly literal and frequently of the character's own making, a key difference between Martin's characters and Tolkien's. The Tolkienian body is a clean and manageable thing. Hobbit dwellings have bathrooms, where the pleasure (not necessity) of bathing is celebrated in song (*Fellowship* 132), but the reader finds no reference to lavatories. A passing mention of Shelob vomiting (*Towers* 946) may be "the only reference to the evacuation of food in the whole work" (Little 27). By contrast, Martin turns the bodily functions of his characters, and the sensory evidence thereof, into something of a feature of his narrative. One of the most striking features of his invented world is its unsanitariness. Quentyn Martell travels on a ship redolent of "piss and rotting meat and nightsoil [...] corpse-flesh and weeping sores and wounds gone bad" (*Dance* 95), a cacophony of smells directly contrasted to the "cleaner" odour created by pigs. The consolidation of Daenerys Targaryen's idealistic conquest of Meereen is stalled by the pale mare, a hellish gastrointestinal illness that leaves its victims "shitting out their lives in stinking streams of brown and red" (554). Even when bodily functions are not influencing the plot, they remain an almost ubiquitous presence in the discourse. Martin displays considerable ingenuity in contriving excuses to depict his characters vomiting (*Clash* 151; *Game* 160; *Storm* 1.105), urinating (*Feast* 171; *Game* 656; *Storm* 1.455) and defecating (*Clash* 717; *Dance* 877; *Storm* 1.415). They also wipe their noses (*Clash* 424; *Dance* 68; *Storm* 1.239), lactate (*Clash* 171; *Feast* 593; *Storm* 2.69), menstruate (*Clash* 685; *Dance* 1,094; *Storm* 2.278), lubricate (*Feast* 548; *Game* 103; *Storm*

1.358) and ejaculate (*Clash* 407; *Game* 476; *Storm* 1.169) with a frequency born of obvious authorial policy. Wounded warriors find their injuries festering theatrically:

> The pus that burst forth was thick and yellow as sour milk. The dusky woman wrinkled her nose at the smell, the maester gagged, and Victarion himself felt his stomach churn. "Cut deeper. Get it all. Show me blood."
>
> Maester Kerwin pressed the dagger deep. This time it hurt, but blood welled up as well as pus, blood so dark that it looked black in the lantern light.
>
> Blood was good. Victarion grunted in approval. He sat there unflinching as the maester dabbed and squeezed and cleaned the pus away with squares of soft cloth boiled in vinegar. By the time he was finished, the clean water in his basin had become a scummy soup. The sight alone would sicken any man. (*Dance* 870)

Tolkien, a combat veteran, incorporates the realities of war into his work (Croft 5). His characters suffer grave wounds and fight for their lives in sickbeds for weeks. But he spares readers any description of what septic matter smells like, let alone one this lurid. Middle-earth is not a place where such matters are discussed. Westeros is. Martin seldom misses an opportunity to remind readers that his characters have bodies, and that bodies have functions, many of them runny and malodourous.

This difference goes somewhat beyond Martin being "more realistic" (Mendlesohn and James 146) than Tolkien. His frequent lavatorial references can certainly be seen as evidence of that quality, though if this is his only intent their sheer frequency would seem to constitute a great overcorrection. An author does not provide a detailed description of diarrhoea "gushing" down an invalid's legs (*Dance* 878) simply because it is authentic; this is a deliberate authorial choice. Indeed, an author does not need to make any reference to bodily fluids in order to create compellingly believable characters. A depiction of a satisfying physical relationship, for example, does not require the author to direct reader's attention to the way in which a phallus "glistened wetly" (*Game* 563) as its owner breaks coitus. Similarly, Martin could have communicated the earthiness of the Lannister encampment at the crossroads without showing Tyrion "shake off the last drops" as he urinates (656). Salladhor Saan reminds Davos Seaworth that the phantasmagorical buildings of Dragonstone, said to be shaped by magic, contain privy shafts (*Storm* 2.158). Realistic or otherwise, the pervasiveness of this discourse hints at authorial preoccupations beyond straightforward authenticity. Martin subscribes to an entirely different medievalist tradition to that espoused by Tolkien. Examination of these two authors in light of Frye's theory of modes demonstrates that they are in fact working at diametrically cross purposes.

Tolkien seldom read modern literature (Carpenter 69–70). From childhood, his reading tended heavily towards the legends and sagas of northern Europe, on which he became a noted authority. There are occasional references to bodily dirt in such literature (*Egil's Saga* 71). But Tolkien's particular hobbyhorses, *Beowulf* and *Volsungasaga*, contain no such discussion. They are evocations of heroic virtues, focussing on idealised depictions of courage, martial prowess and etiquette, with little discussion of anything that might distract attention from such matters. Such a tone does not prevent characters from behaving badly. *Volsungasaga*, concerning Grimhild's manipulation of her children's marriages (26) and the resulting bloodshed (28–31), is as much a tale of spite and skulduggery as Martin's. An (imperfect) analogue from southern Europe, Homer's *Iliad*, finds Achilles desecrating the corpse of Hector (22.396–22.405) just as the Freys do Robb Stark's. But such awfulness is always conducted at a certain pitch of dignity; weapons and armour shine; staves are quoted, esteemed skills practiced, customs observed. The olfactory sense is seldom evoked. Dialogue displays more concern for the stature of the speaker than for plausibility; both Sigurd and Fafnir speak eloquently, calmly and at improbable length after being run through (*Volsungasaga* 18; 30). The result is a sense of looking up to an idealised warrior aristocracy. To further this impression, many of the meaner details of life are elided:

> In *Beowulf*, we see the great hall adorned with woven hangings and filled with joyous and well-behaved celebrants. We would not thank the author for reminding us that there would have been fleas and flies, and dog droppings on the floor. Clothing and bodies would have stunk. Nor would we feel uplifted had the author reminded us that those who got drunk at the feast might not have made it outside to puke, and that drunken warriors were likely to be quarrelsome. (Hume 91)

Resonantly drawn as they are, Beowulf, Achilles and Brynhild are characters, not people. Made of ink and imagination rather than flesh and blood, they do not actually have colons, bladders or uterine linings and need never exercise those anatomical features if their respective authors do not wish them to do so. The abjuration of such discourse contributes to the aristocratic mystique around the characters, ensuring that their defining qualities, good or bad – strength of arm, stoutness of heart, tempestuousness of mind – are not diluted by the biological bathos familiar to the reader. Hume calls this fantasy by subtraction, the editing of a narrative to an extent "extreme enough to call attention to the differences between the reality which is being constructed and those we function by personally" (91). The texts she uses to illustrate her point are those Tolkien grew up with and worked with. In his favourite stories, Hume observes, life is "refined to the heroic simplicities, those pertaining to a gold-adorned life of courage and to the dark patterns of dynastic treachery."

Northrop Frye defines the resulting narrative register as romance or high mimesis, the literary modes in which the author depicts characters who, although mortal, are clearly superior to the reader (33). Tolkien's skill in creating such an impression is one of his strengths as a writer. The departure of Boromir is a case in point, a powerful example of Tolkien editing his narrative to create an idealised, aristocratic impression of his characters. Many of Tolkien's other characters seem to ascend through Frye's modes, contravening the decline towards irony Frye identified in modern literature (34–35). By Hume's estimation, for example, Bilbo "remains" (154) low mimetic while Frodo becomes high mimetic by embracing his place among the likes of Aragorn and Legolas. This estimation actually seems conservative. At his journey's end, the younger Baggins will in fact ascend rapidly into the romantic mode and towards the mythic as he leaves Middle earth as a peer of immortal characters like Elrond and Gandalf. Theoden's prolonged dying farewells (*Return* 1,103–1,104) – a commonplace of heroic literature (Hume 92) – include expressions of regret that he will never be able to properly discuss pipe-weed with Merry. Discourse initially used by Tolkien to characterise hobbits as prosaic wallflowers (*Fellowship* 10–11) is thus infused with high-mimetic grandeur; "someone once chided for small-mindedness" (*Towers* 728) becomes thought of as "lordly" and "magnificent" (*Return* 1,341) for the remainder of his days. Of all the things Tolkien borrowed from medieval literature, perhaps the most subtly powerful was its habit of ignoring the baser realities of human existence in order to concentrate on more resonant matters – that is, its high-mimetic modality. To say Tolkien merely reiterated medieval literary techniques would be a great over-simplification (Flieger 2005 20–21). But he was an authority on literature that, medieval or otherwise, was romantic or high mimetic. A lifetime of reading *Beowulf* and *Volsungasaga* equipped Tolkien to employ Frye's higher modes with particular skill.

Martin "reveres" (Bausells) Tolkien's work, suggesting he is affected by this technique, but he steadfastly refuses to perpetuate it in his own writing. His characters squirt humiliating, humanising fluids out of every orifice. Their world is every bit as grubby:

> It was a vile town, a sty, small and mean and rank with the odors of pig shit and rotting fish. Davos remembered it well from his smuggling days. The Three Sisters had been a favorite haunt of smugglers for hundreds of years, and a pirate's nest before that. Sisterton's streets were mud and planks, its houses wattle-and-daub hovels

> roofed with straw, and by the Gallows Gate there were always hanged men with their entrails dangling out. (*Dance* 143)

The notionally glamorous capital of King's Landing is no cleaner. "You can smell the shit from five miles away," complains Olenna Tyrell in the television adaptation ("The Gift"). Cersei Lannister learns this at closer quarters:

> More refuse showered down from windows and balconies: half-rotted fruit, pails of beer, eggs that exploded into sulfurous stink when they cracked open on the ground. Then someone flung a dead cat over the Poor Fellows and the Warrior's Sons alike. The carcass hit the cobbles so hard that it burst open, splattering her lower legs with entrails and maggots. (*Dance* 996)

It would take a historian of medieval urbanisation to authoritatively pronounce such depictions as "realistic" or not. A viewer of the right television or cinema would, however, recognise it instantly. This is the BBC comedy Middle Ages, a milieu whose creators labour the darkness of the dark ages, portraying the medieval world as a place of ignorance, violence and, above all, dirt. This is a world of muddy marketplaces, plague carts, squalid hovels and ulcerated lepers, where hooded executioners impale severed heads on spikes, chortling torturers turn thumbscrews, bombastic kings roar death sentences and flea-bitten peasants barbeque rats over the ubiquitous pyres of burning witches. The parallels between Westeros and this cartoonish milieu are numerous. Robert Baratheon bears a striking resemblance to the bellowing, bellicose, speculative Richard IV of England played by Brian Blessed in the medievalist sitcom *The Black Adder.* A single episode of this show depicts characters eating rats, rubbing guano on their scalp as a tonic for baldness, being burned at the stake and expiring from plague halfway through a conversation ("Witchsmeller Pursuivant"). Any dungeon in Westeros could easily contain Mad Gerald, the filthy, burbling grotesque played by Rik Mayall in the finale ("The Black Seal"). Ramsay Bolton effectively turns Theon Greyjoy into such a character, renaming him after his stink. Conversely Mord, Lysa Arryn's animalistic turnkey, could be in Westeros on some sort of work exchange from the snail-infested dungeons in which The Black Adder himself is confined. Another such comedy, *Maid Marian and Her Merry Men*, opens its pilot episode ("How the Gang Got Together") with a song bemoaning the mud that dominates medievalist peasant's lives; they literally eat it (cf. *Game* 275) and scrape it from hair that resembles Arya Stark's (329) in its messiness. The filth of Sisterton recalls the "Bring out your Dead" scene in *Monty Python and the Holy Grail*, in which people wallow in muck and can scarcely be bothered observing the difference between a grubby relative and a diseased corpse.

Unlike Tolkien's use of the conventions of Nordic literature, Martin's use of this trope appears to be a case of convergent evolution rather than direct influence. An informed reader, however, would immediately imagine actors Tony Robinson (*The Black Adder's* Baldrick) or John Young (*Monty Python and the Holy Grail's* 'dead' body) among the crowd who jeer Cersei's walk of contrition. Martin perpetuates a recognisable tradition of ostentatious squalor in medievalist literature.

Critics have identified a clear purpose for such rhetoric. The term "medieval" is fluid, used in differing contexts to evoke either antique glamour or primitive barbarity. Flieger observes that an American tourist might return from Europe edified by seeing medieval stained glass, but also complaining about "medieval" plumbing (2005 17). Martin has been quoted rejecting the "Disneyland" Middle Ages he accuses "mainstream fantasy" of often perpetuating (Carroll 4). He offers few specific examples of this mainstream, though his choice of term to describe this putative trend seems apropos. The Disney Corporation's replica castles evoke an "abiding, prespecific, legendary time where fairytales take place" (Bayless 39–40), and are, tellingly, based on edifices such as Neuschwanstein and Hohenzollern Castles in Bavaria (42–43). These palaces are nineteenth-century architectural confections rather than actual medieval fortifications, designed to evoke antique splendour rather than repel assaults from men in chainmail. Disney's creative teams similarly aestheticise history so that viewers can focus on the gilded verities of storybook love. Beautiful princesses need castles that contain a lot of Flieger's stained glass but little of her plumbing, or anybody else's. This is not to indict Disney productions as evasive, any more than to suggest that Elizabeth Bennet is flatly characterised because Austen never makes a talking point of the middens at Longbourn. The Disneyland Middle Ages simply demonstrate Hume's fantasy of subtraction in full effect. A medievalist who perpetuates the grime and odour of the BBC comedy Middle Ages, by contrast, is effectively reassuring the reader that they are not practicing any such neo-medievalism. Dirt is therefore a shorthand rejection of sentimentality, and an established method by which authors can demonstrate and encourage a critical impression of the Middle Ages:

> Those films subscribing to the fantasy of the Middle Ages as a lost organic society will be cleaner than those which see it as barbaric and uncivilised. [...] The insistence on the filthiness of the Middle Ages seems to stem from a need to counter the romanticized nostalgic view of the period, to proclaim its barbarity as a "dark age." (Finke and Shichtman 48)

Hibberd credits Martin with the latter approach, applauding his attempt to "shatter all the romanticised clichés inspired by medieval

Europe and instead depict the period's barbaric reality". In this pursuit, Martin gleefully caricatures medieval corporal punishment; the disembowelled convicts in Sisterton are among the more restrained examples. He also works in almost every conceivable reference to odour and ordure. Again, and contrary to Hibberd's confident assertions about "barbaric realities", questions about how realistic this is should probably be referred to trained historians. The point is that just as Tolkien edits his narrative discourse to recreate the heroic effects of medieval literature, Martin perpetuates a recognisable tradition in *medievalist* literature in order to critique the medieval world. Westeros is not filthy due to realism. Martin's world is awash in ordure for the same reason that directors such as Terry Gilliam order extras to smear mud on their faces – to encourage the impression that the story is set in an unjust, backward time and place, happening to the reader's intellectual and cultural inferiors.

As with Tolkien's rhetoric, this places Martin's narrative in a recognisable position within Frye's theoretical system. It sets up the ironic mode, in which the reader looks "down on a scene of bondage, frustration or absurdity" (34) about which they are better-informed than the characters. Sansa Stark is by no means the only Westerosi to believe her life will be like a song. Martin's characters repeatedly try to apply themselves to matters of interest to the heroes of high mimesis – war, love, statecraft, elegy. Most of the time, when they do, Martin inserts some element of low mimesis, some humble complication that the *Beowulf* poet, practicing Hume's fantasy of subtraction, elides from his story. Such a quiet, dispassionate intrusion expresses life "exactly as [Martin] finds it" (Frye 41), subtly but devastatingly altering the reader's perception of the characters in question, doing so arguably more effectively than showing them behaving evilly or immorally. Attempting to establish themselves as people to be looked up to, the people of Martin's world more often than not end up being looked down upon as vainglorious fools whose arrogance led them to predictable humiliation. Edmure Tully, for example, wanted to give his father a great elegiac departure, but got drunk beforehand, apparently hoping that something would purge the wine from his system in time for him to place his arrow in keeping with high-mimetic convention. This pointedly does not happen, and Edmure looks quite the fool. Tywin Lannister is similarly afflicted:

> He rode his warhorse down the length of the hall and dismounted before the Iron Throne. Sansa had never seen such armour; all burnished red steel, inlaid with golden scrollwork and ornamentation. [a paragraph of further description follows] The Lord of Casterley Rock made such an impressive figure that it was a shock when his destrier dropped a load of dung right at the base of the throne. (*Clash* 817–818)

Tywin's goal here is propagandistic; to invest himself with militarised glory and remind the court who is in charge. His horse has earthier ideas. Acknowledging this would undermine Tywin's dramatic gesture of high-mimetic self-assertion, however. So he pretends not to notice it, and his grandson, awash in samite and rubies, tries to do the same. Lannister propaganda thus collapses. Sansa Stark reports not a king bestowing an honour on a hero, as they clearly intended, but a pair of overdressed snobs pretentiously ignoring the fact that their premeditated stunt has gone pungently awry. Martin continues to mercilessly undermine Lannister's dignity. His death in a privy chamber, "bedrobe hiked up around his hips" (*Storm* 2.497), is "not the way a lion dies" (*Feast* 53). At his funeral, his mourners insist he was "an *extraordinary* man" (119) while the escalating stench of his rotting corpse (115–116; 142; 144) graphically demonstrates the contrary; he is going the way of all flesh. His contracting skin robs him of his prized, characteristic gravitas (114), Margery Tyrell lays flowers at his bier but keeps one to shield her nose (142) and his grandson – the king – bursts into tears and retches (143). Even the statuesque Jaime, standing to attention "as if he had been carved from stone" (115), must bolt from the honour guard to lead Tommen outside "where the air was fresh and clean as King's Landing ever got" (143). One might have thought his family would have foregone a days-long lying-in-state in the Mediterranean climate of King's Landing, but their claims of greatness demand it. The result undercuts those pretentions. Lannister's career demonstrates what happens when straight-faced, high-mimetic pretensions collide with Martin's black-humoured, bathetic irony. Tywin and his mourners are, like Edmure Tully, *alazons*, imposters, ironically struggling to keep up appearances as their author consistently reveals the vacuous pretention of such efforts. The *alazon* is the characteristic protagonist of Frye's ironic mode, and that is the mode in which Martin's narrative characteristically abides.

Social stratification is among the aspects of medieval civilisation Martin critiques in this way. Finke and Shichtman note how in *Monty Python and the Holy Grail* the idealised notion of a divinely mandated king – another high-mimetic trope – is deflated by the observation that a king is recognisable as such simply because "He hasn't got shit all over him" (48–49). Supposedly preordained wisdom is deflated to mere self-perpetuating privilege, the freedom to keep oneself clean in an exaggeratedly dirty world. Martin denies his aristocrats even this comfort, inserting constant reminders that revered matriarchs, shining knights, beautiful damsels and oath-bound brotherhoods are made of the same clay as anybody else. Tyrion Lannister, for example, is a brave fighter, an able ruler and an eloquent speaker, all qualities attributed to Beowulf. But the reader has also seen him urinate (*Game* 656), ejaculate (*Clash* 411) and vomit (*Storm* 2.402), in almost as many words. Thus, it is impossible to see him in the same light as Beowulf or Sigurd, or indeed

Aragorn or Frodo. Likewise, Victarion Greyjoy's festering hand makes a mockery of his conceit that he has conquered death. His grand plans for the future are deeply ironic to readers who know he is suffering a raging infection his maester cannot treat. The red priest Moqorro appears to have solved this problem, though Victarion's own family history includes shocking cases of experimental medicine gone disastrously wrong (*Feast* 26) and at this writing it remains to be seen what will become of him. Victarion has plans – marry the Dragon Queen, overthrow his evil brother, lead his people to greatness – worthy of a high-mimetic hero. Should his infection take hold again, however, he will surely die. He will die mouthing the paeans to resilience and stoicism he learned as a devout follower of the Drowned God, but small good this will do him in the estimation of readers who know he will be defeated by his own short-sighted ignorance, not some great foe. Martin's use of the ironic mode means it is seldom possible to see his characters as the wolves, lions and dragons they see in their mirrors. The king of Westeros may not have shit all over him, but he, his courtiers and challengers are quite literally – and, the reader is encouraged to suspect, figuratively – full of it.

Khal Drogo provides an example. He is an alien creature to his wife, "towering over her" (*Game* 102) "with a face as still and cruel as a bronze mask" (98). Daenerys and Drogo eventually form a constructive, loving relationship, but this takes time, during which Drogo "spent his evenings drinking with his warriors and bloodriders, racing his prize horses, watching women dance and men die. Dany had no place in these parts of his life" (221). Warrior camaraderie, wine, women and song, the greatness of horses – these are grand high-mimetic preoccupations. Odd as Drogo's world is to Daenerys, she finds herself under its protection when Robert Baratheon's plan to assassinate her very nearly succeeds. Drogo is wroth:

> "I, Drogo, *khal*, will do this thing." His voice rose, and he lifted his fist to the sky. "I will take my *khalassar* west to where the world ends, and ride the wooden horses over the black salt water as no *khal* has done before. I will kill the men in the iron suits and tear down their stone houses. I will rape their women, take their children as slaves, and bring their broken gods back to Vaes Dothrak to bow down beneath the Mother of Mountains. This I vow, I, Drogo son of Bharbo. This I swear before the Mother of Mountains, as the stars look down in witness. (573–574)

Note Drogo's tripartite crescendo about raping women, taking children as slaves and plundering Westeros of its idols, the poetic climax "as the stars look down and witness" and the self-assertion of his own name and patrilineal qualifications. This is not a mere statement of intent. Drogo is engaging in high-mimetic oratory, vowing righteous heroic retribution on his foes, an act that contrasts sharply with the ineffectual whinging of his brother-in-law. Having demonstrated repeatedly that Viserys Targaryen is incapable of living up to his absurd regal conceits (35; 96; 223; 382), Martin shows readers what genuine high-mimetic indignation sounds like. This is the foe Robert Baratheon should have targeted, had any hired knife been foolhardy enough to take the contract.

But Drogo is not spared the sort of interrogation Victarion received. He dismisses the flesh wounds he gained fighting Khal Ogo; "This arrow is no more than the bite of a fly, this little cut only a new scar to boast of to my son" (647). His stoic warrior machismo writes a cheque his auto-immune system cannot cash; the wound festers and turns him into a flyblown wreck who will not be telling his son anything. Again, this is where Martin and Tolkien really part company. Frodo Baggins is violated by a magical weapon wielded by Sauron's senior underlings, the "shadows under his great Shadow" (*Fellowship* 67). Such a construction allows Tolkien the narrative tension of traumatic injury without reducing the stature of the stricken with discussion of the sanitary practicalities of emergency medicine; Frodo is wounded by a modally romantic foe and saved by a comparable friend (288–289). Khal Drogo might have found a similar ally in Mirri Maz Durr, had he been sensible enough to follow her advice, but he preferred to trust his own martial fortitude. "I am *khal*," he states, as if his title will protect him; "I spit on pain and drink what I like" (*Game* 650). In Tolkien's story, this may have sufficed. But Martin is writing an ironic narrative, not a romantic one. Bacteria are among the meaner facts of life subtracted (per Hume) from heroic literature. By incorporating them into his narrative discourse, Martin demonstrates the absurdity of high-mimetic pretension. Drogo is an *alazon* as much as Tywin Lannister is, subjected to the frustration and absurdity of which Frye wrote, created, as he described it, via a "dispassionate" (40) low-mimetic intrusion demonstrating the fragility of his self-bestowed dignity.

Martin's bodies do not have to suffer trauma to achieve this effect. In fact, in many cases, a reminder of the straightforward *correct* functioning of a body does just as much damage to a character's modality as does the trauma faced by Victarion and Drogo, as when Alester Florent is thrown in a cell with Ser Davos Seaworth:

> "It is filthy here," Lord Alester said suddenly, "And that odor...what is that odor?"
>
> "The pail," said Davos, gesturing. "We have no privy here. What terms?"
>
> His lordship stared at the pail in horror. (*Storm* 1.353)

The idea of squatting over a pail horrifies Florent, though in the fullness of time he will, just as Ser Davos has. This "very tall, very courtly, and very rich" (*Clash* 547) man, who in the Stormlands campaign wore "red-gold armour, with inlaid lapis flowers" (*Storm* 1.351), is after all as human as his cellmate. Lord Florent has become so caught up in the outward appearances of his station – he unsuccessfully appeals to his family connections for release and apologises to Davos for his appearance (1.350–1.351) – that he appears to have forgotten the inescapable realities of his own body. Notably Davos, a lowborn smuggler who must remind himself periodically of the aristocratic mindset rather than displaying assumptions about it in his focalisation, is spared this treatment. Davos is a low-mimetic character, his absence of pretension valued by his master. It falls to him to essentially give "his lordship" a refresher course in potty training. By the simple expedient of reminding readers that bodily functions take place, Martin exposes the flimsiness of the claims of greatness and wisdom made by the Westerosi aristocracy.

He does the same with Sansa Stark, something of a poster child for the bitter ironies of his narrative. She has been raised on tales of "Florian and Jonquil, of Lady Shella and the Rainbow Knight, of valiant Prince Aemon" (*Game* 532). There may be dungeons in these tales, but the cells do not, one suspects, feature pails to defecate in. This is Westeros's high-mimetic tradition, celebrating idealised courage and love, whose authors are almost certainly practicing Hume's fantasy of subtraction to preserve the dignity of the characters. Sansa has a very clear idea of where she fits into those stories. She is hardly the first adolescent girl, real or fictional, to fall in love with the poetic public image of a boy, though she presents a particularly obvious example of the type. Indeed, given that Martin has laboured Joffrey's puerile obnoxiousness from his second reported speech ("I am a prince. And I grow tired of swatting at Starks with a play sword" [69]), this may be as close as the author gets to becoming one of Frye's "naïve ironists" (41), those who draw explicit attention to their creation of *alazons*. He uses the theme of bodily functions to hammer this particular case home. Sansa understands the division of labour in the chivalric world perfectly well; note her immediate plans to bear Joffrey an heir (*Game* 461–462). Catelyn Stark's subsequent preoccupation with her daughter-in-law's child-bearing hips (*Storm* 1.194; 1.284) is also worth considering here. Cersei Lannister's remarks to the contrary (*Clash* 686) notwithstanding, Sansa clearly understands the responsibilities of an aristocratic wife. Yet, this advice combines with her reading habits to unfortunate effect. She assumed her menarche would be "less messy, and more magical" (687), a pleasant rite of passage into her desired career as a high-mimetic damsel. Martin instead seizes upon this as an opportunity to ram home the unpleasant truths edited from high mimesis. The menarche can certainly be an empowering moment in a woman's life, but Sansa's is portrayed solely in terms of disrupted sleep, cramps and sticky bodily fluids staining everything they touch (683–686). This would be an awful experience even if Sansa were not betrothed to the "little shit"

(*Game* 70) who had her father killed. One cannot imagine that the tale of Florian and Jonquil includes any reference to the fair Jonquil ever arranging "a cloth to wear between her legs" (*Clash* 686). As with Lord Alester Florent, Sansa is not bought back to earth by any mishap, but by a biological process that she, preoccupied with high-mimetic matters, nearly forgot about. Frye's equation is especially blatant here: high-mimetic conceits plus low-mimetic intrusion equals irony.

Martin's ironic modality demonstrates why his novels feel so different from Tolkien's despite sharing a fundamental concern for the moral unpredictability of humanity. Tolkien and Martin are attempting to yank modern fantasy in entirely contrary directions on Frye's spectrum of narrative tone. Tolkien, to be clear, was yanking as hard as Martin. His approach should not be taken (least of all by virtue of being his) as the organic state of modern fantasy. The espousal of Middle-earth by Martin's generation was instrumental in cementing fantasy as a commercial genre (Manlove 1999 57). But Tolkien did not invent the form, and his subtraction of lavatorial discourse therefrom contrasts with some of his predecessors and contemporaries. Jack Vance's *The Dying Earth* (1950) describes plants that fart (18). The heroes of E.R. Eddison's *The Worm Ouroboros* (1922), for all their love of "the high arts of war" (502), possess a sense of humour few hobbits would descend to. They tease an enemy herald for having a tail (23). Besieged, they interrupt the villain's offer of terms with "a deluge of slops and offal and all filth that came to hand" from their battlements; "A bucketful took Corund in the mouth" (184). Such larrikinism inflects Eddison's larger-than-life heroes with a measure of levity, a sense of young men on a rollicking adventure, capable of not just handling life-or-death situations but of enjoying them. Such behaviour would, however, shatter the chill solemnity of Gandalf's rejoinders to the Messenger of Sauron ("it is also the custom for ambassadors to use less insolence." [*Return* 1,164]). For that matter, when Lobelia Sackville-Baggins inveighs against the followers of Sharkey, she tars them with no insult more graphic than "dirty" (1,326). Tolkien's erasure of lavatorial discourse fosters a modal buoyancy; Lobelia's prosaic pride blossoms into righteous defiance. Not all subsequent fantasists have followed suit. Vance's *Lyonesse* (1983) depicts a prince who drools (20), a cook who urinates in his lordship's soup (264), judicial disembowelments (45–46) and an ogre who must visit the privy (234), not to mention a putative protagonist who dies halfway through the first volume of a trilogy. Harry Potter's classmates contend with constipation spells and earwax-flavoured candy. So Martin's lavatorial discourse is not unique. It does, however, serve a clear, pervasive, polemical purpose in his song. It repeatedly undercuts the high mimesis his characters aspire to, sending them hurtling into Frye's ironic mode on a chute greased with substances best not dwelt upon. In this sense, Martin is essentially the American *anti*-Tolkien.

An equivalency between writers is only useful insofar as it illustrates something further about one or another of the authors in question. With that point in mind, however, it is interesting to observe the remarkable parallels between Martin and Terry Pratchett. Despite Pratchett's avowedly comic intent, the two authors have a great deal in common. These commonalities go far beyond the frequently evoked squalor of Pratchett's city of Ankh-Morpork (*Hogfather* 163; *Jingo* 120; *Sorcery* 63). Both frequently play with Frye's modalities, structuring crucial points of characterisation around differentials between what the characters and readers appreciate. Pratchett invests considerable creativity pouring affectionate scorn on the excesses of Frye's higher modes, often by having his loftier characters overlook simple practicalities:

> The air took on a thick, greasy feel, and the deep shadows around Mort became edged with blue and purple rainbows. The rider strode towards him, black cloak billowing and feet making little clicking sounds on the cobbles. They were the only noises; silence clamped down on the square like great drifts of cotton wool.
>
> The impressive effect was rather spoiled by a patch of ice.
> OH, BUGGER. (*Mort* 20–21)

If Death really walks the streets as the cowled skeleton of medieval (or possibly medievalist) folklore, Pratchett reasons, he must be as vulnerable as anybody else to certain mishaps. Death has therefore slipped and fallen on his skeletal backside, taking the gravitas of the mythic mode with him. Such pratfalls are common in Pratchett's world. Grim reapers, stone trolls, witch's covens and even gods lose much of their emotional impact when subjected to the sort of low-mimetic interrogation from which Frye's ironic mode is derived. Pratchett's characters tend to be presented as sympathetic depending on the extent to which they grasp this. By applying this yardstick, Pratchett often creates *alazons* very similar to Martin's.

Such categorisation is often the result of a peculiarly sophisticated form of toilet humour. Like Martin, Pratchett refuses to practice fantasy of subtraction. "You are allowed to make pigs fly," he avers, "but you must take into account [...] the need for people in heavily over-flown areas to carry stout umbrellas at all times" ("Notes from a Successful Fantasy Author" 85). Death takes an apprentice partly because his horse produces dung; "up to [his] knees in horseshit," he needed someone to muck out the stable (*Mort* 47). When a character observes that it must be glamorous to have a baby dragon perched on one's shoulder, dragon-breeder Sybil Ramkin retorts:

> "Oh, it *sounds* nice, I'll grant you. Then they realise it means soot burns, frizzled hair and crap all down their back. Those talons dig in, too. And then they think the thing's getting too big and smelly

> and next thing you know it's either down the Morpork Sunshine Sanctuary for Lost Dragons or the old heave-ho into the river with a rope around your neck, poor little buggers. (*Guards! Guards!* 124–125)

In Ramkin's kennels, "The temperature was terrible, but not as bad as the cocktail of smells" (128). Compare this to Smaug's lair in *The Hobbit*, whose occupant, monstrous though he is, smells Bilbo rather than vice versa (199–200). Smaug is influenced, if not directly inspired, by the dragons of *Beowulf* and *Volsungasaga*, scions of Frye's romantic mode and sources of literary effects that would be spoiled by the sight and smell of animal droppings. Pratchett sets up a "dispassionate construction…born from the low mimetic" (Frye 40–41) around that conceit, innocently pondering what large, volatile animals would actually smell like. In trying to be glamorous, the less astute Discworlders merely end up grubby – *alazons* open to criticism by their intellectual betters both inside and outside the text.

Compare Ramkin's irritation to Tyrion Lannister's at an attempt at fairy-tale glamour in Westeros:

> "Symon says there's to be seventy-seven courses and a hundred doves baked into a great pie," Shae gushed. "When the crust's opened, they'll all burst out and fly."
>
> "After which they will roost in the rafters and rain down birdshit on the guests." Tyrion had suffered such wedding pies before. The doves liked to shit on *him* especially, or so he had always suspected. (*Storm* 1.170)

Doves have digestive systems. Martin invites his readers to judge his characters intellectually based on the extent to which they grasp that this inescapable anatomical point contradicts the attractive symbolism with which human conceit has burdened these unassuming animals. Shae's gushing credulity makes her a perfect *alazon*, closely akin to Ramkin's less astute customers. There are parts of this story she simply has not considered, and Martin, like Pratchett, carefully emphasises her poor grasp of her situation. His vector for doing so – Tyrion – also echoes Pratchett's more astute characters. Like Tyrion, Pratchett's Granny Weatherwax is happy to claim – and arguably abuse – the privileges of her station (*Maskerade* 26–28). She retains reader sympathy as someone who appreciates that it is possible to over-dramatise oneself. "Never pick yourself a name you can't scrub the floor in" (379), she admonishes while digging her new privy, advice that closely echoes Tyrion's reminder to Shae that certain realities cannot be ignored. Similarly, Death sees himself as a sort of eschatological bureaucrat, gets the job done and expresses contempt for pretenders who behave dramatically (*Reaper Man* 239). Martin and

Pratchett both use Frye's ironic mode to explode the conceits of the higher modes, and deploy characters who at least episodically see through those conceits in order to emphasise the follies of those who do not.

The parallels between these two authors continue. Pratchett's mocking of literary convention pointedly stops short of any dismissal of the behaviour those conventions celebrate. Several of his plots involve villains exploiting the supernatural facts around them to selfish or destructive ends, and heroes going to great lengths to set things right. In *Hogfather,* a desire for fame (30) moves the assassin Teatime to use the teeth collected by tooth fairies to control Discworld's children and dispel their belief in their equivalent of Santa Claus, who therefore ceases to exist. Death surreptitiously takes on the duties of the Hogfather. The slapstick of an animate skeleton bumbling his magnanimously literal-minded way through Christmas folklore culminates in an explanation of why he went to that effort:

> "All right," said Susan. "I'm not stupid. You're saying humans need...*fantasies* to make life bearable."
>
> REALLY? AS IF IT WAS SOME KIND OF PINK PILL? NO. HUMANS NEED FANTASY TO BE HUMAN. TO BE THE PLACE WHERE THE FALLING ANGEL MEETS THE RISING APE.
>
> "Tooth fairies? Hogfathers? Little –"
>
> YES. AS PRACTICE. YOU HAVE TO START OUT LEARNING TO BELIEVE THE *LITTLE* LIES.
>
> "So we can believe the big ones?"
>
> YES. JUSTICE. MERCY. DUTY. THAT SORT OF THING. (270)

Those sorts of things are lies, Death elaborates, in that they are not materially verifiable features of the universe. The qualities lumped together under the telling label "humanity" are abstractions that exist only insofar as people have enough faith in them to practice them. Such work is hard and ongoing. Death's unconventional night's work was a stopgap to keep Discworld's children in the habit until Susan could put this "HUMAN THING" (262) to rights. *Hogfather*, among other Discworld novels, is a meditation on how stories shape society for better or worse depending on how they are approached. Pratchett mocks the letter of literary tropes in order to highlight the spirit in which they were – in his inventive estimation – intended.

Martin's story parallels Pratchett's. Deprived of the inherent dignity of high mimesis, his characters must work for the reader's respect. Not all of them bother. This is unsurprising given Martin's scepticism about the power of idealised social institutions to police human behaviour:

> Chivalry was among the most idealistic codes the human race has ever come up with for a warrior. These are men who were sworn to

> protect the weak. Then you look at the reality, and their brutality was extreme. (Hibberd)

The theme of characters failing to live up to chivalric ideals in Martin's work needs little introduction. What is worth noting is that this trend generally results from a genuine – albeit horrendous – misunderstanding of what vows, titles and mottos really are. That is, Martin's unsympathetic characters misread the stories they have told or heard about themselves. Ser Boros Blount mechanically beats a defenceless girl, then gallantly leaps to the defence of her persecutor (*Clash* 442–443), seemingly ignorant of how silly this makes him look. He understands the letter of his vows, but not the spirit in which they were intended, and lazily used them as an excuse for dreadful behaviour rather than a spur to self-improvement. Cersei Lannister always fancied herself a great ruler, but her silly, paranoid regency demonstrates that this conceit never moved her to any of the effort that her father and less-favoured brother obviously put into actually acquiring political skill – she sees herself as having been literally born great. If the political mismanagement of her regency does not settle the matter, then her lavatorial sense of humour – considering rumours of Tyrion working in a brothel "droll" (*Feast* 603) and imagining herself defecating on his severed head (285) – does so conclusively. One cannot convincingly keep one's nose in the air when one's mind is in the gutter. Viserys Targaryen, more straightforwardly, seems to forget he is only a metaphorical dragon. These characters are egregiously overlooking something in Westeros's elaborate traditions of noble warriors, assertive kings and totemic animals. True or otherwise, that folklore contains valuable lessons, but these characters view it as collection of excuses for obnoxious self-assertion. Thus, Martin ensures those characters cannot reproduce those stories; he presents them as *alazons*, victims of irony whose actions exclude them from the exact social class they feel they belong to. As in Pratchett, much of the conflict and suffering in Martin's story stems from people exploiting excuses for self-aggrandisement in stories whose potential as spurs to self-improvement has eluded them.

A number of Martin's characters, however, do think through the stories they lean on. The obvious example is Eddard Stark, whose habit of speaking in pieties (*Game* 20; 110; 295; 341) would be insufferable were it not backed up by his actual behaviour. But he does put the work in, and reader sympathy remains with him as he is confused, disappointed and victimised by those who do not share his disciplined practice of morally accountable warrior aristocracy. Qhorin Halfhand's role in the story is similar, to die in a line of duty he has thought through and takes far more seriously than many of his fellows. Jon Snow's experiences north of the Wall are the opposite of Khal Drogo's in Essos, moving from low to high mimesis. They begin with the bathetic failure of the wildlings to adhere to their fearsome reputation. Craster's Keep is "a midden heap, a pig sty, an empty sheepfold and a windowless wattle-and-daub hall scarce worth the name" (*Clash* 324), Craster himself a petty tyrant rather than a fierce warrior, making an ass of the stories Jon heard from Old Nan. "Perhaps he had not heard the stories" (326), Jon notes, adding a jab of diegetic irony to match that of the heterodiegetic narrator. By the conclusion of *A Clash of Kings*, however, Jon is intoning his shared oath with the legendary Qhorin Halfhand:

> When they were done, there was no sound but the faint crackle of the flames and the distant sigh of the wind. Jon opened and closed his burned fingers, holding tight to the words in his mind, praying that his father's gods would give him the strength to die bravely when his hour came. It would not be long now. (853)

Here are two warriors, grizzled veteran and anxious tyro, reaffirming their vows to die at their posts with no witnesses but a dramatic wilderness of eagles, mountains and "ravines so deep and black they seemed certain to end in some hell" (667). Halfhand has thought though his oath and understands its implications. He is not motivated by malice – "Only fools like Thoren Smallwood despise the wildlings" (690) – but he is quite willing to expend his life to combat his foe, *because that is what he promised to do*. Jon comes to respect Qhorin and his men not for their landcraft or martial prowess but for their ability to keep an oath – that is, to make a story they told about themselves true, even if doing so hurts, as indeed it does. Martin's tale is not a straightforward dismissal of the sort of heroic values evident in ancient and medieval literature. Like Pratchett, he is aware of the potential that notions as honour and duty have for bringing out the good in people. Martin's heroes, therefore, are those who understand they cannot simply "sew some beast upon a scrap of silk" and fancy themselves "lions or dragons or eagles" (*Dance* 31). Like Pratchett he encourages his readers to look up to those who view aristocratic titles, dynastic mottos and chivalric oaths not as licenses but as job descriptions.

As on Discworld, therefore, a particular insight into the nature of stories is required to enjoy the satisfaction and reputations that Westerosi chivalry and aristocracy impart. Such notions are indeed lies, but they are told to encourage moral literacy. Martin, therefore, depicts two distinct strata of characters, differentiated not so much morally as intellectually. Characters such as Boros Blount, Viserys Targaryen and Cersei Lannister either miss the point of their aristocratic identity, or try to bend its technicalities to selfish ends. This behaviour is essentially identical to that of Pratchett's Mister Teatime, whose desire for fame leads him to plan and attempt a folkloric atrocity. Meanwhile, the likes of Eddard Stark and Qhorin Halfhand grasp that society leans heavily upon a handful of abstract conceits and that the core business of any aristocracy – any "rule by the best" – is, by definition, to embody those virtues. Susan Sto Helit, whose desire to be normal (*Hogfather* 24–25) is thwarted by her familial obligation to engage in hair-raising adventures required to re-establish the very concept of normality, does the same in Pratchett's world. As a result, there is something to Johnston's claim (148–150; cf. Saham 62) that Martin's work constitutes a critique, rather than a dismissal, of chivalric ideals. In making his critique, Martin follows exactly the same authorial strategies as Terry Pratchett, and directs reader sympathy to exactly the same caste of characters.

That sympathy is directed in a way that constitutes a final parallel with Pratchett's work. At the climaxes of their stories, Discworlders often find themselves in supernatural situations which Pratchett keeps largely free of bathos. The appearance of the revivified Hogfather (262–269) illustrates the point. Comic similes occur during Susan's ride to save him, but the scene generates more tension than laughter. Flying leaps are reported in terms of aesthetic impact rather than plausibility; magical beings carry their full weight of drama; the staid governess fights heroically and dismisses defeated foes with pugnacious insults. Death becomes "a gaunt figure in a flapping black robe" (265), in no immediate danger of slipping and falling. The pattern continues in other Discworld novels, notably those involving Granny Weatherwax, who repeatedly finds herself in formidably straight-faced moral debates in supernatural spaces about which few jokes can be imagined, much less told (*Carpe Jugulum* 183–186; *Witches Abroad* 275–277). At the sharp end of his narratives, Pratchett abandons irony and begins writing in a close approximation of Frye's higher modes.

Martin follows suit. He employs the ironic mode to reduce the stature of those who miss the point of their stories, but at auspicious moments, his sympathetic characters are permitted a particular brand of dignity. One such instance takes place when Ser Meryn Trant leads a posse to collect Arya Stark from her "dancing master":

> Syrio Forel stepped between them, tapping his wooden sword lightly against his boot. "You will be stopping there. Are you men or dogs, that you would threaten a child?"
>
> "Out of the way, old man," one of the red cloaks said.
>
> Syrio's stick came whistling up and rang against his helm. "I am Syrio Forel, and you will now be speaking to me with more respect."
>
> "Bald bastard." The man yanked free his longsword. The stick moved blindingly fast. Arya heard a loud *crack* as the sword went clattering to the stone floor. "My *hand*," the guardsman yelped, cradling his broken fingers.
>
> "You are quick, for a dancing master," said Ser Meryn.
>
> "You are slow, for a knight," Syrio replied. (*Game* 514)

This is not merely a depiction of a mercenary morally outpacing an anointed knight. Nor is it the ignorant stoicism of Khal Drogo or Victarion Greyjoy, still less the parochial bravado of Desmond (339). Forel grasps, broadly, what is happening here. Yet he does not wet himself, miss his target, fall from his horse or even fumble his lines. Martin provides a clear view of his prowess and panache, a reminder of his name and a report of his pithily devastating indictment of his foe. This is a heroic last stand, a warrior living his code, making sure the stories he tells about himself – "the first sword of Braavos does not run" (515) – are actually true. Syrio Forel is, in short, spared low-mimetic interrogation; he dies an unsullied, high-mimetic death.

So too do Qhorin Halfhand and his men. Indeed, there appears to be something in the water at Shadow Tower, which turns out Watchmen as different from those of Castle Black – the spiteful Alliser Thorne, the oafish Grenn, the nefarious Chett – as Sansa's imagined knights and ladies are to Gregor Clegane and Cersei Lannister. Jon recognises Qhorin by his mere aura and must scamper to keep up with his "long strides" (*Clash* 566–567). As he camps with the Shadow Tower men, Jon makes no observations about their privy pits; Qhorin and his troop do not defecate. What they do instead is share their commander's drive to live up to their own expectations:

> "We are not far from the place the wildlings died," said Qhorin. "From there, one man could hold a hundred. The right man." He looked at Squire Dalbridge.
>
> The squire bowed his head. "Leave me as many arrows as you can spare, brothers." He stroked his longbow. "And see my garron has an apple when you're home. He's earned it, poor beastie."
> *He's staying to die*, Jon realised.
> Qhorin clasped the squire's forearm with a gloved hand. "If the eagle flies down for a look at you…"
> "…he'll sprout some new feathers."
> The last Jon saw of Squire Dalbridge was his back, as he clambered up the narrow path to the heights. (*Clash* 697)

Charged with a suicide mission, Dalbridge does not weep, argue or flee, much less wet himself (cf. *Storm* 1.17). He merely takes a moment to collect his thoughts – a point that reminds the reader of the heart that beats under the black cloak for which he is about to die. He kills the boy inside him and does his duty as a man of the Watch, voicing not one but two witty quips about the situation. Jon Snow, long since cured of any sense of drama or romance about his colleagues or the institution they serve (*Game* 172), suddenly finds one of them behaving exactly like a character in a song. Martin repeats the technique when Qhorin himself dies, endowing Halfhand with the presence of mind to applaud Jon's newfound conscientiousness even as "the blood gushed out of him" (*Clash* 860). For all that Martin peppers his tale with deflations of romantic ideals, for all that he observes that dying warriors "never screamed or begged for mercy in the songs" (*Game* 523), this is not a straightforward dismissal of literary heroism. Martin suspends his prevailing ironic mode in order to dramatise those who genuinely take it upon themselves to live their ideals.

The infamous Red Wedding owes much of its power to the fact that it follows this pattern. Robb and Catelyn Stark claim protection under Westeros's law of guest-right, a code Catelyn labours ahead of time to ensure that Robb (and the reader) understands it (*Storm* 2.99–2.100). This custom is apparently inspired by the codes of hospitality practiced in heroic literature such as Homer's *Odyssey*; the results of Walder Frey's treachery certainly recall those sources. Robb, a young man doing his best to be his absent father's son, goes down staggering towards his mother across the blood-splattered hall of those who have disingenuously exploited his culture's customs, a ghastly reshuffling of the story of Homer's Telemachus. Catelyn lasts some 1,300 words (2.131–2.134) with a quarrel in her back, nine times what Martin allows Tywin Lannister. Blood runs over her hands, not her pubic hair; she retains her presence of mind, power of speech and – which is more than can be said for Lannister – bowel control to the last. Her thoughts include the observation that "She had lived too long, and Ned was waiting," a statement of bullish, assertive Thanatos recalling Leonidas's admonition to his men that after the Battle of Thermopylae they would dine in Hades (Diodorus Siculus 11.9.4). She finally loses her composure by way of an epic simile:

> The tears burned like vinegar as they ran down her cheeks. Ten fierce ravens were raking her face with sharp talons and tearing off strips of flesh, leaving deep furrows that ran red with blood. (2.133)

She is tearing her cheeks with her nails (cf. 2.553), a ritualised gesture of grief depicted by, among others, Aeschylus (*The Libation Bearers* 24–25), the most grandiose of the Greek tragedians. Catelyn's death is a catalogue of high-mimetic tropes, allowed to run their course and achieve their impact. Such rhetoric means the propaganda victory the Starks win in Westeros (*Dance* 285) is anticipated among Earthly observers. Martin's interrogation of the stories societies tell about themselves labours under a pall of cynical irony, but within every cynic lurks a frustrated idealist. The impact of events like the Red Wedding lies in Martin's ability to get his readers sharing his frustration. Like Pratchett, he accomplishes this by spiking his irony with episodes that evoke the higher modes from which he borrowed his ideals.

At heart, Martin's fantasy is not morally innovative. His characters, though sometimes labyrinthine examples of moral ambiguity, are part of a long tradition of such creations in modern fantasy. Mervyn Peake, J.K. Rowling and J.R.R. Tolkien all depict evil as a human problem, using magic to highlight the issue rather than settle it. Indeed, Tolkien codifies the use of fantasy contrivances as points of contrast by which authors and readers can Recover such matters from the contempt born of familiarity, identifying this as a core function of the literary fantastic going back to the birth of Anglophone literature. Rather than bucking this trend, Martin in fact reiterates it is a particularly clear manner. The "looming catastrophe" (Garcia and Antonsson x) of the Others accentuates the destructive folly of the game of thrones, providing a textbook example of Tolkienian Recovery. What makes Martin's work distinct from Tolkien's is not his moral universe but his adoption of Frye's ironic mode. Tolkien's power lies partly in his well-informed command of high mimesis, clearing away the meaner realities of human existence in order to focus attention on the more resonant matter of where good and evil come from. Concerned with the same core issue, Martin nevertheless takes exactly the opposite approach, dunking characters into irony via constant low-mimetic intrusions upon the glamorous conceits they cling to. His readers look down on a society of grubby, indignant *alazons* tragicomically scrabbling for what little dignity their creator allows them in his rigorous interrogation of their claims of moral authority. This closely parallels the authorial strategies of Terry Pratchett, whose smelly dragons, earthy witches and accident-prone pale riders similarly deflate Frye's higher modes and the pretentions of those who fail to grasp the purpose of such notions. In their scepticism, however, Martin and Pratchett clearly share a regard for the ideals – courage, duty, honour – which those modes celebrate, and for the power of stories to promote that behaviour. Both authors therefore carefully deploy high mimesis to glorify their morally literate characters. That is to say that in both the Discworld novels and *A Song of Ice and Fire*, the narrative eye of God helps those who help themselves. The great stories of the past can come true, but only for those who grasp their actual purpose. This concern shows Martin doing the same thing as Tolkien, Pratchett and indeed all resonant fantasists – he is writing about what humanity is, and how it gets that way.

2 "Enough about Whores" – Sex and Characterisation

Upon his arrival in King's Landing, Eddard Stark faces an immediate headache. He must organise the Tournament of the Hand, an extravagance and more a treat for King Robert than his incoming aide; "Seven hells, Ned," the king says when the grand day arrives, "I want to *hit* someone" (*Game* 298). The tournament is a celebration of high-mimetic virtues, of courage, martial prowess, largesse and lineage. As such, however, it furthers Martin's modally ironic critique of such values. Someone has to pay for this. The pageantry strains the finances of the realm and the civil order of the capital, which are Eddard's problems, not Robert's, neatly underlining the latter's observation that "The king eats and the hand takes the shit" (44). But, notes Petyr Baelish, it has its benefits:

> "Every inn in the city is full, and the whores are walking bow-legged and jingling with each step."
>
> Lord Renly laughed. "We're fortunate my brother Stannis is not with us. Remember the time he proposed to outlaw brothels? The king asked him if perhaps he'd like to outlaw eating, shitting and breathing while he was at it. If truth be told, I oftimes wonder how Stannis ever got that ugly daughter of his. He goes to his marriage bed like a man marching to a battlefield, with a grim look in his eyes and a determination to do his duty." (265)

The council laughs, except Stark, who concludes the meeting by wearily noting "I have heard quite enough about whores for one day" (266). Readers could be forgiven for agreeing with him. References to sex, commercialised and otherwise, are as prominent a feature of Martin's text as those to dirt and odour. Stannis in fact gets off rather lightly in this regard. Renly's sex life is the basis of an abiding point of narrative tension and almost everybody else has their sexual mores bared, at least briefly, for the reader's consideration. Even seven-year-old Bran Stark's innocence is signalled by his confused observation of Queen Cersei's infidelity (80). Other children are more precocious, something Cersei either fails or refuses to grasp:

> "My son is too young to care about such things."
> "You think so?" asked Tyrion. "He's thirteen, Cersei. The same age at which I married."
> "You shamed us all with that sorry episode. Joffrey is made of finer stuff."
> "So fine he had Ser Boros rip off Sansa's gown."
> "He was angry with the girl."
> "He was angry with the cook's boy who spilled the soup last night as well, but he didn't strip him naked."
> "This was not a matter of some spilled soup – "
> *No, it was a matter of some pretty teats.* (*Clash* 480)

Tyrion Lannister keeps the last observation to himself, but he is only a focaliser for Martin's heterodiegetic narration (Napolitano 43). This voice allows Martin to show Tyrion's appreciation that his thirteen-year-old nephew is abusing his authority to satisfy his emerging curiosity about the female form and also to remind readers that such insight stems in significant part from the Imp's own partiality for pretty teats. The fact that this invented culture includes a slang term for the sexualised female breast demonstrates that this authorial focus is entirely conscious.

Such discourse has naturally attracted attention, particularly as it has found its way into *Game of Thrones*. Shortly after the premiere of the show reviewer Myles McNutt coined the term *sexposition* to describe the supposed practice of the show's writers sweetening the pill of expository dialogue by pairing it with sexual imagery. The idea that this discourse is a marketing exercise, a sop to unsophisticated audiences, is very much part of the reception of the series (Frankel 2014 7–8). *Entertainment Weekly* has quoted Maisie Williams, who plays Arya Stark, joking that the show's opening music should be embellished with a lyrical refrain: "Death and boobies, death and boobies, death and boobies." On her show *Funny Girls*, comedian Rose Matafeo addressed Martin directly on the point – "We get it, George. You've never actually kissed a girl." As the show's success has invigorated interest in Martin's books, his sexual discourse has become a focus of scholarly attention as well. Much of the feminist criticism that Martin's tale has received to date has focussed on the carnal politics of Westeros. Frankel has noted that Martin's women "rule with their bodies" (2014 7), gaining power through carnal subjection to a patriarchal regime. She thus queries the extent to which the prominence of female characters actually results in their strength or empowerment. The matter of sexual violence in Westeros has particularly come under interrogation. Such criticism is obviously warranted. At the risk of callous understatement, sexual violence is an unpleasant and emotive business; those who would perpetuate it in fiction had best have an explanation prepared for why they would confront their readers in that way. The purpose of this chapter is to examine the themes of sex and sexual violence in Martin's narrative, and to reveal that the former is not gratuitous, and the latter not glorified. As Alyssa Rosenberg has observed, Westerosi sex serves as a sort of moral litmus test – "it's sexual misconduct that signifies monstrosity" (17).

Rosenberg is onto something here. As with Martin's discussion of medievalist filth, his depiction of his character's sex lives, consensual and otherwise, is simply too prominent to be passed off as an exercise in realism. Such discussion contributes to the ironic critique of aristocratic values identified in the previous chapter. Low-mimetic intrusions on the self-bestowed dignity of his aristocratic characters remind readers that these grand folk are as human as the peasantry they presume to rule. A character's sexual imagination often serves to demonstrate the strength, or weakness, of their grounds for such presumption. With this point in mind, Wolfgang Iser's phenomenological model of reading becomes relevant to the discussion. Although Martin's sexual discourse is frequently graphic, its central purpose is to create shadowy, semi-formulated areas of narrative discourse. Some of Martin's most vivid characters owe their impact to the hints about their overall personality raised by descriptions of their sexual behaviour. As readers ponder such ambiguities they are, per Iser, drawn into Martin's creative process. He directs such engagement, furthermore, in a manner that parallels the authorial strategies of the classic Gothic novelists. Concerned, like Martin, with the perceived barbarities of history, Gothic authors typically illustrate their point by contriving situations in which those barbarities are visited on characters who display discernibly modern manners and attitudes, and can thus appreciate the enormity of what they were suffering. Martin uses sexual behaviour to set some of his characters up in similar positions, highlighting the crimes of others. Put simply, he uses sex as a way of encouraging readers to consider the way his characters interact with his world.

That world is not a pleasant one. "Hyperviolence" note Finke and Shichtman, has also "always been a cinematic convention of the medieval, part of our fantasy of the Middle Ages as a barbaric past" (59) Martin, interested in depicting the "extreme brutality" (Hibberd) attributed to medieval regimes (Hackeny 133), draws on this tradition. His world is one of "chaotic cruelty" (Napolitano 52). Having used dirt to explode the notion that the various aristocracies of his world are any sort of breed apart, Martin then has them presumptuously dole out shocking forms of corporal and capital punishment. The Wise Masters of Yunkai stone runaway slaves (*Dance* 728–729). Dothraki horselords maim those they view as impudent (*Game* 224) and are ingenious in circumventing the sanctuary of Vaes Dothrak (482–483). The lords of Westeros have miscreants flogged (*Storm* 1.56) burned (*Dance* 946–952) and disembowelled (143). King Joffrey offers a notionally seditious singer the privilege of choosing between losing his fingers or his tongue (*Game* 721). Such unselfconscious violence combines with the bathetic humanisation of Martin's lavatorial discourse to extend his ironic critique of medieval aristocracy by demonstrating the flimsiness of their claims of inborn moral authority. Western literature has a long history of allowing (mostly) men of a certain stature to get away with violence. The Roman hero Aeneas vengefully kills Turnus (*Aeneid* 12.946–12.952); the Nordic smith Volund, captured and put to work by King Nithuth, kills his captor's children and makes trinkets from their eyes (*Volundarkvitha* 24–25); the Polynesian hero Maui slows the sun by matter-of-factly beating it into submission. Such behaviour takes place in accordance with the truths of the heroic code; one who imprisons a smith capable of working wonders is asking for trouble. As established in Chapter 1, however, most of Martin's characters lack such illustrious modality, and thus come across as people who simply do not value human life particularly highly. Note the pettiness of the spoils Ser Gregor Clegane takes from the Riverlands – "a little gold, a little silver, a great sack of copper pennies and a dented goblet set with garnets that two soldiers almost came to blows over [...] a dozen pigs, a cage of chickens, a scrawny milk cow and nine wagons of salt fish [and] one girl prettier than the others" (*Clash* 376–378). For all his stature, Clegane is a small man, not even a particularly ambitious thief. As such his cartoonish acts of violence – beheading the pretty girl when she causes problems, for instance – become all the more appalling. Less nakedly villainous characters get something of the same treatment. Ser Vardis Egan's worst crime is his humourlessness. When tasked with facing Tyrion Lannister in trial by combat, however, he objects not because such duels are juristically nonsensical but because there is no honour in killing the physically incapable Lannister (*Game* 408). Attempting to demonstrate morality, Egan instead provides a modally ironic indication that he values a courtly nicety ahead of human well-being. Although careful not to dismiss chivalry out of hand (Hackney 135), Martin emphasises that the moral authority of his invented aristocracy is as suspect as their sanitation.

As Rosenberg asserts, sexual misconduct is a major component of this "indictment of corruption and inhumanity" (27). Joffrey's order to have Ser Boros Blount strip Sansa Stark makes discomforting sense when it is recalled that Joffrey has "always liked" Sansa in that particular dress, which is "tight across her chest" (*Clash* 440). He later confirms his interests by publicly groping her at her wedding (*Storm* 1.386). A teenage boy can be forgiven an interest in a female counterpart's anatomy up to a point, but Joffrey's willingness to abuse his authority in this regard furthers the impression of a morally bankrupt, unfit monarch. The same is true of the king's illustrious grandfather. Tywin Lannister is the head of one of Westeros's great houses, proverbially wealthy, a gifted politician famed for restoring his family to greatness after his father let their reputation falter (*Storm* 2.332). Yet as established in the previous chapter, Tywin receives a sustained modal dressing-down throughout the story, denied high-mimetic grandeur in both life and death. His sex life and sexual imagination contribute significantly to this authorial invective. The presence of Shae in Lannister's bed on the last night of his life dispels much of the mystique he wove around himself; this dour stoic, who never remarried after the death of his wife and who judged his son's libertinism so sternly (*Storm* 1.66), will disport himself with a prostitute behind closed doors. Are we really then to believe Shae was his first such liaison? And did she come to him willingly? She may have done. Even assuming she acted purely on her own commercial interests, however, Lannister has a history of abusing his authority in sexual contexts, arranging and supervising the gang-rape of Tyrion's first wife, a crofter's daughter to whom Tywin did not care to be related (*Game* 443). This is an act of supreme, violent snobbery, revealing a horrifying deficit of the quality he believes he is safeguarding; he is happier as the master of a pack of rapists than as the father-in-law of a peasant. It also demonstrates his willingness to utilise the fouler aspects of his culture to his personal advantage. The stunt relied on his guards being prepared to force themselves on a fourteen-year-old girl, which distressingly proves to have been the case. Tywin is a lord of violence, an enabler of atrocity, and every inch the viper Eddard Stark compares him to (41–42). Tyrion's explanation of this incident is in fact one of the first sustained discussions of Tywin, serving as a pointed corroboration of Stark's opinion. By the time Tywin actually appears, 150 pages after Tyrion tells this story, he is therefore already cemented in the reader's mind as a villain. His subsequent follies – refusing to admit that bringing a horse indoors might be unhygienic – demonstrate the brittleness of the persona he hides behind. His tryst (contract?) with Shae settles the issue; this man can have his eye caught by exactly the same pair of pretty teats that turned Tyrion's head. Martin's depiction of Lannister's sexual imagination moves his critique of the man up a gear. The Warden of the West is not merely a pretentious fool like Khal Drogo but an actively hypocritical villain, an *alazon* of a particularly despicable type, devoid of the moral authority he pretends to. Sex, indeed, sells, and Martin has used it to sell his readers someone they love to hate.

Although this example obviously vindicates Rosenberg, sexual discourse can be used to reinforce a positive image of a character. The introduction of House Stark is a good example. Early depictions of the family include several images – a father telling bedtime stories (*Game* 12), squabbles between sisters (65–66), teenagers conspiring to feed their elders white lies (91), siblings slipping each other contraband (93), an imaginative lad off in a world of his own (74–76) – that would be wholly apropos in a domestic sitcom such as *Full House* or *The Simpsons*. *Game of Thrones* charmingly extends this with Catelyn wordlessly delegating Robb to put the misbehaving Arya to bed ("Winter is Coming"). Such domesticity is only very rarely (*Dance* 86; *Feast* 35) shown among Martin's other houses. Davos Seaworth loves his kids but is only ever shown advising the grown ones on their public careers. Martin takes care to depict the Starks not just as a power bloc but as a family, parents raising children, characters designed to provoke knowing smiles from readers who enjoyed such upbringings themselves. Only Catelyn's spiteful antipathy for Jon Snow (*Game* 90) mars this. Catelyn also, however, provides information that helps solidify her family's wholesome image:

> Her loins still ached from the urgency of his lovemaking. It was a good ache. She could feel his seed within her. She prayed that it might quicken there. It had been three years since Rickon. She was not too old. She could give him another son. (55–56)

Rather than reporting Eddard's bodily fluid in a way that undercuts his dignity, Catelyn exalts in its presence and biological purpose. These are not the thoughts of an alienated woman coldly performing an aristocratic duty. For all that Catelyn resents Jon, she clearly still desires Eddard and values their liaisons as both recreational and procreative exercises. Though this unflinching depiction of the physical realities of sex might seem to contradict the wholesome domesticity of the Starks, it actually furthers that picture. In strict low-mimetic terms, a family is a result of two people engaging in an act that makes them emotionally and physically vulnerable to each other. Depictions of fictional parents doing so with consideration for each other thus connote the integrity of the families they lead by putting to rest any potentially disquieting questions about the origins of those domestic units. To draw an example from the world of television, the "active, even playful" sex life of Marge and Homer Simpson (in the episode "Whacking Day", for example, they banter slyly over their preferred tempo of coitus) has been cited as evidence that *The Simpsons* valorises conventional domesticity (Neuhaus n. 2). It demonstrates that for all their bickering, the family they lead owes its existence to a relationship of love and respect. The healthy married sex life of the Starks – all but unique in Westeros – does the same for them. As in Springfield, this raises potential questions about domestic hegemonies. But in a world where the game of thrones frequently overwhelms the supposedly lofty principles of a medievalist aristocracy, this closely observed ability to uphold some rather more familiar standards of behaviour goes a long way to explaining the Stark's resilient stock of reader sympathy. One suspects that, given the choice, Catelyn would have preferred that this matter not be illustrated quite so graphically; Marge Simpson has never had to deal with post-coital leakage. But this intrusion on her dignity provides physical evidence for the soundness of her family. Martin uses the low-mimetic realities of human sexuality to solidify an image of the Starks as people to be identified with.

This use of sexual discourse is part of a broader theme in Martin's work, and one that furthers his authorial purposes. His aforementioned use of violence adroitly demonstrates the moral deficits of Westerosi society. Competing indications of virtue are vital to prompting emotional engagement, however; a story cannot merely document conflicting agendas. Antagonists must be variegated, however subtly, on a moral spectrum (Hogan 93–94). But Martin cannot simultaneously indicate virtue by simply having certain characters behave more humanely than others. To have a faction of morally assured heroes oppose one of murderous villains would be far too obvious, capping reader involvement rather than encouraging it (Iser 283). Martin is therefore careful to avoid this. The Starks lie to protect each other (Fallis 21–23), conduct warfare with questionable cause (Corrigan 59–60) and pick and choose what crimes they condemn (Hahn 81–82). Sansa, criticised both within the text (*Clash* 739) and without (Johnston 139) for her romantic naiveté, animatedly debates how best to display severed heads (*Game* 458). Such discussion, coming from a eleven-year-old child, demonstrates the ubiquity of Westeros's culture of violence. As Iser argues, however, authors with such concerns cannot confine their narratives to "the penetration of those false appearances that mask all social vices" – as provided by the supposedly abstemious Tywin Lannister's tryst with Shae – which would leave the reader with the "possibility that our superiority is also based upon a misunderstanding" (35). Rather they must prompt the reader to consider and construct models of virtuous behaviour. Such prompting cannot, says Iser, come from the putative subject of the narrative since that discourse is fully formulated by the author (36). Rather the narrative must "shade off" (31) into areas of implied content with which authors can "gently guide" (37) readers towards conclusions the author wishes them to reach. The game of thrones therefore cannot function effectively as an indictment of a flawed regime without some accompanying indication of humanity, and simply having one power bloc conduct the game decently will not convincingly provide this. Catelyn Stark's post-coital contentment, however, illustrates in striking terms that there is at least one respect in which the Starks are conducting themselves more decently than their opponents. Her docility in her arranged marriage may detract from her feminist credentials, but her sex life solidifies an image of moral authority. This is not an isolated example. Fitting naturally into Martin's established pattern of low-mimetic constructions, Martin's game of beds runs parallel to the game of thrones, providing an alternative, implied moral spectrum with which the author can discreetly keep readers orientated in his indictment of bloodthirsty aristocratic presumption. It contributes to the resonance of the tale because it prompts genuine, ongoing engagement in what might otherwise be a 4,500 page (and counting) prose pantomime about smelly, vainglorious idiots lopping each other's appendages off.

Cersei Lannister is an excellent example. Her focalising contributions to *A Feast for Crows*, ceaselessly labouring the chasm between her self-image as a Machiavellian strongwoman and her mismanagement of the kingdom, await future classroom use as textbook examples of Frye's ironic mode. "A thousand years from now," she thinks to her father on his bier, "when the maesters write about this time, you shall be remembered only as Queen Cersei's sire" (*Feast* 115). She then promptly proves herself wrong, as demonstrated when the banker Noho Dimittis complains of having spoken to the Master of Coin six times:

> "Speak to him a seventh time," Cersei suggested pleasantly. "The number seven is sacred to our gods."
>
> "It pleases your grace to make a jest, I see."
>
> "When I make a jest I smile. Do you see me smiling? Do you hear laughter? I assure you, when I make a jest, men laugh."
>
> "King Robert – "
>
> " – is dead," she said sharply. "The Iron Bank will have its gold when this rebellion has been put down."
>
> He had the insolence to scowl at her. "Your Grace – "
>
> "This audience is at an end." Cersei had suffered quite enough for one day. "Ser Meryn, show the noble Noho Dimittis the door. Ser Osmund, you may escort me back to my apartments." Her guests would soon arrive, and she had to bathe and change. Supper promised to be a tedious affair as well. It was hard work to rule a kingdom, much less seven of them. (*Feast* 389)

Her brothers both have lively wits, but the reader must think fairly carefully to come up with any instances of Cersei telling any effective jokes. The last sentence solidifies Cersei's status as an *alazon*; she is, of course, doing anything but ruling seven kingdoms. Martin's first three volumes each provide a first-hand picture of what running a truculent realm actually looks like, and Eddard, Tyrion and Tywin all have cause to complain about workload. Cersei spends her time pursuing personal vendettas, ducking questions, inflaming problems, fracturing alliances and maintaining cosmetic semblances of *noblesse oblige* – wearing the right frocks, smiling the right smiles – rather than actually getting anything done. Her deflection of Noho Dimitis simply leaves a problem to fester, comparing poorly with, for example, Tyrion's industrious preparations for the Baratheon attack on King's Landing. Even within her chosen purview, her self-centredness is striking, as when this supposedly grieving daughter complains inwardly about having to wear unflattering mourning-dress to her father's funeral (111). Naked and shivering on the steps of Baelor's Sept, she is still rejecting Petyr Baelish as low-born

(*Dance* 991), clearly not cured of her pride in the slightest. Cersei has enough low cunning to achieve power, but she has no idea what to do with it, partly because of her uncritical belief that she was born great and will ipso facto make a great ruler.

Were he simply producing a prose pantomime, Martin's presentation of this destructively vain snob could stand on its own as a black-humoured clown act. Again, the medievalist sitcom *The Black Adder* provides an example of such a character. Its speculative Richard IV stamps around his castle roaring threats of violence, ramming swords through doors ("Witchsmeller Pursuivant") and forgetfully sending notes of sympathy to the relatives of people he has just killed ("The Queen of Spain's Beard"). The result generates laughter, but little reflection. Martin clearly hopes to inspire a degree of intellectual and emotional engagement in his story, however. He does so by providing glimpses of Cersei's participation in and commentary on the game of beds, placing her on a second moral continuum that shades away from the putative subject matter of his tale. This plays a major part in Martin's evocation of her folly. Her proto-feminist grievances against Westerosi patriarchy (*Clash* 291; 702) are deflated by striking dismissals of other women. She excoriates Lollys Stokeworth for "getting herself raped" (*Feast* 117), theorises that lowborn women "bled like pigs" on their wedding nights (462) and gracelessly compares Septa Moelle's hymen to leather armour (728). In light of such perceptions, her subsequent reflection that "women were always the cruellest where other women were concerned" (*Dance* 994) sharply underlines her obliviousness, intimating the lack of method in her madness. Her relationship with Jaime has an effect precisely opposite to Catelyn Stark's marital contentment, demonstrating the unwholesome origins of her family, though that in itself appears to be the mere tip of a sinister iceberg. She claims a seemingly mystical connection to Jaime, describing him as a part of her own identity (*Game* 468), yet when he is captured she turns very quickly to her biddable cousin Lancel for sex (*Clash* 405–407). This implies that her relationship with her brother stems less from affection for Jaime than from a narcissistic preoccupation with that which affirms her own beauty ("I don't look as much like Cersei this way," notes Jaime after having his head shaved, "She'll hate that" [*Storm* 1.24]). Indeed Martin, by providing glimpses of Cersei torturing the infant Tyrion to assuage her fury at being warned of the potential negative consequences of beauty (*Feast* 472), seems to be discreetly encouraging an impression that her obsession with her appearance is genuinely unhealthy. This has some unsettling implications for her children. Joffrey, she recalls, had "such lovely lips" (*Dance* 998). This is conspicuous given how few other people she regards as beautiful. – "No man," she recalls, "had ever made her feel as good as she had felt when he took her nipple in his mouth to nurse" (*Feast* 206) – an odd comparison. All this is surely guiding the reader towards a worrisome possibility; had he not died, might Joffrey have become another target of his mother's libido? Might this still await Tommen, or perhaps Myrcella? By raising such questions without answering them Martin is able to prompt the reader to start wondering exactly where the toxic follies of this fool might end, and indeed where they might have begun. Cersei becomes a resonant villain because Martin has used her sexual imagination to delegate some of the most troubling aspects of her capacity as such to the reader, exactly as Iser argues authors must do (51).

By comparison Jaime comes out fairly well. He drops Cersei because of her infidelity rather than the incestuousness of their relationship, but drop her he does, in the process switching his energy from insulting Brienne of Tarth's appearance (*Storm* 1.19) to lecturing his squire on treating camp followers decently (*Feast* 506). This culminates in him considering Cersei's hysterical plea for rescue from her comeuppance long enough for a snowflake to melt on the parchment (761) before rejecting the request. His feelings for Cersei linger, but are not strong enough to sting him into the violent action he once espoused so casually. Where Jaimie's sexual imagination solidifies an impression of a man trying to reconnect with moral standards, however, Cersei's drops troubling hints of chronic intellectual, moral and indeed psychological deficits.

Sandor Clegane's sexual imagination also shades off in a way that demonstrates a great deal about why readers care about this character. Why they would do so is a valid question. The Hound is recognised as a vicious brute by everyone who passes comment upon him, a reputation he makes no attempt to suppress or counteract. His chief purpose in Martin's first two volumes is to harangue Sansa Stark about the iniquity of the world she lives in:

> "There are no true knights, no more than there are gods. If you can't protect yourself, die and get out of the way of those who can. Sharp steel and strong arms rule this world, don't ever believe any different."
>
> She backed away from him. "You're awful."
>
> "I'm honest. It's the world that's awful." (*Clash* 684)

Such pronouncements could serve as cinematic title cards signalling Martin's sceptical medievalism – exactly the sort of didacticism that Iser decries as offering the reader no involvement in the creative process. The cause of Clegane's spite – his grudge against his monstrous brother – is made clear fairly early in the story (*Game* 293–294). During the Battle of Blackwater, however, Clegane somehow finds his way to Sansa Stark's bedroom, where he suddenly becomes more complex:

> He yanked her closer, and for a moment she thought he meant to kiss her. He was too strong to fight. She closed her eyes, wanting

> it to be over, but nothing happened. "Still can't bear to look, can you?" she heard him say. He gave her arm a hard wrench, pulling her around and shoving her down onto the bed. "I'll have that song. Florian and Jonquil, you said." His dagger was out, poised at her throat. "Sing, little bird. Sing for your little life." (*Clash* 783)

A literary scene in which a man forces a woman onto a bed at knifepoint can develop in only a finite number of directions. Yet when Sansa sings a hymn to mercy, Sandor bursts into tears and melts away, leaving her shaken but unhurt. Discomforting as it is to consider the effect of an attempted rape on the perpetrator rather than the victim, this is a fascinating nuance to Clegane's character. In Westeros, where wartime rape is accepted either casually (27; 801) or fatalistically (739), his instinct to commit such an act is predictable. After all, he actively associates himself with the moral shortcomings of the medievalist regime. His inability to go through with the attack, however, sharply differentiates this self-described butcher in Martin's medievalist abattoir (683) from the army straining at the gates a mile away. It calls into question the precise purpose of his claims about the awfulness of the world. Are they the exaltations of a pantomime cynic or the complaints of scared, scarred, confused little boy coping with a profound sense of injustice, a frustrated idealist who once believed in chivalry strongly enough to play with toy knights just as Sansa sang of them? Is this similarity, perhaps, what drew Clegane repeatedly to Sansa? Did the Hound want a *friend*? If so, obviously, he pursued her wrongly, and Martin is careful not clarify the point by having him embark on any broader moral awakening – later, in distress, Clegane wishes he had gone through with the attack (*Storm* 2.464). But the reader is forced to reconsider his statements and motivations in light of a startling qualification on his oft-stated willingness to be part of a problem. The attack perhaps makes most sense considered as an attempt by Clegane to reassert a defensive self-mythology as he flees from a battle being waged with a weapon – fire – that he fears and seeks sanctuary with a friend he hates to admit he wants. The attempt fails. Clegane calls himself a dog, but dogs are, as Varymyr Sixskins observes, "almost human" (*Dance* 9). The scene in Sansa's bedroom turns one of Martin's most vicious medievalist dogs from a clown in a pantomime to the sort of hint at virtue that Iser holds is necessary to make narratives genuinely effective moral indictments.

The sexual discourse of Martin's song therefore promulgates the sort of engagement required by Iser's phenomenological model of reading. Martin's primary subject matter, the game of thrones, is an indictment of a violent, unjust social order. Such an indictment can only fully function in the presence of competing implications of virtue, but making certain characters blameless in that regime would be exactly the sort of stifling compositional over-determination Iser cautions against.

Martin therefore offers sexual morality as an alternative spectrum on which to variegate his characters. Such discussion thus becomes a secondary narrative running parallel to the game of thrones, allowing readers to conjure with characters who might otherwise flatten out into a crowd of tragicomic buffoons and pantomime villains. This grants the readers a creative stake in the characters and therefore deepens their emotional connection to the story. Readers looking for public bases on which to judge these characters would be better-advised to observe to what goes on behind closed doors – or rather, the doors Martin carefully leaves ajar.

The effectiveness of this manner of characterisation is evident in Tyrion Lannister. Martin's favourite focaliser by sheer page count, Tyrion is also a secure fan favourite, which could be seen as odd given that the "twisted little monkey demon" (*Clash* 288) is in no way innocent of cartoonish medieval violence. This point can be demonstrated by comparing Tyrion to another variety of twisted little demons in fantasy fiction, J.R.R. Tolkien's orcs. The agents of a greater evil, the orcs are nevertheless moral beings. Shippey demonstrates how they "recognise the idea of goodness, appreciate humour, value loyalty, trust, group cohesion and the ideal of a higher cause than themselves, and condemn failings from these ideals in others" but have fallen, possibly irretrievably, into bad habits as a result of "their inability to judge their own actions by their own moral criteria" ("Orcs, Wraiths, Wights" 186; 189). Shippey explains this soberingly realistic shortcoming – "They have gotten into their state as willing collaborators with evil through initial weakness or necessity, reinforced by fear, and made to seem more palatable or even admirable by the steady, dulling use of a rhetoric of smartness and shrewdness". That rhetoric often takes the form of off-colour humour; orcs jape and laugh frequently, possessed of an active culture of black comedy (186). Compare this with Tyrion's instructions on how to deal with Symon Silver Tongue, the singer who tries to use the Imp's relationship with Shae to blackmail him:

> "Give him three days, then inform him that Hamish the Harper has broken his arm. Tell him his clothes will never serve for court, so he must be fitted for new garb at once. He'll come with you quick enough." He grimaced. "You may want his tongue, I understand it's made of silver. The rest of him should never be found."
>
> Bronn grinned. "There's a pot shop I know in Flea Bottom makes a savory bowl of brown. All kinds of meat in it, I hear."
>
> "Make certain I never eat there." Tyrion spurred to a trot. He wanted a bath, and the hotter the better. (*Storm* 1.433)

Tyrion "grimaces" at the task he is ordering, clearly aware of its implications, but gives the order anyway, then trots home to cleanse himself like Macbeth at the well. Like orcs, he and Bronn are moral beings who know what they are doing is disgusting and do it anyway, deflecting the gravity of their actions with dark humour. Such behaviour is also comparable to that of the Mountain's Men when similar crimes are ordered. "One of the captives was always begging for food," Raff the Sweetling admits, "so Ser said to give him roast goat" (*Feast* 453). So Tyrion is guilty of grave crimes, equal in most respects to those of Gregor Clegane's men, and like those men – or Tolkien's orcs – offers little defence for his actions beyond some defensive, trivialising jokes. Yet the Mountain's Men are villains receiving scant sympathy as Arya Stark and her enablers (Jaqen H'ghar, Sandor Clegane) begin to cut a swathe through them, whereas Tyrion remains a character in whom readers have an ongoing investment. Are his jokes really good enough to excuse cold-blooded, self-interested, premeditated murder? Judged by his conduct in the game of thrones, Tyrion would seem to be as guilty of medievalist savagery as anybody else in the story.

His conduct in the game of beds, however, is vastly different. His habit of consorting with prostitutes is risky behaviour. Laying aside moral objections as subjective, it is surely uncontroversial to observe that prostitution places one participant in a sexual encounter at the disposal of another, heightening the risk of objectification and abuse present in such situations. Tyrion is guilty of this. Compare his immediate appraisal of Shae's erotic appeal ("she was doe-eyed and slim, with small firm breasts and a smile that was by turns shy, insolent and wicked") with his relief that she can convincingly conceal her opinions of him (*Game* 655–656). When he slaps her during a subsequent quarrel, her only recourse is a "wooden" apology for being "impudent" (*Clash* 580). The blow illustrates the inequity of the relationship. Yet, Tyrion's focalisation of the episode is devoid of any indignation at the presumptuousness of a woman he is not paying for her opinions. Instead, Martin uses his authorial access to Tyrion's thoughts to communicate immediate contrition; "I never meant to strike you. Gods be good, am I turning into Cersei?" The tale of Tysha spills out, a clumsy but genuine attempt to explain why Shae's jibe about his father upset him so much. To be very clear, none of this makes Shae's cheek feel any better. But it does show that Tyrion finds his own actions unacceptable, which wholly differentiates him from his father. Tywin dismissively calculates that Tysha was "well paid for her day's work" (*Storm* 2.498) – adequately remunerated, he reasons, she had no reason to complain about her treatment. Laying aside the fact that Tysha was not a prostitute at all, this is the sort of objectification that prostitution can prompt when viewed sufficiently cynically by patrons. Tyrion is clearly capable of lapsing into a similar frame of mind himself. But upon doing so, he is disturbed by his own actions and falls over himself to account for them. With this point in mind, it becomes harder to ignore that he ordered the murder of Symon not to protect his reputation but to shield Shae from his family's hypocritical retribution.

Tyrion's concern for the consequences of his actions on ladies of the evening is a pattern of behaviour. After the prostitute Alayaya takes a flogging intended for Shae, he commends the girl's bravery, castigating himself for not appreciating the danger he put her in (*Storm* 1.56), and later offers what compensation he can, regretting his inability to apologise in person (1.172). One cannot imagine many of her other clients, even those who have jade bracelets to pass out, behaving this way. Bronn and Oberyn Martell both merely praise Alayaya's professional skills (1.172; 2.334). Raised in a culture that attaches spiritual significance to carnality (*Clash* 216; *Feast* 595), she may value such compliments. But Tyrion is the only person to describe her as brave, an adjective he also applies to Shae (*Clash* 581), and not a quality one looks for in a mere bedwarmer. This is a considerable mercy compared to the medievalist attitude of some members of his family to retainers hired for their female anatomy. "You're just a milk cow," Oberyn reports Cersei informing Tyrion's wet-nurse. "Be quiet or I'll have my father cut your tongue out. A cow doesn't need a tongue, only udders" (*Storm* 1.525). Cersei clearly took to animalising the lower orders very early in life. Tyrion seemingly never quite developed the habit. He uses the services of prostitutes, and in doing so is occasionally, odiously, culpable in their abuse (*Dance* 337–338). This does not reflect well on him, but his attitudes towards such abuse differentiate him from his family. His abuses of the prostitute-client dynamic are those of a flawed man forgetting himself, not a medievalist monster.

Tyrion's wont to humanise the dehumanised extends to the bedmates forced upon him. Tywin engineers his son's wedding to Sansa Stark in order to further his construction of a Lannister empire (he has the Westerlands and, through Joffrey, the Crownlands; having Sansa as daughter-in-law will secure the North). Preoccupied with such matters, he specifically tells Tyrion that "The girl's happiness is not my purpose, nor should it be yours" (*Storm* 1.268). But Tyrion does, almost instinctively, value Sansa's happiness:

> "You did not ask for this marriage, I know. No more than I did. If I had refused you, however, they would have wed you to my cousin Lancel. Perhaps you would prefer that. He is nearer your age, and fairer to look upon. If that is your wish, say so, and I will end this farce." (1.385)

In fact, Sansa is considerably better off with Tyrion than his cousin. Lancel has proved himself eminently tractable in sexual matters (*Clash* 405–406). Confronted with his fearsome uncle's repeated demands that

Sansa be impregnated by a Lannister, Lancel would no doubt have done his dynastic duty, and probably enjoyed it, without much concern for Sansa's desires. Tyrion, by contrast, takes his wife's carnal rejection of him on the chin and respects her wishes that the marriage remain unconsummated, despite taking the rebuff, quite accurately, as another example of the aesthetic discrimination that has dogged him all his life (*Storm* 1.394). From a phenomenological standpoint, therefore, he is cleverly nuanced. Tyrion is a sort of embedded journalist in the narrative, unpretentiously reporting on the pretensions, follies and crimes of the other characters. Martin cannot make this obvious by leaving him blameless in the game of thrones. Thus, the Imp orders Symon Silver Tongue's murder, authorises the roundup of the Antler Men in the knowledge of the fate that awaits them (*Clash* 649) and unapologetically sets Blackwater Rush afire, killing hundreds of spear-carriers whose only crime was backing the wrong stag. But it will take more than another jibe at his appearance to move him to force himself on a pubescent girl. He is a flawed man, but one who is still playing by certain rules. It is indicative of Martin's authorial habits that the Imp's bottom lines are sexual in nature.

Shae, sadly, does not play by Tyrion's rules. Even before she sells him to his enemies in exchange for the fragile promises of Cersei (*Feast* 58), she is already accruing points against herself. This is not a reference to her line of work. Martin sometimes depicts prostitutes as uncouth (*Dance* 230) but rarely as immoral. The staff of Chataya's, the Peach and the Happy Port are nothing less ethical than professionals meeting a demand. Pycelle's tryst with a pliant young retainer (*Clash* 370) raises more questions about the supposedly celibate maester's personal conduct than that of his companion. Petyr Baelish, in whose dubious protection Jeyne Poole is whipped and "trained" (*Dance* 582–583) and who placates Lyn Corbray with "gold and boys and promises" (*Feast* 385), is another example. Where these boys come from in homophobic Westeros is not stated. Littlefinger's implied complicity in forcing or tricking people into the sex industry neatly underlines his celebrated untrustworthiness. Hizdahr zo Loraq's unconcern for his missing wife is demonstrated when Barristan Selmy finds him abed with a woman "trained in pleasure" (*Dance* 1,029) whose volition to the evening's festivities is not conclusively established. Westeros's sex industry thus reflects poorly on its customers, not its vendors. Shae, however, may be the least sympathetic of Martin's prostitutes. How she began her work is unclear, simply because she cannot keep her story straight. Initially asserting that she fled home after her father attempted to begin an incestuous relationship, she later claims she left to avoid domestic labour (*Clash* 580). The former explanation makes her a victim, the latter rather less of one, particularly in a low-mimetic universe where pots need scrubbing. It is up to individual readers to decide which story they find convincing. Either way, when camouflaged as one of Lollys Stokeworth's maids, she develops a decidedly ugly opinion of her mistress:

> "Sleep's all she ever wants to do, the great cow. She sleeps and she eats. Sometimes she falls asleep while she's eating. The food falls under the blankets and she *rolls* in it, and I have to clean her." She made a disgusted face. "All they did was *fuck* her." (705–706)

The reader is well aware that they fucked her "half a hundred times," without her leave, and left her to stagger home naked and impregnated (542). Shae's use of a plural pronoun to describe Lollys's attackers demonstrates that she also knows this. Given her purported reasons for fleeing home, this lack of sympathy for Lollys is deeply peculiar. It in fact merits comparison with the attitudes of Tolkien's orcs, whose hypocrisy is the first point Tom Shippey identifies when describing their evil as "an exaggerated form of recognisably human behaviour" ("Orcs, Wraiths and Wights" 183; 187). Supposedly fleeing sexual abuse herself, Shae remains of the opinion that others should grin and bear it. A best-case analysis suggests she is much like Cersei, her lack of empathy for the brutalised Lollys the result of an inability to relate the attack on her mistress to any broader pattern. The worst-case scenario paints her as closer to Tywin, a cold-hearted individual unable to grasp the suffering of others. Neither reflects well on her. This opinion probably explains why Tyrion retains reader sympathy even after he repays her treachery with death. Tyrion is a libertine, but unlike his concubine he has no patience or sympathy for sexual violence, rescuing Sansa from Joffrey's sexually motivated beating (*Clash* 443) and ordering that Bronn and his sellswords commit "no more rapes!" (642) Viewed in light of Martin's emerging pattern of using sex to encourage readers to construct speculative models of virtue to solidify his indictment of vice, the couple's climactic encounter in Tywin's bedroom could be abstractly described as a voice of reason silencing a voice of assent to Westerosi rape culture; a hobbit killing an orc. Shae as guilty of exactly the crime – the fatalistic acceptance of sexual violence – that Tyrion knows to be wrong and does his best to curtail.

The cases examined above reveal an interesting theme. The sexual mores of Martin's characters provide indications of their respective ability to transcend their brutal regime. Tywin Lannister's premeditation of the gang-rape of Tysha demonstrates an apathy for the lowborn; he barely sees his daughter-in-law as having an individual identity (*Storm* 2.498). He is very much a creature of the milieu he inhabits, an agent of the violent, presumptuous culture Martin indicts. So too is Cersei. Her comments about other women demonstrate her inability to connect her own proto-feminist frustrations to any broader pattern, and her solutions to problems – casually threatening to have Margaery Tyrell's tongue removed (*Feast* 607) and vowing to "pile dead dwarfs ten feet high" (268) in pursuit of Tyrion – are classic examples of medievalist violence. Cersei feels the pain of medieval injustice, but she responds simply by perpetuating it (Carroll 67). Shae, likewise, has not only a clear sense of what she is willing to put up with herself, but also a lack of sympathy for other victims of this regime. This decisively alienates the reader; she illustrates the problem rather than addressing it. Martin's villains are creatures of their regime, accepting, perpetuating and often utilising the unpleasant sexual mores of their imperfect world.

By comparison other characters consistently transcend the injustices or this grim medievalist world. Again, Catelyn Stark's apparent contentment with an arranged marriage complicates any attempt to frame her as a feminist heroine. Yet that contentment contrasts with the responses of Cersei, or her own sister Lysa, to similar situations. Both those women, cheated of the men they romantically daydreamed about (*Feast* 405–406; *Storm* 2.540) had their husbands killed, perpetuating traditions of medievalist brutality. Neither prospers as a result. Catelyn has eschewed such violence, rolled up her sleeves and gone to the effort of cultivating a healthy, happy family. She has been wronged by Westerosi patriarchy, but the best revenge, as they say, is living well. Sandor Clegane's sexual imagination also sets him apart from the violent world he inhabits. Sansa has been warned, all too credibly, to expect no mercy from Stannis's army (*Clash* 739); she receives it from a man who has just spent the last book and a half gloating about how he has none. It would be wrong to praise Sandor for not committing rape; he owes Sansa a profound apology. Yet that apology, were it to eventuate, would have some credibility; the episode both highlights the problem Martin writes about and qualifies the Hound's willingness to contribute to it. Meanwhile Tyrion, culpable in some dreadful crimes, nevertheless has some crucial redeeming qualities. The reader can only hope that Tywin's query "Is the Stark girl made differently?" (*Storm* 1.438) is rhetorical; at the very least, it demonstrates once again his and his family's unlovely habit of considering women in solely anatomical terms. Tyrion's breakage of this habit and deferral to Sansa's wishes, against the dynastic imperative, show his innocence of the frantic drive for self-replication identified as one of the key malaises of Westerosi culture (DeCoste 226). He is less of a contributor to this problem than a well-informed witness to it. This point, as much as anything, probably accounts for the resonance of the character with readers. Tyrion's libertinism is not an instance of an author endowing a character with feet of clay in an attempt to make him interesting, and still less an excuse for titillation. It is an extensively nuanced example of a broader pattern in the narrative. In Martin's song, a character's sexual imagination signals their relationship – instigator, perpetuator, assenter, circumventor, malcontent, witness for the prosecution – to his discomforting milieu.

The marriage of Khal Drogo and Daenerys Targaryen is another example of this. Drogo should be a monster. He is a fictionalisation of Attila the Hun, looting and pillaging in accordance with pejorative depictions of steppe cultures (Larrington 192). On his wedding night, however, he makes a patient, careful, notably successful attempt to judge the desires of his terrified teenage bride through a language barrier (*Game* 102–103). This is one of the handful of occasions in which the screenwriters of *Game of Thrones* can be said to have genuinely erred in their interpretation of Martin's narrative, since their version of the episode simply depicts him compelling Daenerys into his desired coital posture ("Winter is Coming"). Frankel quotes actress Emelia Clarke, who portrays Daenerys, claiming credit for this change, which was made on the basis that she and her collaborators wanted "a bit more reality" (2014 150) in the development of the relationship. Clarke's statement raises a potentially interesting point as to which is more realistic, a woman falling in love with her rapist, or a Dothraki warrior with a thigh-length braid (a hairstyle not earned with sweet words and gentle touches) deciding to treat a particular woman with respect. Again, however, Martin's objective with all this sex is not realism, but the casting of his characters in certain lights, the interrogation of their moral authority and establishment of their position within the various savage regimes they inhabit. Whatever his personal history, Drogo clearly understands that a handsome wedding gift (*Game* 100–101) will not suffice to begin his relationship with his *khaleesi* on the right foot. It appears to be culturally imperative that their marriage be consummated, but he carefully ensures that the encounter takes place at a pace she is physically and emotionally comfortable with. This not only makes the development of a constructive, loving partnership between the couple believable; it also marks Drogo as oddly out of step with his culture. This impression continues in his public conduct. He does not subscribe, for example, to the Dothraki custom of sharing his wife with his bloodriders (379). When Daenerys objects to Dothraki rape culture, he applauds her assertiveness rather than defending the gratification of his warriors (646). Jhogo and Quaro, somewhat to their credit, overcome their misgivings and follow her instructions before Drogo even gives the order (643–664). The sexual mores of Drogo's *khalassar* are in fact in a state of rapid reform from the sexual violence identified as typical of Dothraki culture (97–98).

Daenerys's role in bringing about this change stems largely from a swiftly developing sense of sexual self-confidence. Married off as soon as biologically viable, she has little sense of her own desires, "always assuming" (29) that she would marry Viserys when she came of age. Her evolving ability "to find pleasure even in her nights" (222), and to take charge in looking for it, are key indicators of her receding culture shock during her time with the Dothraki. Uncomfortable with their traditional coital posture, she turns back around and looks into Drogo's eyes as she rides him "as fiercely as ever she had ridden her silver" (229) and has him calling out her name rather than complaining about being dehumanised or emasculated. By setting the tone and pace of such an encounter Daenerys demonstrates clearly that she is no longer an objectified victim. Widowed at fifteen, furthermore, Daenerys pursues an active post-marital sex life. She masturbates (*Storm* 1.325), experiments with bisexuality (2.418–2.419), rejects the advances of an unattractive man (2.14) and confronted with a likelier lad, pursues him, takes an active role in their lovemaking (*Dance* 668), and achieves some apparently rather demonstrative orgasms as a result (661). Her conquest of Slaver's Bay is begun out of pity for the Unsullied, whose indoctrination begins with the sexual violation of castration (*Storm* 1.326). She also gives as good as she gets when sexually harassed by Prendahl na Ghezn of the Stormcrows, scotching Strong Belwas's typically medievalist offer to cut the mercenary's tongue out (2.6). Daenerys is hardly innocent of such violence. But her sexual imagination closely recalls that of an idealistic, self-possessed, heterosexual twenty-first-century teenage girl, open-minded, indignant at injustice and unimpressed by presumptions on her affections, but with discernible tastes in men – confidence, it is known, being sexy – and open to temptation by a little of what she fancies. This attitude towards sex stands in sharp contrast to the dry ritualism of the Meereenese who, apparently preoccupied with the reproductive purpose of sex, wish her to submit to a ceremonial gynaecological examination before her wedding to Hizdahr zo Loraq. Her response (to refuse their scrutiny because "*Khal Drogo found no fault*" with her anatomy [*Dance* 558]) is a feminist misstep, but a strikingly realistic one; it will hardly be the first time a young woman has inadvertently referred to the male gaze to support an assertion of her own dignity. To readers in regular contact with female teenagers, Daenerys will seem as familiar as the squabbling Stark daughters are to parents of younger girls. The sexual conduct of Daenerys and Drogo marks them as curiously out of the time Martin is evoking.

Precedent for such anachronism can be found in the Gothic tradition. Gothicism emerged out of a perception of a fundamental break between the Middle Ages and the post-medieval world, and a desire to examine the effect that the perceived iniquities of medieval civilisation had on those subjected to them (Byron and Punter 8). It is through that examination that the scheming baron, the hooded torturer and the raven-haunted garret became tropes of unsympathetic medievalism. By creating Roose Bolton, the Tickler and the maester's use of ravens in place of carrier pigeons, Martin perpetuates all of these. He also employs a common Gothic means of rhetorical anachronism to amplify the effects of these dark ideas. The typical Gothic novel depicts protagonists who are exemplars of well-intentioned modern mores, then uses plot contrivances to subject these folk to the vicissitudes of the medievalist world. Mighall describes the genre as staging

> a confrontation between the heroine of Richardson and a villain taken from the Jacobean stage, who embodies the past and all its terrors. The modern heroine or hero (the reader's counterpart who is equipped with an appropriate sensibility and liberal principles) is located in the Gothic past, forced to contend with the supposed delusions and iniquities of its political and religious regime. It is the conflict between the civilised and the barbaric, the modern and the archaic, the progressive and the reactionary which provides the terrifying pleasure of these texts. (9)

The perceived abuses of the past make their greatest impact, says Mighall, when visited upon those who do not wholly belong to the delusional, iniquitous regime from which they spring. Such characters are not only easier to relate to, their sensibilities highlight the follies and cruelties they encounter. Though hardly a conventionally Gothic author, Martin repeatedly uses this device. What Rosenberg describes as "monstrosity" (19) in his tale might well be reconsidered as medievalism. That is, the villains are those who belong more precisely to the medievalist milieu he evokes, while heroes are those who somehow resist or transcend it. Sexual misconduct identifies the extent to which one is a part of the world of "chaotic cruelty" Martin depicts, or, alternatively, the extent to which one is simply living in such a world. Spector observes that the sexual violence of Westeros is invariably "uncomfortable rather than titillating" (185), underscoring a medievalist vision that owes more than Martin may consciously appreciate to the Gothic tradition.

Tywin Lannister's abuse of Tysha is not the only example. Hackney (133) identifies Ser Gregor Clegane, with some qualifications, as one of Martin's more historically plausible medievalist grotesques. His crimes – taking advantage of a joust to commit murder (*Game* 286), employing a torturer (*Clash* 376), compelling Vargo Hoat to eat his own extremities (*Feast* 453) – constitute a mordant burlesque of Westeros's culture of violence. His sexual mores darkly underline this capacity. He responds to a request ("him being an anointed knight and all") that he intervene in the sexual harassment of a girl by escalating the situation to a pack-rape which he then trivialises with a horrendous joke (*Clash* 423–424). His confession to the rape of Elia Martell (*Storm* 2.401) is identified by Rosenberg as a "triumphant reaffirmation" (23), devoid of contrition. Where the Hound's sex life reveals him as almost human, therefore, the Mountain's turns him into – pun intended – part of Westeros's harsh, immoral landscape. Other characters follow this pattern. Varamyr Sixskins, devolving into the anthropophagous big bad wolf of the Haunted Forest, fondly recalls stalking desirable women in beast form until they take the hint – "Some came weeping, aye, but still they came" (*Dance* 8). Viserys Targaryen, the most unhinged of Martin's medievalist *alazons*, seeks to copulate with Daenerys before her wedding to preserve the family tradition of dynastic incest (83). Daenerys's wishes in this regard are unformulated, but Viserys would hardly have respected any veto she might have issued. Then there are the Boltons, a family whose viciousness is the subject of chilling rumour even within Westeros (*Game* 556). Roose practices the medievalist canard of *jus primae noctis* (*Dance* 499–500). Ramsay ensures that his family's ghoulish reputation is well-founded, a pursuit that extends to his marriage to Jeyne Poole:

> A tear ran down her cheek. "Tell him, you tell him. I'll do what he wants ... whatever he wants ... with him or ... *or with the dog* or ... please ... he doesn't need to cut my feet off, I won't try to run away, not ever, I'll give him sons, I swear it, I swear it..." (794; emphasis added)

Rather than simply demonstrating Ramsay's dehumanising savagery in the elaborately formulated game of thrones, Martin shades it off into the parallel game of beds, in which readers are impressionistically guided to decide for themselves that Ramsay truly is a creature of Westeros's dark age, a monster on the order of Walpole's Manfred or Hugo's Frollo. Not all characters categorised in this way are male. Cersei recalls her sexual elusions of King Robert thusly:

> Ten thousand of your children perished in my palm, Your Grace. [...] Whilst you snored, I would lick your sons off my face and fingers one by one, all those pale sticky princes. You claimed your rights, my lord, but in the darkness I would eat your heirs. (*Feast* 549)

This may be the most ironic act in Martin's novels to date. Robert is a dreadful husband on numerous counts, but if mere contraception was Cersei's aim she had alternatives, and indeed has used them (*Game* 469). The reader has already seen Asha Greyjoy take control of her fertility in this way (*Feast* 191). Cersei imagines that her particular method of contraception grants her special dignity and power in a patriarchal system; she is getting her own back, recovering something of her decision-making agency in a system that treats her like "a brood mare" (*Storm* 1.265; another example of the Lannister wont to dehumanise the female). In fact, compared to Greyjoy's pharmaceutical nous, this gloating confines the Queen to a very particular and ironically self-anointed role in Martin's tale – as a medievalist groesque, a nocturnal, child-eating ogress, as much a monster from Old Nan's stories as Drogon or Varamyr. Carroll (77) uses this act to identify Cersei as a monstrous female, which is a fair point, but not to link her to the chaotic, irrational, Gothic medievalist world to which she belongs. In this graphic, emotive way, Cersei betrays herself as part of the problem.

As Mighall observes that problem achieves full effect when visited on characters of a discernibly modern stripe. Such characters provide the suggestions of virtue necessary for full phenomenological engagement with indictments of faulty mores (Iser 35–36). The unmaking of Robb Stark demonstrates this. Much of his story is dedicated to revealing the truth of Jaime Lannister's observation (*Clash* 720) that, once low-mimetic intrusions are admitted, high-mimetic values serve only to create contradictions. The intrusion that ruins Robb's career is his adolescent sex drive. Just as horses defecate, teenagers have urges, which may well boil over if a pretty (*Feast* 749; *Storm* 1.190; 1.194; 1.284) friend offers comfort at a stressful time. His resulting alternatives – break a marriage contract or consign Jeyne Westerling to ignominious devaluation in a patriarchal sexual economy – are both abstract impositions of Westeros's obsession with patriarchal, high-mimetic propriety, demands of a regime Martin is criticising. The militarism of that order gives Walder Frey access and intuitive recourse to violent revenge for the Young Wolf's perceived insult. Jeyne, who temporarily eludes commodification by marrying the sympathetically anachronistic Robb, nevertheless also endures the results of an inhumane medievalist mindset. She suffers not only widowhood but an atrocious breach of trust, doped with contraceptives by a mercenary mother negotiating a more lucrative betrothal (*Feast* 749–750). Note furthermore how little these two care for their medievalist identities. Jeyne amiably rejects her royal title (*Storm* 1.282) while Robb banishes Grey Wind, his dynastic totem, to the kennels because the wolf unnerves his in-laws (1.197). One suspects that, like the Gothic heroines Mighall refers to, they would have been far happier among their readers, who would not punish them for being what Martin has taken pains to portray them as – a couple of kids doing what comes naturally. Again, Martin uses sexual discourse to sell his tale of conflict between relatable human beings and an invidious regime from the imagined past.

That the Westerosi see Robb's consideration for Jeyne as unusual highlights Martin's discussion of another of the perceived iniquities of history, the sexual double standard. Without being so complacent as to suggest that society has left this practice as far behind it as it has crossbows, crenelations and heads on spikes, it is certainly a feature of Martin's medievalism. Robert Baratheon, the very model of boorish, militarised aristocratic presumption, reveals his wandering eye before he has had time to sit down in Winterfell (*Game* 38). This attribution, so early in the story, essentially inaugurates the game of beds, Robert's marital indiscipline contributing significantly to an impression of a profligate, neglectful potentate. Cersei has little recourse in the face of his repeated infidelities (and abuses) but faces execution if hers are discovered.

Similarly Catelyn Stark must accept the presence of Jon Snow, while Lysa Arryn must abort her illegitimate child at the instigation of her father (*Storm* 2.540), seemingly prompting a lifetime of harrowing neurosis and ill judgement. Hoster Tully's apparent deathbed contrition (1.35) offers scant comfort to a daughter forced to contend with a patriarchy. Westerosi women are supposed to be content with the sort of ethereal sentimentalities that Sansa Stark was raised on, while men are permitted, to a large extent, to indulge their baser desires.

As demonstrated by the presentation of Robert as a blustering ass, Martin's depiction of this inequity is hardly an endorsement. The introduction of the Ironborn in *A Clash of Kings* also demonstrates the point. At a first reading of Martin's first volume readers might only barely remember Theon Greyjoy, "a lean dark youth of nineteen who found everything amusing" (*Game* 13) hovering at the edge of the Stark family circle. Beyond medievalist bloodlust – he urges the execution of the captured Jaime Lannister (676) – he exhibits only one clear personality trait, though a telling one:

> Two serving wenches stood beneath the sign of the Smoking Log, the local alehouse. When Theon Greyjoy called out to them, the younger girl turned red and covered her face. Theon spurred his mount to move up beside Robb. "Sweet Kyra," he said with a laugh. "She squirms like a weasel in bed, but say a word to her on the street, and she blushes pink as a maid. Did I ever tell you about the night she and Bessa..."
>
> "Not where my brother can hear, Theon," Robb warned him with a glance at Bran. (384–385)

As the examples of Robb, Jeyne and Daenerys prove, Martin is not one to blame teenagers for exploring their sexuality. When Theon steps forward as a focaliser in *A Clash of Kings*, however, his fondness for Kyra and her ilk turns to bludgeoning contempt. His first act is to demand fellatio from a "stupid girl" (152) the better to spare himself from her "mindless prattle" (153). When she points out that as a result of their liaison her father will "call me names and hit me" he fastens his trousers and wanders off, noting that she and her father should feel honoured to be raising a king's bastard (155). Note that this is the diametric opposite of Robb's behaviour. In *A Clash of Kings* Theon reconnects with his cultural roots in the Iron Islands, which imply a particular view of heterosexual relations:

> "Once I might have carried you home as a prize, and kept you to wife whether you willed it or no. The ironmen of old did such things. A man had his rock wife, his true bride, ironborn like himself, but he had his salt wives too, women captured on raids." (153)

Westeros quietly tolerates male sexual profligacy; the Iron Islands celebrate concubinage as a cultural touchstone. This, says Rosenberg, makes mainland Westeros "look like a feminist paradise" (20) in comparison. Larrington (73–74) draws comparisons between the Islanders and the historical Vikings, which would locate them at a much earlier stage in medieval history than the rest of Westeros, the material and intellectual cultures of which closely evoke those of the Wars of the Roses (Lowder xiii; Pavlac 8–9; Walker 71–72). These people are therefore "more" medieval than those they raid, more primitive, more savage and, inevitably, more blatant in their sexual misconduct. Theon's capacity as a lusty young man cross-pollinates with this license in an unlovely manner. His treatment of the captain's unnamed daughter demonstrates what kind of man he is, and his ignorant flirting with his sister (*Clash* 343–344) quickly establishes his short-sighted impulsiveness. That attribute leads to his treacherous, silly occupation of Winterfell, during which he assuages his frustrations, it seems, the only way he knows how – leaving sweet Kyra sobbing, her neck and breasts covered with bruises and bite marks. Theon shoved her from the bed and threw her a blanket. "Get out" (731–732). Kyra blushed rather than scowled at him in *A Game of Thrones*, suggesting he was gentler in their previous encounters. As he aligns himself with more abjectly medievalist factions in Martin's universe, therefore, his sexual manners sharply decline, because in the past, he does not have to say please and thank you. Robb Stark could have done the same – he could have slipped away from The Crag a bachelor without upsetting anyone outside the impuissant House Westerling – but he did not, because Robb is, per Mighall, not a truly medieval character. Theon is and behaves like it in bed. This continues after his comeuppance, when he is then reduced to that commonplace of unsympathetic medievalism, the mad, filthy, mutilated starveling. Martin underlines this status with a sexual dimension as Ramsay Bolton makes Reek complicit in his abuse of Jeyne Poole (*Dance* 581–583). Sympathy for Reek only starts to meaningfully accrue when he takes part in Jeyne's rescue. Theon's sexual manners deteriorate as he embraces a medievalist identity; his redemption hinges on his rejection thereof by way of the rescue of a victim of sexual abuse.

The immediate point of comparison is with Theon's sister, Asha. Where Theon's focalising chapters – those under his own name at least – are dedicated to establishing his Cersei-like hubris, Asha is pragmatic and sensible, celebrated by Frankel (2014 59) and Carroll (99) as one of the few fully developed heroines among a crowd of qualifiedly feminist figures such as Catelyn Stark. The odd thing about this is that Martin has his readers cheering on arguably the most competent proponent of the misogynist Ironborn cause. Balon Greyjoy has at least two salt wives (*Feast* 23), meaning Asha more than likely has half-siblings resulting from rape. As a capable fighter and reaver, she is complicit in the reduction of other women to that status. Her capacity as a warrior, married to her axe and suckling her knife (*Clash* 356), appears to be contingent on her father's approval (*Feast* 25), this being extended after he gave up on Theon as feminised by his time on the mainland (*Clash* 167). Her expedition, against her father's orders, to rescue her mutilated brother was invented for television ("The Laws of Gods and Men"), and does not appear in Martin's version of the narrative. Her military career is thus arguably a matter of a patriarch spotting and utilising talent, not really any more feminist than Tywin Lannister seeking to re-engage Cersei's fertility to forge an alliance. The key point to remember about Asha, however, is that she reverses the Westerosi sexual double standard that her family exalts in, and that this decision is all her own. Her "wretched ruin" (*Dance* 642) of a husband holds no interest for her. Her interest in her lover Qarl is unashamedly physical; she enjoys his "soft, smooth skin," "downy" pubic hair, responsive nipples, and "swimmer's body [...] with not a scar upon him" (*Dance* 391). Laying aside the issue of Asha's rather pointed feminisation of Qarl the Maid, she wants his body and gets it, counting him as her favourite of her various transitory lovers without expressing any shame about those others. She lost her virginity to a man she happened to fancy, practices contraception learned from a female woods witch rather than a patriarchal maester (*Feast* 191) and rejects the mooning romantic Tristifer Botley at knifepoint (192). What she has reversed is not the political or martial marginalisation of women, but the sexual double standard. Perpetuating the violence of the game of thrones but substantially redeemed by her conduct in the game of beds, Asha is probably the closest thing to a female equivalent of Tyrion Lannister.

This raises an interesting point about the female libido in Martin's world. In asserting their desires, several female characters rebel against the expectations of their communities. Sometimes they do so while simultaneously espousing those expectations as common sense. Ygritte observes that "a true man steals a woman from afar, t' strengthen the clan" (*Storm* 1.365) but did not have to sleep with Jon Snow any more than she had to twiddle her thumbs while he worked up the courage to execute her. Like his half-brother, Jon is not wholly of the medievalist regime, at least not the bandit-like existence of widling reavers, and will not "take" a woman just because the opportunity arises. Ygritte in fact only raises the issue because of Jon's – to her mind bizarre – tardiness in claiming his supposed rights, and ends up prodding the shy, inexperienced teenager into bed entirely on her own initiative. The parallel with Asha is clear. Ygritte sees something desirable in the crow-come-over, goes after it and gets it, leaving neuroses about propriety to him. As he catches on she becomes vocally appreciative of Jon's adolescent experimentation (1.364), which serves as a levelling device between the two, dispelling the notion that she needs to "show" (1.358) him anything. This is not an atavistic abduction like that of Munda by Longspear Ryk (*Dance* 817), endorsed as fitting by Munda's father, but a young couple, like Robb and Jeyne, blowing off steam in tumultuous circumstances. Later Gilly, initially seen pathetically offering Jon sexual favours in exchange for protection from her abusive father (*Clash* 335), makes all the running in getting Samwell Tarly's breeches open (*Feast* 592–593). Like Ygritte she is acting on her own desires, an obvious point of rebellion against a background so heedless of what women want that those in authority dismiss labour pangs as trivial (*Storm* 1.444–1.445). Gilly's actions aboard the *Cinnamon Wind* demonstrate clearly the role of female desire in these books. In asserting themselves sexually – not by force, but by initiative and demonstrated pleasure – characters like Ygritte and Gilly give an impression of not being entirely of their regimes.

Of course, they are not part of those regimes, but subjects thereof. This is a patriarchy; the constrained roles and opportunities Westeros offers women are part of Martin's unsympathetic medievalism, made explicitly so by Randyll Tarly's observation that "the gods made men to fight and women to bear children" (*Feast* 238). Wildlings allow women to fight, but Ygritte's observation about bride-theft demonstrates that women are seen as resources north of the Wall as well. Martin is open to criticism for his deficit of uncomplicated, uncompromised female opponents to this regime. Ygritte sees bride-theft as perfectly sensible. Cersei Lannister has internalised Westerosi misogyny rather than overturning it (Carroll 67); Catelyn Stark has to an extent lucked into a comfortable niche in the sexual economy; Arienne Martell and Melisandre "parody" (Frankel 2014 136) rather than exercise political power via their feminine wiles; Sansa Stark's narrative purpose is to endure and witness patriarchal barbarism rather than oppose it (a role that incidentally parallels that of the great Gothic heroines; Day 19); Asha Greyjoy, Arya Stark and Brienne of Tarth seek agency by aping masculine militarism rather than, say, attempting to matriculate at the Citadel. This could be a problem. Conversely, this collection of compromised female characters can be seen as symptomatic of Martin's desire to present the reader with something more engaging than a medievalist clown act. To this end, he cannot actually afford to have a perfect model of feminist self-assertion loose in Westeros any more than he can have one power bloc behave demonstrably more morally than the others. She would be too obvious a ralling point for the readers. Martin's women are engaging, per Iser, partly because of their feminist faults. The effectiveness of this technique is evident in Frankel's climactic concession (2014 184) that no conclusive feminist verdict can be made about these books. Individual readers must weigh each concession to patriarchy against the accompanying opposition to the regime and decide for themselves which women to sympathise with.

Nevertheless characters must be variegated on a moral spectrum to be engaging (Hogan 93–94), and Martin uses the game of beds to do this with regard to this aspect of his world. For Olenna Tyrell, feminism is part of her broader contempt for the courtly rigmarole she so deftly navigates:

> "You Starks were kings once, the Arryns and the Lannisters as well, and even the Baratheons through the female line, but the Tyrells were no more than stewards until Aegon the Dragon came along and cooked the rightful King of the Reach at the Field of Fire. If truth be told, even our claim to Highgarden is a bit dodgy, just as those dreadful Florents are always whining. 'What does it matter?' you ask, and of course it doesn't, except to oafs like my son. The thought that he may one day see his grandson with his arse on the Iron Throne makes Mace puff up like...now, what do you call it?" (*Storm* 1.82)

To accuse another noble of whining, admit one's own claim on one's ancestral seat is "dodgy" and allow that a king even has an arse are all affronts to Westeros's medievalist dignity. Olenna attaches little importance to the practice of "knocking men off horses with a stick" (1.81) or a regime based on such pursuits. Her jocular iconoclasm has a distinct sexual component. She may not quite be the funky grandma portrayed on screen – Benioff and Weiss's Olenna upbraids Tywin Lannister for his homophobia ("The Climb"); Martin's clamps down "crisply" on any discussion of her grandson's relationship with Renly Baratheon – but she does have very clear ideas about her own sexual destiny. "They tried to marry me to a Targaryen once," she recalls, "but I soon put an end to that" (1.81). How she managed this is unstated. Eventually parcelled out to Luthor Tyrell, she found him "A kind man, and not unskilled in the bedchamber, but an appalling oaf all the same" (1.84). To a true medieval dynast, skill in the bedchamber amounts to fecundity. Walder Frey, fielding an army out of his breeches, subscribes to this metric. So too does Aeron Greyjoy, counting his father a great man for fathering nine sons (*Feast* 22–23). Olenna compliments her late husband despite being only a mother of three. The implication is surely that Luthor Tyrell, like Eddard Stark and Khal Drogo, had some regard for his wife's desires and some ability to meet them. For that reason, she persevered with him. From a woman who somehow manoeuvred her way out of a match with a Targaryen (which would surely be the dream of a wholly compliant female dynast) this point is telling. It contributes significantly to the storybook image of Highgarden. The Red Keep, Casterly Rock, Craster's Keep and Pyke are all Gothicised as venues of sexual wrongdoing. In Highgarden, as in Winterfell, children are engendered as one might hope they would be; from a joyful collaboration rather than an act of abuse or a mechanical accretion of dynastic assets. Whether the

Tyrells wanted Sansa for her inheritance or not, she could have found a happy ending with them; their familial seat is, in one small but very significant way, the fairytale castle Sansa imagines. Like Daenerys and Ygritte, Olenna transcends her regime via her sexuality. The common theme between the fur-clad warriors of the Frostfangs, the brocaded politicians of King's Landing and the robed gynaecologist-mystics of Meereen is the commodification of female fertility. In this situation, any independent, remotely healthy expression of the female libido becomes a sort of guerrilla action, on the part of both the woman in question and the author who created her.

Martin's sexual themes are even evident among those incapable of the act itself. As Cersei points out in a rare moment of acuity (*Clash* 702), Varys's apparent absence of physical desires contributes to his inscrutability. The writers of *Game of Thrones* have picked up this ball and run with it. Benioff and Weiss's Tormund Giantsbane is considerably humanised by his abiding crush on Brienne of Tarth ("Book of the Stranger"). Their Podrick Payne, aged up to late adolescence, is an instinctively generous lover ("Walk of Punishment"). Meryn Trant is a paedophile ("Mother's Mercy"); Missendei recalls Kraznys mo Nakloz in terms suggesting he was as well ("Oathbreaker"). And, of course, Littlefinger delivers copious sexposition while auditioning Ros (a character, indicatively, invented for television) in his brothel ("You Win or You Die"). Viewers turning to Martin's books will be disappointed, however, in their search for anything remotely pornographic. Instead, they will find a literary theme that transcends both marketing and a straightforward indication of how ghastly Westeros is. Martin has employed sex skilfully to inflect his critique of that ghastliness. Frank as that discourse is, it is often staged in a way that begs questions, inviting the reader to consider ambiguities and thus drawing them into the creative process. Readers are then guided to the conclusion that some of Martin's characters are indeed creatures of an uncivilised, inhumane regime, while others – pointedly a number of his female characters – are merely living in and coping with it. In short, sex sells *A Song of Ice and Fire* not because it leaves nothing to the imagination, but because it gives the imagination something to do.

3 "Look with Your Eyes" – Immersion and Thinning

What emerges from the previous chapters is a picture of *A Song of Ice and Fire* as a medievalist problem novel. Martin uses the ironic mode and the phenomenological model of reading to guide the reader in a sustained indictment of a medievalist regime beset with cynicism and self-interest. Incessant claims of nobility, precedent, institutional rectitude, ceremony and moral authority bespeak a people with a very clear sense of propriety, a strong fondness for the glamour of the "Disney Middle Ages," but the characters seem largely incapable of living up to such aspirations. The king lacks the initiative to rise to the dignity and diligence he knows his station demands. His bodyguards, behind their symbolically spotless raiment, are oafs and ruffians disengaged from precisely the standards of behaviour that knightly oaths are intended to ingrain. The Night's Watch is in a similar state. It has long since degenerated into a penal colony whose current commander can maintain discipline only by discreetly accepting the flouting of certain auspicious elements of the Watch's oath of office (*Game* 757). The first estate is ill-equipped to serve as any moral anchor. The sept at Castle Black is manned by a hopeless drunk, while there is a widespread perception (*Clash* 802; *Dance* 333) – accurate in at least one case (*Storm* 1.533) – that the clergy harbour pederasts in their midst. The Old Gods, devoid of clerics and therefore potentially resistant to human peccadilloes, also have nobody to assert the morality they promote. The Boltons keep to the old ways, promising a quiet land and people, but that land echoes to the screams of the flayed and the lamentations of the raped. Roose Bolton eventually kills Robb Stark for career advancement. His compatriots are shocked by this (*Dance* 285; *Feast* 383) but can do little to prevent it. Social rules have become licenses for bad behaviour rather than safeguards against it. Words have indeed become wind. These people cannot trust in what they trust in.

This indictment can only function, however, in light of the notion that the bruised reeds of medievalist protocol and institution ought to have some validity. To that purpose, Martin's narrative discourse is shot through with references to and insinuations of a cleaner, nobler past of morality and good sense. The Night's Watch was not always a joke.

The regard that Eddard Stark has for it is an anachronistic remnant of the respect it commanded in society at large in the days when it attracted knights and heroes instead of poachers, rapists and dynastic jetsam. King Baelor the Blessed built a grand sept in King's Landing, adhered rigidly to the teachings of the Faith and pushed his people to follow suit. The results were mixed, but they stemmed from the fact that the king believed in something, a sharp contrast with the lip service Joffrey and his bruisers pay to the chivalry they supposedly exemplify. And the Targaryen dynasty, the blood of Old Valyria, once soared and swooped through the skies on the dragons that adorned their banners – genuinely special people rather than decrepit, unhinged bullies like Viserys and his father, or indeed the blustering, obese stag who deposed them. The Kingsguard are in a sorry state, but Ser Barristan Selmy still "lent honor to any man he served" (*Game* 745). In terms of Martin's ironic critique of the conceits of men like Tywin Lannister, Barristan's monastic lifestyle bears this out:

> His bedchamber was a small cell off the queen's apartments, originally slave quarters; his furnishings consisted of a bed, a chamber pot, a wardrobe for his clothing, even a chair should he want to sit. On a bedside table he kept a beeswax candle and a small carving of the Warrior. Though he was not a pious man, the carving made him feel less alone here in this queer alien city, and it was to that he had turned in the black watches of the night. (*Dance* 912)

Though mention of a chamber pot seemingly undercuts Barristan's dignity, it actually safeguards it. Unlike Tywin Lannister, whose dramatic ride into Joffrey's throne room reaches a bathetic end, he refuses to practice Hume's fantasy of subtraction. He knows he is human and admits it. Much like Barack Obama's admission to having used cocaine in his youth, Barristan's unpretentious, business-like admission that he has an anus renders him substantially immune to attempts to use the point to humiliate him. The reader is instead touched that he seems impressed by the fact his bedroom, containing all he owns in the world, contains – luxury of luxuries – a chair. What Barristan got up to in his salad days, meanwhile, connects him to the game of beds. The Kingsguard are notionally celibate. The inability of most of them to maintain that standard (*Feast* 212–213) demonstrates the doubtful status of the institution. Barristan keeps his vow, being devoted to the memory of a beautiful damsel who got away many years earlier and subsequently committed suicide after suffering a stillbirth (*Dance* 1,024). The high-mimetic tragedy of Ashara Dayne solidifies the air of elegiac dignity that surrounds Barristan. He does not need aristocratic pretensions, because he is not pretending. He is the genuine article, Barristan the Bold, one of Sansa's romanticised paladins standing soundly to attention in a slouching institution. But he is also Barristan the Old, white of hair and perhaps the last of his kind. Barristan serves faithfully, but primarily as a reminder of what has been lost.

The purpose of this chapter, and the one following, is to explain how Martin utilises the imperatives of the fantasy form to encode this impression of fading, dissipating glory into his tale. This sense is a crucial factor in the appeal of the story. The lack of clearly definable heroes and villains creates an interest in Martin's work commonly held to be lacking in other fantasists. As demonstrated in Chapter 1, that perception is flawed; this genre thrives on moral ambiguity. That Martin receives this sort of praise, however, demonstrates how effective he has been in conveying this moral unpredictability to the reader. An examination of his work in light of the critical apparatuses erected around modern fantasy will demonstrate that he achieves this sense not by disregarding or innovating genre conventions, but by adroitly utilising them. Martin approaches and discharges his responsibilities as a fantasist in a way that ensures the fallibility of his characters is not just a matter of narrative incident, but of the approach he compels the reader to take to the narrative matter itself. This chapter will explain how Martin's general method of exposition creates this sense of dissipation; the following will use the same critical theories to demonstrate some of the ways in which he emphasises it.

Human institutions are not all that has been reduced or debased. Martin's entire written world appears to be a shadow of its former self, subject to a precipitous decline from previous glories. The maesters are in various minds about the current efficacy of magic, but there is a consensus that it was once unambiguously effective. Maester Luwin relates a history of diminishing and etiolation to Bran Stark; that of the coming of the First Men, their attack on the children of the forest, and their reduction of these nature spirits to partners in a treaty, the great Pact (*Game* 713–714). He later ruminates on the long-term consequences of this seeming tractability of these wondrous creatures to human agency:

> Perhaps magic was once a mighty force in the world, but no longer. What little remains is no more than the wisp of smoke that lingers in the air after a great fire has burned out, and even that is fading. Valyria was the last ember, and Valyria is gone. The dragons are no more, the giants are dead, the children of the forest forgotten with all their lore. (*Clash* 401)

This theme is a noteworthy point of contact with the modern fantasy tradition as a whole. Modern fantasy is abidingly concerned with what critic John Clute terms "thinning," by which he means "the passing away of a higher and more intense reality" (942). He cites Tolkien's

The Lord of the Rings, chronicling the elegiac closing movements of "eons of slow loss" as an example, but the leitmotif of a fantasy world somehow fundamentally lacking in fantasy, somehow less magical than it once was, is widespread. Jack Vance's *Dying Earth* cycle, set in a time "when Earth is old and the sun is about to go out" (*Rhialto the Magnificent* 579) demonstrates the point. Wizards have somehow lost access to some nine-tenths of the magic they once knew (*The Dying Earth* 5), and squabble over the remainder. Brian Stableford (305) cites Vance's work as the *locus classicus* of the trope, but it did not begin with him. Mervyn Peake's Gormenghast Castle is riddled with marvellously bizarre architectural follies and grandiose artistic flourishes, but all are neglected and crumbling (*Titus Groan* 148); nobody has built, decorated or maintained any part of that castellated universe in generations. Among Martin's contemporaries, Susanna Clarke sets *Jonathan Strange and Mister Norrell* in a Regency England endowed with a history of successful "practical magic," but a history only; at the novel's commencement nobody has actually cast a spell in living memory, and antiquarians who study the matter scoff at the idea Mister Norrell might possess the means to do so (25). The pattern extends to audio-visual fantasy. George Lucas's original *Star Wars* trilogy takes place in a galaxy where the rationalistic Empire, with its fascistic faith in the blunt coercive power of the Death Star, has all but destroyed the order of warrior-mystic Jedi Knights, paragons of "a more civilised age" when martial prowess was exercised with "elegant" weapons and moral literacy. The Gothic fantasy television series *Carnivalé* (2003–2005) begins with an expository monologue:

> Before the beginning, after the great war between heaven and hell, God created the earth and gave dominion over it to the crafty ape he called man. And to each generation was born a creature of light, and a creature of darkness, and great armies clashed by night in the ancient war between good and evil. There was magic then, nobility, and unimaginable cruelty. And so it was until the day that a false sun exploded over Trinity, and man forever traded away wonder for reason. ("Milfay")

The show depicts the second and third sentences of that tale in action; it was cancelled, its storyline incomplete, before the episodes telling of the false sun could be produced. But for its fortunes in programming the tale is very similar to Martin's. The notion that the written world has undergone some galling rationalisation of mystique, and now abides in a state of unglamorous loss, is one of the leitmotifs of modern fantasy. Clute particularly associates this thinning with "low fantasy," fantasies not "elevated in their literary style" (David Langford 597). Martin's concerted use of the ironic mode would seem to place him squarely in the latter category. In fantasies like Martin's, Clute observes, "rarely does the world provide venues unthreatened by one or more of a huge range of diminishings and dismissals of the old order" (942).

Luwin's assessment of this situation is overly pessimistic, as the children of the forest do still exist, but one of the purposes for which they eventually appear is to corroborate most of the maester's tale (*Dance* 527–528). Leaf's story is a textbook example of one of the manners in which this thinning of the world can be effected – "the crushing advent of *homo sapiens*, which exterminates the old fauna and drives the inhabitants of Faerie into wainscots" (Clute 942). The theme was later reiterated by the Targaryens. Dragons carry a mystique that is far more important than their capacity as weapons. The story of Daenerys's dynasty closely parallels the opening monologue of *Carnivalé*. There was wonder then. Tyrion Lannister's "morbid fascination" (*Game* 116) with the beasts transcends fear. Finding their skulls in the cellars of the Red Keep he is "awed" (117) that such creatures could have ever existed. There was also nobility; the Targaryens were demonstrably grander beings than their foes in the conquest, able to exist in partnership with these astonishing creatures. And there was "unmaginable cruelty," the burning alive of the Lannister host at the Field of Fire, an atrocity scarcely possible in Tyrion's own day (though Tyrion himself comes close at the Battle of Blackwater) and certainly not by such grand instruments. But the Targaryens forgot that dragons were not kin to other livestock and sought to domesticate them, confining them to a barn in King's Landing – a grand barn perhaps, "with iron doors so wide that thirty knights could ride through them abreast" (*Storm* 1.109), but a barn nonetheless. Treated like cattle the dragons ebbed and died. This is a perfect instance of Clutean thinning. The loss of the great reptiles represents, per *Carnivalé*, a final trading away of wonder for reason.

The trading away of nobility is worthy of particular attention. When they died, the dragons rendered a particular kind of practical demonstration of aristocracy impossible. Aristocracy means "rule by the best" and has been largely abandoned in the primary world for humanitarian reasons stemming from the notion that nobody is, in fact, born best, or at least nobody can agree on exactly how to measure that quality. Fantasy literature commonly uses the fiats of the supernatural to set up practicable aristocracies, less to promote such regimes in reality – a common misconception among the genre's detractors – but as experiments in how the existence of such institutions would affect society. Given the preponderance of thinned universes, such experiments typically take the form of investigations into how the *absence* of such institutions would affect societies in which they once existed. George Lucas's Jedi Knights, almost extinct in his original trilogy, demonstrate the point. So too do Martin's Targaryens, who gave Westeros its dragons. This is not to credit them with moral superiority or an innate right to rule. But it does make them, in Frye's terms, modally romantic, differentiated fundamentally from the other families they ruled. They mismanaged their gift, however, and became just another dynasty, less stable than most, reduced from romance to high mimesis, and thence to Viserys's snivelling irony. Robert Baratheon's revolution has not, predictably, produced any practical aristocracy, any rule by individuals who can be demonstrated to be somehow intrinsically exceptional. In fact what Robert has really demonstrated is that in the absence of any such order, attempts to re-establish such a regime boil down to the right of might. His brother Renly is one of many to follow his example (*Clash* 319–320). With the supposed embodiment of treasured virtues now decades deep in an essentially unresolvable squabble over non-existent authority, society at large is perceived as lacking moral direction (378). In both human and cosmological terms, this is a thinned world, a perfect example of twentieth-century fantasy's concern less with wondering over magic than with considering the consequences of its loss.

Martin encourages this impression in large part via his approach to the imperatives of his genre. Critic Farah Mendlesohn observes that "all literature builds worlds, but some genres are more honest about it than others" (59). Literary space is fundamentally blank until words shape it; doing so to effect is the central job of the author (Attebery 1992 51). Writers who choose to use fantasy to achieve that impact face a particular challenge in that their work by definition includes something with which the reader is fundamentally unfamiliar (15). Such contrivances must be explained. None of Martin's readers has ever travelled from Winterfell to King's Landing, heard of the Rat Cook, tasted sourleaf, smelled Flea Bottom, felt the Dornish sun or seen a zorse, a weirwood or the violet eyes of Old Valyria. Martin's knights are not historical knights – or rather individual cavaliers are inspired by various different stages in the development of historical chivalry (Hackney 142). The reader needs guidance in how to interpret these men. Braavos certainly has "many affinities" (Larrington 147) with medieval Venice, but it is *not* Venice, and nor it is pretending to be. It is Braavos, a city no reader has ever been to, which must be built from its lagoon bed up along with the rest of Martin's world. In her book *Rhetorics of Fantasy*, Mendlesohn explains how the decisions an author makes when addressing this imperative have a pervasive influence on the reader's reception of the tale. She delineates four broad methodologies for explaining a fantasy world:

- Portal-quest fantasy, in which the reader follows the protagonist as they move from an environment they understand into one they do not and learn about their new situation from one or more guides. The reader learns alongside them.
- Immersive fantasy, in which the reader observes the assumptions of focalisers who already understand their invented world. The reader

assembles the world themselves by analysing the context in which the characters discuss their surroundings.

- Intrusion fantasy, in which characters familiar with a world develop a sense of an exception to or contravention of that understanding. The reader observes an investigation of that exception, typically with the objective of expelling it.
- Liminal fantasy, in which an ostensibly ordinary narrative proceeds on the understanding that there is something supernatural taking place on the fringes or in the background, colouring the narrative with fantastic implications about which the focaliser is often wholly blasé (xix–xxiv).

Most fantasies fall into one or another of these categories. Baum's *The Wizard of Oz* is a portal-quest, with Dorothy's new environment explained to her (and the reader) by natives. Stevenson's *The Strange Case of Dr. Jeykll and Mister Hyde* is an intrusion, driven by the sense the good doctor's friends have that there is something objectionable about his odd new associate. Some fantasies go through phases in which the author employs different Mendlesohnian methods. Tolkien's two major novels begin as immersive fantasies, elucidating the Shire as if reminding the reader of something overlooked. It is "of course, absurd" (*Hobbit* 5) to suggest that one of Bilbo Baggins's ancestors married a fairy. The implication is that the reader knows why this is absurd but the existence of a forgotten civilisation of hirsute burrowing trenchermen is not. Once outside the Shire, however, the hobbits know Middle-earth no better than the reader. Tolkien's invented world thenceforth takes shape via explanations from figures like Gandalf and Aragorn, which turn the stories into portal-quests. With its plethora of focalisers, *A Song of Ice and Fire* is another such polyglot. Different focalisers employ different Mendlesohnian strategies. Analysis of these strategies highlights a great deal about Martin's world-building, including the manner in which he evokes the thinning that is such a fundamental part of his written world.

It might be argued that Martin is writing a portal-quest. Leaving Winterfell the Starks clearly move from an environment they know into one they do not, and receive advice – from Varys, Petyr Baelish and Sandor Clegane – about how things work. They fail to heed that advice, to their cost. At home, Eddard maintains a particular, strict code; his inability to cope with the moral climate of the south, despite Varys and Littlefinger patiently walking him through it, destroys him. The same is true of Sansa, whose chivalric idealism ends with her topless and bashed at Joffrey's feet. By contrast, Arya heeds Syrio Forel, looks with her eyes rather than her assumptions, and keeps her head above water, albeit barely. Arya's capacity to learn new rules, and thus cope with her new environment, arguably typifies the character development demanded by this form of fantasy.

Categorising *A Song of Ice and Fire* as such is problematic, however. Portal-quests hinge on the protagonist being ignorant of the trans-portal world, and thus in need of the guide's explanations. The Starks are simply too well-integrated into Westeros for this. Eddard is not venturing into an unknown world when he moves south; he is returning to a place he has already seen, fought over and bled for. He knows Renly Baratheon and has reason to mislike Petyr Baelish and be suspicious of Varys (*Game* 185–186). Even in Winterfell, the Starks are not separate from Westeros. They are Wardens of the North; they receive ravens just like everybody else; they know and respect the Night's Watch enough to be concerned about its difficulties (21). Bran's initial plan to join the Kingsguard (73) is a lofty but feasible ambition. He is a non-inheriting son of the king's most trusted brother in arms; for him eventually to attend Robert makes perfect sense. That the reader learns about the Kingsguard from Bran, rather than any of the royal party visiting Winterfell, also demonstrates the problem with calling this a portal-quest. The Starks provide as much information as they hear. Once on the Kingsroad Eddard begins reminding Robert of details of their rebellion while Robert updates him on the activities of Jorah Mormont (106–111). The shared burden of exposition shows that neither man is fundamentally better-informed about the world than the other. This trend continues as Martin expands his cast of focalisers. Few of those who build Westeros require the explanations by which a portal-quest world takes shape.

Instead, the bulk of Martin's world-building follows the conventions of Mendlesohnian immersive fantasy. His characters talk about Westeros's numerous differences from Earth as if there was nothing unusual about them, and readers reverse-engineer a picture of the world by analysing such discourse. Mendlesohn (62) compares such fantasies to science fiction; Orwell's *Nineteen Eighty-Four* certainly demonstrates the technique. Orwell provides a clear example in the opening sentence of his novel – "It was a bright cold day in April, and the clocks were striking thirteen" (5). Focaliser Winston Smith is not amazed at clocks striking thirteen; rather, he sees it as banal. This activates what Mendlesohn calls the "irony of mimesis" (59) an authorial alarm signal whereby the reader is invited to construct the world by analysing what the focaliser accepts as normal. Martin's favourite focaliser starts doing this in his third paragraph:

> He massaged some life back into [his legs] and limped heavily to the table where the septon was snoring softly, his head pillowed on an open book in front of him. Tyrion glanced at the title. A life of Grand Maester Athelmure, no wonder. "Chayle," he said softly. The young man jerked up, blinking, confused, the crystal of his order swinging wildly on its silver chain. "I'm off to break my fast.

> See that you return the books to the shelves. Be gentle with the Valyrian scrolls, the parchment is very dry. Ayrmidon's *Engines of War* is quite rare, and yours is the only complete copy I've seen." (*Game* 83)

Tyrion Lannister knows Grand Maester Athelmure was dull, what a septon is, and the significance of Chayle's crystal pendant. He knows the respect due to Valyrian scrolls and offers an expert opinion on a rare title. The world takes shape as the reader assesses and considers the assumptions evident in his discussion of what a literate Westerosi should apparently know. The result is typical of Martin's expository technique, which prompts the reader to draw a series of inferences from the assumptions evident in the narrative matter. Geography as well as culture takes form in this way. Martin uses the common post-Tolkienian device of endowing his novels with paratextual maps, a device Mendlesohn associates with portal-quest rhetoric (14). Journeys across such maps allow guides to continue talking, naturalising their world-building patter. The focalisers of immersive fantasy do not have guides, however, and as such form their own impressions of landscape and location:

> Sansa shuddered. They had been twelve days crossing the Neck, rumbling down a crooked causeway through an endless black bog, and she had hated every moment of it. The air had been damp and clammy, the causeway so narrow they could not even make proper camp at night, they had to stop right on the kingsroad. Dense thickets of half-drowned trees pressed close around them, branches dripping with curtains of pale fungus. Huge flowers bloomed in the mud and floated on pools of stagnant water, but if you were stupid enough to leave the causeway to pluck them, there were quicksands waiting to suck you down, and snakes watching from trees, and lizard-lions floating half submerged in the water, like black logs with eyes and teeth. (*Game* 135)

Readers, caught up in Martin's medievalism, might view the stubby grass symbols on the map of central Westeros accompanying the novel as an indication that the Neck is some sort of moorland. Thanks to Sansa, they learn it is more of a jungle or mangrove, rife with gargantuan plants and riverine animals "like black logs with eyes and teeth." Note how Sansa relays this information only *after* she has experienced this jungle first-hand and formed an opinion on it. Martin does not show her visit, only her memory thereof. Readers learn about most of this world by assessing the reports of those who already know it.

Martin's use of immersive rhetoric is one explanation for why many observers, particularly those who consume their fantasy audio-visually, see his world as unusual. Most televisual examples of immersion have been space operas such as *Star Trek* or *Battlestar Galactica*, texts categorised (helpfully or otherwise) as once removed from fantasy. Audiovisual adaptations of fantasy texts have gravitated strongly towards portal-quests. The cinematic iterations of *The Lord of the Rings*, the *Harry Potter* cycle and C.S. Lewis's Chronicles of Narnia are cases in point. The 2006 television adaptation of Pratchett's *Hogfather* demonstrates the trend by breaking the novel's immersive rhetoric with a guide-like expository voice-over. The original *Star Wars* trilogy also perpetuates the portal-quest form. To somebody accustomed to such texts, a fantasy without a guide will naturally appear disorganised, disorientating, and devoid of the sort of authoritative moral direction that portal-quests provide. (Mendlesohn 5) If Glinda tells Dorothy to follow the Yellow Brick Road, she had best get moving; she has no frame of reference to refute her guide, and the world-building, and with it the story, is paralysed until she gets with the program. Lacking guides, immersive focalisers lack any authoritative direction on where the story is going, and so does the reader. Reviewing *A Dance with Dragons* Grossman likened Martin's world to "a political jigsaw puzzle, and somebody just turned the table over, and everybody is on the floor scrabbling for pieces" This is fair comment, but it springs from an approach that is not fundamentally innovative. To say so is not an accusation of unoriginality but a spur to further analysis. As Mendlesohn notes (xviii), a shrewd writer will employ the techniques that guide the reader to engage with the narrative in a manner that serves their authorial ambitions. Martin, as established in earlier chapters, is embarked on an interrogation of the capacity of institutions to shape and guide morality. To this end, he has constructed a thinned, etiolated world that seems to have lost its moral compass. He also wants to draw his readers into an investigation rather than to simply clutch their pearls at his indictment of the situation. The capabilities and imperatives Mendlesohn associates with immersive fantasy are wholly apropos to what Martin is attempting.

The device bears comparison with Iser's phenomenological model of reading. Immersive rhetoric is made up of "*pointers*, glimpses of a world that hint at something more concrete" (72) and draws the reader into the world-building process in a manner that Iser would recognise. Tyrion's reference to Grand Maester Athelmure is a case in point. It shades off into the implication that there are successions of maesters and archmaesters, some of them famously boring and others presumably more interesting. This creates a sense that the narrative discourse constitutes the tip of an iceberg, a random sample extracted from a broader body of knowledge. The engaged reader immediately starts conjuring with these notions, reconstructing a world from an accretion of hints rather than the sort of explicit description characteristic of portal-quests. Martin demonstrates this with his introduction of the Nine Free Cities of Essos.

The first time the reader sees of any of these places it is through the eyes of someone who clearly knows it well:

> Dany went to her window and looked out wistfully on the waters of the bay. The square brick towers of Pentos were black silhouettes outlined against the setting sun. Dany could hear the singing of the red priests as they lit their night fires and the shouts of ragged children playing games beyond the walls of the estate. (*Game* 26)

Daenerys's lack of surprise that her window looks out into a non-existent locale spurs the reader to manufacture the introduction she does not supply. Their reading of the place therefore becomes an interrogative exercise as they try to assemble the information Daenerys does provide into a coherent literary impression. Such information is composed of Mendlesohn's "pointers," and the fifty-eight words quoted above provide plenty with which to begin filling the blank space created by Daenerys's assumption. The city is made of brick rather than the medievalist stone of Winterfell. It is a port. It exhibits marked income inequality; wealthy inhabitants live in walled estates rather than castles. It is home to red priests who sing at night fires. This liturgy is different from those described by Catelyn Stark, who contrasted her husband's animistic religion with her own faith in a creed (19–20) that stands as Martin's equivalent of medieval Catholicism (Wittingslow 114). Hundreds of pages later the reader will meet some of these red priests and build on this point. Daenerys's reverie, however, reveals only that the Pentoshi observe a religious tradition distinct from that of Westeros. Daenerys's host Illyrio Mopatis is striking before he even wobbles into view. The names the reader has seen so far – Robert, Catelyn, Will, Castle Black, Winterfell, White Harbour – are seldom more than a phoneme away from those of modern English. *Illyrio* is a comparatively weird collection of syllables, as is *Pentos*. They are clearly products of a different linguistic tradition to that practiced at Winterfell. Illyrio deals in dragonbone (*Game* 25), a substance comparable to spices and gemstones. This is the first reference to dragons in the narrative, and raises the question of exactly what animals exist in this world. Pentos is clearly a very culturally distinct place from the environs of Winterfell. Martin does not sit anybody down and explain this. He simply has Daenerys think about things she is already familiar with. Readers reverse-engineer Pentos from the pointers she provides, moving from detail to general picture – the opposite, Mendlesohn notes, of a typical expository process in either fiction or fact (75). Presenting his world this way, Martin creates work for the reader, but by undertaking that work they gain a creative stake in the world-building process, as Iser observes of phenomenological reading. If Martin's world seems so vivid to so many of his readers, it is because they built it, in part, themselves.

Once an author starts building a world this way, that world can get very large very quickly. Pentos is one of nine Essosi cities Daenerys has visited in her travels "from Braavos to Myr, from Myr to Tyrosh, and on to Qohor and Volantis and Lys" (*Game* 28). More blank spaces are thus created, initially characterised solely by her grouping them with Pentos. The reader stands by for further information about those communities, which does trickle in over time. The small council chamber in King's Landing is decorated with Qohorik tapestries, recognised as such at a glance by Eddard Stark (185). Clearly, the artistic traditions of Qohor are known in Westeros. Eddard later entrusts Arya to the tutelage of Syrio Forel, a Braavosi, who gives some information about his home. Daario Naharis, with his blue beard, enamelled nails and butter-coloured lace, is "flamboyant even for a Tyroshi" (*Storm* 2.5). His compatriots, sprinkled sparingly throughout Martin's narrative (*Dance* 277; *Feast* 601; *Game* 33), corroborate Daenerys's association of Tyrosh with bold colours. When the narrative returns to the Free Cities, there is a period of portal-quest rhetoric (*Feast* 98–105) as Yorko proudly rows Arya Stark into his home town. This gives way, however, to further immersion. Martin reveals Braavos through the eyes of Cat of the Canals. A day in the life of Cat reveals the tumult of Braavos. She knows the Long Canal, which passes "the green copper domes of the Palace of Truth and the tall square towers of the Prestayns and Antaryons before passing under the immense grey arches of the sweetwater river to the district known as Silty Town" (570–571). Cat is familiar enough with Braavosi culture that she need not reiterate to herself the exact roles the Prestayns and Antaryons play in city life. Readers surmise it themselves. She also knows the names of Braavosi plays (572) the reputation of the roof rats, the relative locations of the Chequey Port, Drowned Town and the Ragman's Harbour (573–574), that the Braavosi watch eel fights (576) and revere an odd caste of pseudonymous courtesans (577–578). And of course she knows that at the end of the day she can always sell her shellfish at the workplace of more approachable prostitutes (581–582). Cat provides a knowing, well-versed view of a lively press of subcultures, neighbourhoods, creative traditions and institutions, one much more clearly and lavishly focalised than any of the other Free Cities. There are eight more of these places scattered around Essos. References to Tyroshi dyes, Qohorik tapestries and ginger-flavoured Norvoshi wintercakes (40) imply that each of the other Free Cities is as complex as Braavos. Martin's narrative need never go to Lys or Tyrosh for those places to be characterised by their comparability to the colourful bustle Cat observes. Such cities are not simply dots to make invented maps look interesting; they stand, partially obscured, in the phenomenological shade at the edge of Cat's immersive rhetoric, given enough life to lend credibility to comparisons with the tumult of Braavos but otherwise left to the reader's imagination. "A good immersive fantasy creates the world by writing it in such a way that noncomprehension of what is written and said becomes part of the mortar of the immersion," states Mendlesohn. "What is not said is as important as what is" (73). This process creates the celebrated depth and breadth of Martin's world.

To combine the said and the unsaid in this way, Mendlesohn observes, requires the presence of "concentric shells" of narrative (68). To create the unsaid, an immersive world must operate "as if it is impervious to outside influence" (59). There can be no reference to the reader's world, no indication that the world the focaliser knows is a mere literary artefact. For a focaliser to specifically say their world is different from Earth would turn the assumptions that activate the phenomenological process into the rigid explications of a portal-quest. There must therefore be a translucent shell protecting the written world from outside influence. In order to build the world in that context, however, the focaliser must encounter things that seem noteworthy from their position of competence, examples and issues to consider in relation to their implied knowledge and thus create Mendlesohnian irony. Tyrion's learned appraisal of Winterfell's library and Cat's off-hand remarks about Braavosi Palace of Truth are examples. There must therefore be a second shell within the first, in which the narrative is actually taking place. The focaliser must sit between these two shells, their gaze directed inward to the smaller shell and caught by the exceptions to, variances from, and opportunities to exercise their existing knowledge. Mendlesohn illustratively likens this to a bain-marie or double-boiler (79); the story sits in the inner chamber and is prepared for reader consumption by the heat exerted upon it by the focaliser's inspection from the outer.

The need to arrange a narrative in this way accounts for the convergent evolution between Cat of the Canals – Arya Stark – and another fantasy character, Lyra Belacqua of Philip Pullman's *His Dark Materials* trilogy. The similarities between these two girls are remarkable. Both are raised in privilege, but seemingly happier among humbler folk. Both are apathetic about their gender, and thus the despair of their respective governesses. Both have a very clear sense of justice which they enforce via amoral pugnacity. Both form partnerships with terribly dangerous, pathetically solitary male alcoholics (Arya with the wine-guzzling [*Storm* 2.454] Sandor Clegane, Lyra with the ethanol-chugging [*Northern Lights* 180–181] Iorek Byrnson). Both above all are accomplished imposters whose capacity for convincing fibs is a major motivating force in their respective plots. Some of their similarities, such as their common willingness to kill and eat birds (*Game* 694; *Northern Lights* 67), are coincidental, but others emerge from the fact that they have been given essentially identical tasks in an immersive fantasy. Pullman's trilogy is mostly a portal-quest, but one that departs from a fantasy of Oxford that takes shape via an immersion that fills two-fifths of his first volume. Lyra's idiosyncrasies serve to construct the Mendlesohnian bain-marie that allows that immersion to take place. Comparing some examples of this in relation to Arya doing the same demonstrates that the similarities between the two girls stem from their common narrative responsibilities. It also serves to demonstrate some key strengths of Mendlesohian immersion, which in turn illustrate how this narrative species is so propitious to the creation of thinned worlds.

Lyra's thoughts on gender illustrate the point. Pullman depicts a society of tightly defined gender roles. Women are frequently encountered in maternal or caregiving roles but rarely elsewhere. Lyra's mother Mrs Coulter, "hungry for power," cannot pursue it herself; she must do so by cultivating relationships with the right men (*Northern Lights* 374). Her gender dictates her actions. It is therefore interesting that Lyra initially seems to have little sense of gender; her governess must force her into feminine attire "with many threats" (37; 64–65) for visits by her absentee parents. She has been raised in the "grand and stony and masculine" (76) Jordan College, though she has reached an age when the Master is flustered by the idea of a pubescent girl under his roof. She needs, he insists, "Female guidance."

> The word *female* only suggested female Scholars to Lyra, and she involuntarily made a face. To be exiled from the grandeur of Jordan, the splendour and fame of its scholarship, to a dingy brick-built boarding-house of a college at the northern end of Oxford, with dowdy female Scholars who smelt of cabbage and mothballs like those two at dinner! (71)

Among the restrictions on female activity in this world, clearly, is a patronisingly token acceptance of women in education. Looking at the issue of gender from outside Lyra is able to demonstrate something of her world's attitudes to it in ways that activate the irony of mimesis and therefore put the reader to work on reverse-engineering a world from the assumptions evident in what they are told. Pullman thus communicates the status of women in his invented world to his readers by charging them with the phenomenological exercise of assembling Mendlesohnian pointers. An important facet of the dystopian totalitarian theocracy of which he writes therefore becomes apparent via Frye's "sophisticated," rather than naïve irony – "the naïve ironist calls attention to the fact that he is being ironic, whereas sophisticated irony merely states, and lets the reader add the ironic tone himself" (Frye 41). Or herself. Espying this point, the reader is immediately on guard for further pointers, approaching the narrative with a sceptical, appraising eye they would probably not be using if they were simply being told things as in the manner of a Mendleoshnian portal-quest. Pullman achieves this effect by having

Lyra share the assumptions of her world but making her only partly subject to them, placing her between the two shells of Mendleoshnian immersion.

Arya does much the same. Like Lyra's Oxford, Westeros is a patriarchy, and few of the other cultures Martin describes are greatly different. With patriarchy comes the imposition of expectations of appropriate female behaviour. Although Sansa Stark seems to embody the ideal of Westerosi girlhood, it is her sister who illustrates what that ideal is, by reflecting on the matter from outside:

> Sansa was two years older; maybe by the time Arya had been born there had been nothing left. Often it felt that way. Sansa could sew and dance and sing. She wrote poetry. She knew how to dress. She played the high harp *and* the bells. Worse, she was beautiful. Sansa had gotten their mother's fine high cheekbones and the thick auburn hair of the Tullys. Arya took after their lord father. Her hair was a lustreless brown, and her face was long and solemn. (*Game* 66)

This early commentary communicates a sense of envy that Arya rarely mentions thereafter. Her subsequent observations of Sansa instead demonstrate the sort of casual contempt common between temperamentally mismatched siblings. Martin may have intended a nuance to their relationship that has not panned out in practice. Nevertheless, Arya's perception of her sister's courtly graces from a position to one side of this orthodoxy means that the Mendlesohnian double-boiler heats up; Arya's critical distance from an issue allows Martin to draw attention to one of the attributes of his world. Arya continues to look with her eyes while others communicate their assumptions:

> "What were you doing to that cat, boy?" Myrcella asked again, sternly. To her brother she said, "He's a ragged boy, isn't he? Look at him." She giggled.
>
> "A ragged dirty smelly boy," Tommen agreed.
> *They don't know me, Arya realised. They don't even know I'm a girl.* (329)

Tommen walked into the great hall at Winterfell arm-in-arm with Arya (47). His subsequent inability to recognise her demonstrates that Westerosi expectations of female behaviour are very deeply ingrained. Arya's discovery that she can pass for a boy means that this aspect of her society is "observed by somebody interested in their surroundings" – interested enough to give the matter some conscious thought – "but who already knows what [she] is seeing" (Mendlesohn 78). Arya's interrogation of the point from a position outside the norms of her society allows Martin to communicate Westerosi patriarchy the same way Pullman does the misogyny of Lyra's Oxford. It is a Mendlesohnian pointer, something the reader must think through and analyse. That analysis exemplifies the sort of sceptical, interrogative reading process immersive focalisation demands of its observer.

Lyra and Arya do the same with another common issue in their respective worlds – social stratification. Pullman's depicts a class system of almost medievalist rigidity. He contrasts the wealth and grandeur of Jordan College (34–35), a major socioeconomic power in his invented Brytain, with the plight of those not privileged to be associated with such institutions. His plot begins with a poignant anecdote about the deprived Tony Makarios being entranced by the glamour of Mrs Coulter and thus shanghaied into a magical atrocity (40–43). While movement between these strata appears almost non-existent, Lyra can observe both at close quarters. She lives at the College, regarding "visiting professors and eminent scholars from elsewhere with pitying scorn, because they didn't belong to Jordan" (35). But she spends most of her time getting up to no good with the urchins of Oxford:

> Lyra and her peers were engaged in deadly warfare. First, the children (young servants, and children of servants, and Lyra) of one college waged war on those of another. But this enmity was swept aside when the town children attacked a collager: then all the colleges banded together and went to battle against the townies. This rivalry was hundreds of years old, and very deep and satisfying. (36)

Lyra's pugnacious adventures among her playmates demonstrate the stratification of her world. Pullman has, again, placed his focaliser in an unconventional position, one in which Lyra can take an important feature of her world for granted but also record it as noteworthy because she herself stands slightly to one side of it. Again, the Mendlesohnian bain-marie is simmering; crucial aspects of the narrative discourse become apparent in the inner chamber via the observations of someone carefully positioned in the outer. Pullman reports his world in a manner that preserves the irony of mimesis and thus encourages readerly interrogation of the consequences of a sinisterly totalitarian regime.

Martin uses Arya for exactly this purpose. As noted in earlier chapters, the stratification of society is one of the key aspects of his medievalism. Tyrion Lannister finds the democracy of the hill clans ("even their women were allowed to speak") absurd (*Game* 587). Characters such as Davos Seaworth and Varys are unusual in their ability to occupy multiple niches in a very rigid social order (*Clash* 138; 577). Arya does the same thing instincively, as a matter of temperament. Her father somewhat eccentrically interviews one of his vassals each night over dinner, and

> Arya had loved nothing better than to sit at her father's table and listen to them talk. She had loved listening to the men on the benches too; to freeriders tough as leather, courtly knights and bold young squires, grizzled old men-at-arms. She used to throw snowballs at them and help them steal pies from the kitchen. Their wives gave her scones and she invented names for their babies and played monsters-and-maidens and hide-the-treasure and come-into-my-castle with their children. (*Game* 211)

Born into privilege, Arya nevertheless instinctively engages in exactly the sort of plebeian horseplay as Lyra, getting filthy without a thought (*Game* 136; *Northern Lights* 36), accepting treats from smallfolk (Arya's fondness for peasant scones compares precisely with Lyra's for gyptian gingerbread [*Northern Lights* 54]) and making friends with servants like Mycah, heedless of propriety. This experience proves invaluable. Knowing that she can pass for a "scrawny naked girl scrubbing her rags" (*Game* 336), as well as a boy, Arya eludes the forces of the Lannister coup and hides in Flea Bottom.

> She had tried talking to the children she saw in the street, hoping to make a friend who would give her a place to sleep, but she must have talked wrong or something. The little ones only looked a her with quick, wary eyes and ran away if she came too close. Their big brothers and sisters asked questions Arya couldn't answer, called her names and tried to steal from her. Only yesterday, a scrawny barefoot girl twice her age had knocked her down and tried to pull the boots off her feet, but Arya had given her a *crack* on the ear with her stick sword that sent her off sobbing and bleeding. (696)

Arya's plebian persona is imperfect, but her honest efforts to engage with the urchins of King's Landing turns them into a Mendlesohnian pointer, an instance of sophisticated irony. The reader must again make sense of what they are reading. They cannot do so in this instance without grasping that the militarised aristocracy exemplified by Eddard Stark and Robert Baratheon is not the be-all and end-all of Martin's written world. He achieves this effect in the same way Pullman demonstrates the negative consequences of a reflexively conservative totalitarian theocracy: by having large sections of his narrative focalised by someone who understands, but stands slightly aside from, the social assumptions that many of his other characters exhibit, and can thus make them explicit points of narrative record. It is probably no accident that Arya is the only character to have focalised chapters in all of Martin's first five volumes.

Her practical, unpretentious analysis of Westerosi society is crucial to his authorial aims.

The fact that immersive narrative requires readers to think through points of narrative discourse has emotive as well as expository potential. Readers experience what is strange, striking, or unsettling about the written world not from their own perspective, but from that of the character, following their thought processes and being drawn into their emotional responses (Mendlesohn 70). In a sense, where the portal-quest "tells", immersive rhetoric, bound by the impermiability of the outer of the two concentric shells, must "show", and do so through the eyes of the character. This is a powerful enough device that Mendlesohn sees the need to pause her analysis to specifically state she does not see immersive rhetoric as fundamentally superior to the other forms she discusses (71). Martin and Pullman use the shared, arguably definitive capacity of Arya Stark and Lyra Belacqua for imposture to avail themselves of this device at important points in the story. Lyra discovers what a "severed child" – an unsettling idea that has been haunting Pullman's narrative for 200 pages (22; 46; 122) – actually is when separated from her portal-quest guides. All people in Lyra's world have a totemic animal daemon, and the Gobblers, the villains in whose pursuit she quests, have contrived a way of magically separating people from these creatures, a spiritual maiming for which Lyra has no frame of reference. At the sight of the hapless Tony Makarios, therefore, her trademark gumption and courage both nearly fail her.

> Her first impulse was to turn and run, or to be sick. A human being with no daemon was like someone without a face, or with their ribs laid open and their heart torn out: something unnatural and uncanny that belonged to the world of night-ghasts, not to the waking world of sense.
>
> So Lyra clung to Pantalaimon and her head swam and her gorge rose, and cold as the night was, a sickly sweat moistened her flesh with something colder still. (215)

The gravity of this atrocity is crucial to the impact of Pullman's story as a whole. To ensure the reader takes his point, therefore, he does not have Lyra receive an explanation. Instead, he presents her thought processes as she works it out for herself. The effect of this on the reader is crucial; rather than being told this is revolting, the reader follows Lyra's line of reasoning and appreciates her distress. Using this device to deepen the pathetic spectacle of Tony, Pullman later has Lyra adopt an assumed identity when she is captured by the Gobblers herself. This shifts her back from portal-quest rhetoric to the outer chamber of the immersive Mendlesohnian boiler, observing the operations of the villains and working things out for herself. This draws the reader into the nauseating trauma of the attempt to "incise" her:

> And she kicked and bit more passionately than ever, until the man holding her gasped and let go for a moment – and she was free, and Pantalaimon sprang towards her like a spark of lightning, and she clutched him to her fierce breast, and he dug his wildcat claws into her flesh, and every stab of pain was dear to her.
>
> "Never, never, never!" she cried, and backed against the wall to defend him to her death.
>
> But they fell on her again, three big brutal men, and she as only a child, shocked and terrified, and they tore Pantalaimon away, and threw her into one side of the cage of mesh and carried him, struggling still, around to the other. There was a mesh barrier between them, but he was still part of her, they were still joined. For a second or so more, he was still her own dear soul. [...] The great pale silver blade was rising slowly, catching the brilliant light. The last moment in her complete life was going to be the worst by far. (278–279)

Rather than being told how terrible the experience of incision is, readers receive a first-hand account of how it feels from someone who (via her encounter with Tony) knows what is happening. This is made possible by Lyra's assumed identity as the foundling Lizzie Brooks, to whom her captors will not explain anything directly and who must work things out for herself. This obliges the readers to do so themselves based on the discourse she provides. Perhaps paradoxically, Lyra's critical distance, preserved by her capacity as an instinctive fabulist, sets up a situation of emotive immediacy for the reader, who in their necessary analysis of the narrative discourse feels her pain rather than receiving a diagnosis of it.

Arya's succession of assumed identities sustains her Mendlesohnian immersion, to much the same effect. Arya's chapters generally begin by demonstrating the passage of time and the changing of circumstances, communicating the ironic normality of whichever new identity Arya has adopted. Her chapter as Cat of the Canals is the obvious example, but a more emotive one occurs after her capture in the Riverlands:

> There was no place to hide, no tricks to play, no way to be safe.
>
> One girl shared a soldier's bed three nights running; the Mountain picked her on the fourth day, and the soldier said nothing.
>
> A smiley old man mended their clothing and babbled about his son, off serving in the gold cloaks at King's Landing. "A king's man, he is," he would say, "a good king's man like me, all for Joffrey." He said it so often that the other captives began to call him All-for-Joffrey

> whenever the guards weren't listening. All-for-Joffrey was picked on the fifth day. (375)

It is not until the following page that Martin demonstrates what "being picked" amounts to, though even then this is still not directly stated. Instead, Martin notes that "the Tickler asked the questions" and reports Chiswyck's opinion that "Tickler makes them howl so hard they piss themselves" (376). By reverse-engineering these comments, and taking into account Martin's para-Gothic medievalism, the reader surmises that Gregor Clegane is torturing his prisoners. As he often does in Arya's chapters, Martin begins the tale of her captivity by carefully re-establishing Mendlesohnian irony of mimesis. The narrative prompt he offers to help readers fill that vacuum is not a statement of an emotional state, but a case history, forcing the reader to follow an argument. As readers relate specific examples (All-for-Joffrey) to general context (conditions in Gregor's slave train), they become drawn into Arya's thought processes, following her reasoning for her sense of fear, helplessness and lost individuality. Martin narrates a crucial aspect of the tale – the unselfconscious brutality of warfare in a stratified society in which certain individuals are not required to account for their treatment of certain others – in such a manner that the reader sees them as striking not from their point of view, but from Arya's. This is the same fortunate paradox Pullman uses when describing Lyra's near-incision; the critical distance of the focaliser deepens the effect of their focalisation.

This recurs at Harrenhal after Roose Bolton takes the castle. Bolton is unlike Gregor Clegane, who Eddard knew only by reputation (*Game* 303). He is, as far as Arya knows, a loyal Stark bannerman, at least casually acquainted with her family. As she bears a close resemblance to her father (66), she might have revealed herself in the hope of being reunited with her mother. Instead, she warily calls herself Nan and serves as Bolton's cup-bearer. This gives her ample chance to observe subsequent developments in Harrenhal. As with her chapter in Clegane's slave train, her report picks up some time into Bolton's regime at the castle:

> The cook was spared (some said because he'd made the weasel soup), but stocks were hammered together for pretty Pia and the other women who'd shared their favours with Lannister soldiers. Stripped and shaved, they were left in the middle ward beside the bear pit, free for the use of any man who wanted them.
>
> Three Frey men-at-arms were using them that morning as Arya went to the well. She tried not to look, but she could hear the men laughing. The pail was very heavy once full. She was turning to bring it back to Kingspyre when Goodwife Amabel seized her arm. The water went sloshing over the side onto Amabel's legs. "You did that on purpose" the woman screeched.

> "What do you want?" Arya squirmed in her grasp. Amabel had been half-crazed since they'd cut Harra's head off.
>
> "See there?" Amabel pointed across the yard at Pia. "When this northman falls you'll be where she is." (*Clash* 801)

Amabel threatens to violate Arya with a broom when her prediction bears out, calibrating herself grotesquely in the game of beds. She is a creature of Martin's world, the very model of a gibbering medievalist harridan. By contrast, Arya remains in the outer chamber of the boiler, positioned by her alias to observe Amabel's world with critical distance. Her unease at sexual violence, recoiling from a rape and turning instead to fantasise about joining the crows eating the heads on the walls (800), contributes to keeping the reader on side with her as Martin increasingly reveals her childlike capacity for uncomplicated hate (she answers Amabel's threat with one of death, just as Lyra does to those who do not accord the maimed Tony due respect [*Northern Lights* 220]). Martin shows the grisly consequences of the Bolton takeover long enough after the fact that Bolton's punishment of Pia has become part of Arya's everyday routine. The reader must then make sense of the ghastly sights that she sees as normal by treating them as Mendlesohnian pointers, by relating them to broader trends and reading them as indications of what is so disastrously wrong with this society. Corporal and sexual abuse, both startling demonstrations of Westeros's culture of violence, are depicted in a way that encourages the reader to see them directly through Arya's eyes. Like Lyra's, Arya's ability to fabricate new identities contributes to her ability to present the iniquities of a Martin's cynical, morally dissipated medievalist world.

Much of the similarity between Arya Stark and Lyra Belacqua is therefore attributable to their focalising perspective from between the two concentric shells of a Mendlesohnian immersion. This also activates the emotive potential of this world-building technique. That potential comes from a point Lyra and Arya have both repeatedly demonstrated: readers of this method of fantasy exposition follow arguments rather than receiving instructions. This pulls the reader into the world-building process, forcing them to appreciate reasoned points of view and demonstrable states of mind (Mendlesohn 70). A reader of Arya's experiences in Harrenhal sees the gruesome violence of this Gothic ruin as part of the daily grind of living there, not as anything particularly strange. Reflecting on this, they appreciate the callouses forming on this ten-year-old soul. The vividness and immediacy of the experiences reported by Arya and her compatriots contributes significantly to the verisimilitude of Martin's world.

It also contributes to the sense of etiolation and exhaustion of that world – as Clute puts it, its thinning. Mendlesohn associates immersion with that leitmotif (61). This is because the heat of the immersive double-boiler is that of an interrogative gaze (69). Note how, in the preceding comparison of Arya and Lyra, focaliser and reader alike are analysing the written world. Already fundamentally familiar with their world, characters cannot credibly wonder at discoveries. What is noteworthy is not the celebration of the new – which would be "the equivalent of remarking to someone of one's own species 'My, you're a *human*!'" (76) – but the rationalisation of the familiar. The narrative matter they generate therefore inescapably takes the form of a critique. Immersive focalisers need not dislike what they see, but they cannot take it at face value (68). "Instead of fulfilling the mission that has been bestowed upon them by higher forces," observes Trębicki, the protagonist "becomes an antagonist in relation to his/her microcosm, both critical and evaluating" (52). A generator of narrative discourse situates their perceptions in relation to past experiences and broader bodies of implied knowledge, an exercise inherently requiring critical distance (Mendlesohn 65). Pullman's Lyra, for example, lays out a concise case, based on previous observations, for her esteem for the plebian matriarch Ma Costa (*Northern Lights* 54–55). Martin's focalisers similarly explain their world by discussing what they see in light of what they know. Catelyn's concession of the beauty of her husband's ancestral sword (*Game* 21), Illyrio Mopatis's reassurance of Viserys that his violet-eyed sister looks "regal" (30) and Tyrion Lannister's warning "Be gentle with the Valyrian scrolls; the parchment is very dry" (82) also demonstrate the pattern. Characters establish the cultural debt Westeros owes to Valyria by presenting existing knowledge to rationalise their impressions. Immersive worlds make sense because they are built from the reports of those making sense of them.

But the cost of sense is wonder. Manlove defines wonder, in the context of fantasy literature, as "anything from crude astonishment at the marvellous, to a sense of "meaning-in-the-mysterious" or even of the numinous" (1975 7), and cites its contemplation as a key defining feature of the genre. Harry Potter's amazement as his chocolate frog jumps out the train window is wonder; so too at the more profound end is Keats's contemplation of his Grecian Urn. Modern fantasy is essentially a latter-day continuation of the Romantic tradition, being centrally concerned with mysteries posited at the centre of humanity's relationship with the world. Portal-quest fantasies, demanding faith in the guide, are ideal for provoking such mystique. Immersive fantasy all but inescapably meditates upon its absence. Mystique implies faith, a voluntary suspension of analysis and willingness to accept something as what it appears, claims, or is claimed to be. Such concessions cannot be made in a world that exists as an assembly of reasoned observations and logical deductions. Timeless, Romantic verities are not valued *per se* but serve as critical tools, contextualising the focaliser's attempt "to analyse what he *actually* sees" (Mendlesohn 69). "Your honor as a Lannister is worth less than *this*" (*Clash* 717), sneers Catelyn Stark as she tips over Jaime Lannister's pisspot, invoking an abstract verity to observe its absence. Honour, loyalty, religious faith and the divine right of kings are, similarly, departure points for Jaime's rejoinders, which horrify Catelyn ("*I do not want to know this*" [720]) because his mockery of a society clattering through the empty shells of its ideals is so credible. This accruing of credibility by arguing away from, rather than towards, sacred truth is the "backward undoing of the tapestry-web of God's science [which] works with its back to him" ("The Truth" 25) decried by George MacDonald, the Victorian Christian Romantic who has more claim than most to have instigated the modern fantasy tradition. Readers assembling Mendlesohnian pointers follow precisely this epistemology. They know the Qohorik tapestries in the council chamber are costly imports because they know, roughly, what and where Qohor is, which they know because it is comparable to Pentos, which they know is distinct from the North, which they know is part of the Seven Kingdoms ruled from the council chamber. All signification is contingent, hiving away from the organic certainties of Romanticism (Bould and Vint 107). Spells are made to be broken. To read a tightly-constructed immersive fantasy is to "start with what is and watch it crumble" (Mendlesohn 113), to collude in the trading away of wonder for reason, the narrative of thinning.

A comparison between the presentation of a magic sword in a portal-quest fantasy and an immersion illustrates the point. First, the portal-quest version:

> Dumbledore reached across Professor McGonagall's desk, picked up the blood-stained silver sword, and handed it to Harry. Dully, Harry turned it over, the rubies blazing in the firelight. And then he saw the name engraved just below the hilt.
>
> *Godric Gryffindor.*
>
> "Only a true Gryffindor could have pulled *that* out of the hat, Harry," Dumbledore said simply. (*Chamber of Secrets* 333–334)

Harry Potter's focalisation never queries the statement of his learned portal-quest guide. The sword is magic; he is a *true* Gryffindor. By contrast, Davos Seaworth is rather more suspicious of Lightbringer, Stannis Baratheon's magic sword, which supposedly identifies him as the successor to the legendary Azor Ahai. Deferential to Stannis, Davos observes the ostensible enchantment of the sword via its immolation in the heart of the burning effigy of the Mother taken from Dragonstone's desecrated sept. "Devan knelt with Byren Farring and rolled up the king's burnt and blackened sword in the leather cloak. *The Red Sword of Heroes looks a proper mess*, thought Davos" (*Clash* 136). His dubious reflection on this artefact comes in the course of a chapter substantially about Davos's reservations about his king's fiery new creed; his suspicion of Melisandre (133), his dubious reception of R'hllorian apocrypha from Salladhor Saan (140–142) and his warnings to Stannis that this will be a public-relations disaster (147). Davos takes little at face value. He is still interrogating Lightbringer as Stannis uses it to make him a lord; "The air shimmered around it, and no jewel had ever sparkled so brilliantly. But when Stannis touched it to Davos's shoulder, it felt no different than any other longsword" (*Storm* 1.498–1.499). Lightbringer has, as of the conclusion of *A Dance with Dragons*, yet to be demonstrated as anything more than a parade-ground prop. Stannis's brother dismisses it as such (*Clash* 434) and the blazing light it emits when Mance Rayder is executed (*Dance* 158) is undercut by the fact that the blood of kings is in fact *not* shed at the Wall (Rattleshirt burned, not Mance) and later by Melisandre's stated pyrotechnic trickery (479). Whether the sword is magical or not, the analytical tone of discussion about it undercuts the sort of emotive power Stannis and Melisandre want it to have. Such dicourse denies the reader the sort of Romanticist certainties that Harry and his readers enjoy by taking Dumbledore's word. The result, as noted earlier, is an immediacy and vividness of focalisation. Almost inescapably, however, magic is deprived of the innocent faith it requires to truly take effect. What emerges from this method of fantasy exposition is not the discovery of the wonders of a fantasy world but disenchantment, the breaking of spells, the rationalisation of glory, and the interrogative thinning of the world (Mendlesohn 113).

Authors can put this particular mode of meditation to constructive effect, however, and Martin is one who does so. Daenerys Targaryen, for example, is a carefully constructed immersive focaliser. Sections of her story resemble a portal-quest. Her journey to Vaes Dothrak and sojourn in the city, abetted by consultations with the faultlesssly well-informed Westerosi orientalist Jorah Mormont, might be analysed as examples of the form. Yet her great shift in the first volume is not geographical, but familial: her evolving relationship with her embryonic dragons. Mormont (innocently) misinforms her on this matter, pleading with her not to undertake the ritual that hatches them (*Game* 773). Daenerys works this ritual out herself, meditating on her own fondness for heat (29), the auspicious cause of death of a brother she knows to be unworthy (225) and the imperviousness of the eggs to fire (572–573). She is in Mormont's debt for his insights into the Dothraki, but her shift to a state of knowledge and agency that can change the world comes not through listening to a guide but by ignoring one and testing a hypothesis of her own formulation. Syrio Forel would approve of this girl. Daenerys manufactures narrative discourse not by trusting what she is told but by looking with her eyes, considering what she sees, and making logical deductions.

Doing so in Astapor she interrogates some of the Mendlesohnian pointers she focalised in Pentos. Among the slaves at Khal Drogo's Pentoshi residence is a man with "the copper skin and dark almond eyes of a Dothraki, but his face was hairless and he wore the spiked bronze cap of the Unsullied" (*Game* 32). Daenerys recognises this panoply when she sees it. Her lack of explanation activates the phenomenological effect of immersive focalisation; somewhere in this world some martial caste or order known as the Unsullied exists. Little more is said about them until Jorah Mormont suggests Daenerys buy some Unsullied of her own, telling her of the Three Thousand of Qohor (*Storm* 1.117–1.119) to support his point. This tale of long ago ("four hundred years ago or more"), resembles that of a portal-quest guide; such figures will often present history as matter of essential truth rather than as the discipline of interpretation and critical debate practiced in Earthly universities (Mendlesohn 13–14). Kraznys mo Nakloz does the same. His eight-page sales pitch (*Storm* 1.312–1.319) is a remarkably sustained, dictatorial exposition. But Daenerys is not passively receiving Kraznys's patter. By pretending to be ignorant of High Valyrian and speaking through an interpreter while understanding everything the slavemaster says, she is actively gathering data about the Astapori slave trade. Kraznys sounds like a portal-quest guide because he thinks he is one, explaining something to an ignorant sunset savage, when in fact he is the rube and she the calculating mind taking the measure of him. Like Arya's imposture in Harrenhal, this provides critical distance from which she can appraise, rather than simply receive, her world.

That distance has the same effect as Arya calling herself Nan; the reader sees things from her point of view. Daenerys is displeased with what she finds, and upbraids Jorah Mormont for bringing her to such a "vile sty":

> "They sell eunuchs, not men. Eunuchs made of brick, like the rest of Astapor. Shall I buy eight thousand brick eunuchs with dead eyes that never move, who kill suckling babes for the sake of a spiked hat and strangle their own dogs? They don't even have names. So don't call them *men*, ser."
>
> "*Khaleesi*," he said, taken aback by her fury, "the Unsullied are chosen as boys, and trained – "
> "I have heard all I care to of their *training*." Dany could feel tears welling in her eyes, sudden and unwanted. Her hand flashed up and cracked Ser Jorah hard across the face. It was either that, or cry. (*Storm* 1.326)

She manages to contain herself during Kraznys's pitch, for the sake of keeping up her interrogative pretence, but in private, Mormont becomes the recipient of her pent-up distress. Her recollections of Kraznys's ironically prideful patter focuses on the foulest aspects of his work, the dead babies and puppies. The reader follows the thought processes of a character who has grown up with slavery struggling to deal with the true enormity of something she may not have thought too much about before. This pulls those readers into Martin's world-building process. Daenerys has seen the Unsullied in the Free Cities, and knew they were eunuchs; clearly she did not know all the details. Martin reports her cunning assembly of clues and shocked analysis of them as she rides back to her ship through the brick-dust of Astapor, "old and crumbling," populated by nose-picking gutter-rats and aristocrats "like some troupe of demons escaped from the seventh hell" (1.322–1.323), shocking and garish but also shabby and unglamorous. The outburst Mormont absorbs stems from her investigation of what paid for Astapor's chintzy affectations – Kraznys's over-deployed raspberry perfume, the passing aristocrat's absurd hairdos - and what the guards who watched her as she slept in Illyrio Mopatis's estate (*Game* 108; Robert's intelligence comes from an eyewitness) endured as children. The presentation of a puzzling-out of an industrialised atrocity taking place in the phenomenological shade of Martin's world makes the Unsullied strange and tragic not from the reader's perspective, but from Daenerys's.

This serves a further-reaching purpose than getting the reader to appreciate what motivates her crusade though Slaver's Bay. It breaks a spell. Like any good infomercial narrator, Kraznys is selling Daenerys an idea as much as a product. His goal in mutilating and brutalising thousands of boys, he explains, is the creation of "The lockstep legions of Old Ghis come again" (*Storm* 1.315). He is offering the sunset savage the chance to buy recreated wonders, functioning reiterations of his decrepit people's vanished glories, chattels that will behave like the fabled and idealised Three Thousand of Qohor. The contempt in his comments to Missandei are all directed towards his client; his pride in his wares appears wholly genuine. Daenerys is not content to accept Jorah Mormont's tale about the Three Thousand, however, or the slave-trader's assertion that he has bullied these boys into becoming such fabled warriors. Her subsequent critical observation of these purported cockless wonders demonstrates they have actually retained much of the individuality Kraznys claimed to have thrashed out of them. Grey Worm is indeed "tireless," but he is also "quick to learn" (*Storm* 2.2), a quality Kraznys explicitly assures Daenerys he no longer has (1.319). Stalwart Shield hires prostitutes to cuddle him, seeking surcease of the traumas of his upbringing (*Dance* 35–36). An accretion of properly informed observational intelligence shows that *Kraznys has failed*, that people cannot be forcibly moulded into glorious symbols any more than they can be cajoled into that status with a white cloak. The reader is perhaps relieved, but the case demonstrates that the interrogative approach of the immersive focaliser disenchants their subject. Focaliser and reader alike are engaged in a fundamentally critical process – focalisers relating what they see to what they know; readers analysing the results of that process. Very rarely does an immersive fantasy reach any truth, any literary equivalent of a unified field theory of the written world. If faults are not found, then functions are still revealed to be contingent on other matters, themselves likely contingent upon something else, and so on ad infinitum (Bould and Vint 107). The wonders of a fantasy world cannot remain wholly wonderful if they are presented via a process of logical argument, since wonder occurs when logic fails. Immersive fantasies are hostile to the sorts of organic, symbolic verities that characters like Kraznys cling to; the necessary reading process involves poking holes in them, hemming them in, and thinning them out.

Martin's evocation of a tired, diminished, slouching world is therefore not simply a matter of his depiction of kings, bureaucrats and soldiers behaving badly. The manner in which he presents such depictions contributes significantly to that picture. Of the twenty-four significant focalisers (discounting those of his prologues and epilogues) in Martin's first five volumes, twenty-one are engaged in Mendlesohnian immersive rhetoric. The exceptions are Bran Stark (who is undertaking a Mendlesohnian portal-quest), Jon Snow (who experiences a Mendlesohnian intrusion) and Samwell Tarly, who functions largely as an adjunct to Jon. Martin deploys these characters effectively, as will be discussed in the following chapter, although their purpose is to provide codas to an interrogative method of fantasy exposition. Characters like Arya, Daenerys and Davos build their world by thinking things through and working things out. In some cases, like Arya's, this serves the purpose of bringing a startling, emotive immediacy to the narrative, as the reader, following Arya's thought processes, sees things as noteworthy and horrible from her perspective rather than their own. Dystopian conditions are therefore brought home to the reader as they follow an argument. In other cases, such as that of Daenerys and Davos, the effect of this is to call wonders into question, to apply logical deduction and critical distance to things they are being asked to accept as unquestionable. That exercise forms the preponderant bulk of Martin's narrative discourse and is passed onto the reader in their phenomenological effort to create a picture from the pointers Martin supplies. The Romantic certainties of the modern fantasy tradition are thus called into question. The manner in which he explains Westeros encodes a sense of thinning and dissipation into the very process by which the reader assembles the written world.

Characters who speak in certainties tend to come across either as *alazons* or people hiding something, although such people are seldom focalisers. Kraznys mo Nakloz is, for all his deplorable faults, not trying to swindle Daenerys; he thinks the Unsullied will work as advertised. He does not live to see his wares prove him wrong, but he is thoroughly cashiered by subsequent events. He lives and dies a fool. Melisandre is a figure of opaque absolutes and unfathomable agendas, Davos Seaworth thinks, a dangerous idiot at best and an evil witch at worst. It is only in *A Dance with Dragons* that the reader discovers she is attempting to advance a sincere religious crusade, one that tellingly requires her to continue searching for answers – to continue her engagement with and investigation of the world rather than drawing a line under it, as Selyse Baratheon seems to have done (474–477). The same shift occurs, intriguingly, to Brienne of Tarth, whose protestations of chivalry make her – unanointed as she may be – one of the most genuine knights in Westeros, and also one of the most starry-eyed:

> "Winter will never come for the likes of us. Should we die in battle, they will surely sing of us, and it's always summer in the songs. In the songs all knights are gallant, all maids are beautiful, and the sun is always shining." (*Clash* 317)

Catelyn Stark pities Brienne for her naivete, as well the reader might; through Catelyn's eyes she comes across as a genuine *alazon*. Note also her insistence on Romanticised truths, and her language of warmth and light, both direct parallels with the fiery catechisms spouted by Melisandre. This timbre continues during Brienne's ill-fated mission to escort Jaime Lannister to King's Landing "It is a rare and precious gift to be a knight," she informs her irreverent captive, "and even more so a knight of the Kingsguard. It is a gift given to few, a gift you scorned and soiled" (*Storm* 1.158). As soon as she is promoted to focaliser, however, Brienne begins thinking analytically, relating her mission to find Sansa via interrogative observations. Her idealism remains, as does the courtly language she uses to express it ("*Be not afraid. I shall not rest until I've found you*" [*Feast* 79]) but note how carefully she appraises Creighton Longbough and Illifer the Penniless, the two hedge knights she meets early in her journey; "*If I fear the likes of these, I had as well swap my longsword for a pair of knitting needles*" (66–67). The post-war malaise settling over southern Westeros, its refugees and stragglers, are focalised by someone logically thinking through what they see, activating both the immediacy and interrogative bent of Mendlesohnian immersion. Very often, the introduction of a new focaliser deepens Martin's narrative not by adding a conflicting agenda, but by adding further layers of analysis to the stripping away of illusion, the winnowing-down of the invented world to what is really there.

Sansa Stark is a particularly interesting case of this movement in action. The last Stark to start recording her observations (this does not happen until she has left Winterfell), Sansa appears at first glance to be there to draw attention to Martin's prevailing modal irony. She is scandalised by the thought that her half-brother "Jon's mother had been *common*, or so people whispered" (*Game* 138) and cannot understand how she and Arya can possibly be sisters. Her emphasis underlines her, initially, as a dreadful snob, the sort of character Martin reveals Cersei Lannister as being in *A Feast for Crows*. What is interesting is that this character is disabused of her courtly illusions while Cersei pig-headedly clutches at her own. This movement suits Martin's purposes. Although she lusts after Romantic certainties, Sansa is an immersive focaliser. This combination of an active longing for emotional truth and an expositional obligation of intellectual analysis combines to make her one of Martin's most effective evokers of Clutean thinning.

Sansa's second outing as a focaliser is a textbook case of immersive rhetoric:

> They watched the heroes of a hundred songs ride forth, each more fabulous than the last. The seven knights of the Kingsguard took the field, all but Jaime Lannister in scaled armor the color of milk, their cloaks as white as fresh-fallen snow. Ser Jaime wore the white cloak as well, but beneath it he was shining gold from head to foot, with a lion's head helm and a golden sword. Ser Gregor Clegane, the Mountain That Rides, thundered past them like an avalanche. Sansa remembered Lord Yohn Royce, who had guested at Winterfell two years before. "His armor is bronze, thousands and thousands of years old, engraved with magic runes that ward him against harm," she whispered to Jeyne. Septa Mordane pointed out Lord Jason Mallister, in indigo chased with silver, the wings of an eagle on his helm. He had cut down three of Rhaegar's bannermen on the Trident. The girls giggled over the warrior priest Thoros of Myr, with his flapping red robes and shaven head, until the septa told them he had once scaled the walls of Pyke with a flaming sword in his hand. (*Game* 284–285)

Sansa's observation of the Tournament of the Hand serves two purposes, the first being expository. This is the first real indication of the scope and intricacy of Martin's invented aristocracy. It is also the first mention of two subsequently pivotal secondary characters, Gregor Clegane and Thoros of Myr. Both are call-backs to previous points of world-building. Gregor Clegane is the brother of Sandor, already well known, while Thoros is one of the red priests Daenerys heard in Pentos (26). Sansa also introduces tertiary characters who have an interesting habit of poking their heads back into the narrative. Jason Mallister is later mentioned among Jorah Mormont's conquests as he wooed his beloved Lynesse (*Clash* 180), informs the Starks of Balon Greyjoy's death (*Storm* 2.62) and surrenders his castle, Seaguard, to the Freys under threat of his son's life (*Feast* 645). Nevertheless he is sparingly characterised.

He gets an equivalent of Tyroshi hair-dye – Seaguard features the Booming Tower, named for its great bell (*Clash* 162) – but little else. Two paragraphs later Sansa sees Jalabhar Xho, who is similarly neither a character nor a subplot but a piece of world-building décor. Xho's job is to be mentioned in lists of people – fugitives from the King's Landing riot (*Clash* 535), guests at Sansa's wedding (*Storm* 1.386), Margaery Tyrell's trumped-up infidelities (*Feast* 658) – that build a sense that King's Landing is a bustling, cosmopolitan hive of intrigue and diplomacy. Martin uses the same strategy to create Westerosi aristocracy as he does to build the Free Cities.

The tournament also draws particular attention to Sansa herself by constituting a significant alteration in the way Martin catalyses the interrogative engagement that immersion encourages. Invoking Wayne Booth's analysis of irony, Mendlesohn observes how a sharp shift in narrative voice draws attention not only to the facts of the written world (as Arya does in Braavos) but to the manner in which it is being built (79). Such "sudden departures" from an author's established way of writing "should have alerted every reader to an ironic shift" (Booth 68) and thus prompt an interrogative reading. Sansa's observation of the tournament is an example. She observes a competition in which great men can prove their greatness in controlled conditions and in the height of their aristocratic finery. Hume's fantasy of subtraction is in full effect. The day climaxes (as Frye [44] observes high mimetic comedy tends to do) with Sansa's integration into her imagined organic society, "beauties she had dreamt of all her life and never dared hope to know" (*Game* 289), when she falls in love with Joffrey as only a eleven-year-old can. This exercise in giddy self-mythology clashes with the episode that immediately proceeds it. At the Inn at the Crossroads, Sansa's mother surveys the heraldry of the patrons for an altogether more serious purpose, to calibrate the coercive leverage she has to order the arrest of Tyrion Lannister for the capital offense of which she sincerely believes him to be guilty (283). Such level-headedness is characteristic of Catelyn. She explains the confluences of personal and political concerns to her husband (56), refuses to rise to Walder Frey's slight of her father's funeral (*Storm* 1.475) and identifies Renly Baratheon's wartime tournament as "madness" (*Clash* 309) Scarcely an *alazon*, Catelyn brings a utilitarian, low-mimetic practicality to aristocratic etiquette. Even before her confrontation with Jaime Lannister at Riverrun, her immersive demystification prompts the reader to see such tartuffery as Sandor Clegane's ribbon around a sword, the inherently precarious politeness of an armed society. She takes these matters appropriately seriously. Martin then quickly replaces her careful, clinical diction at the Inn – "Is Lady Whent a true and honest friend to my father, Lord Hoster Tully of Riverrun?" (*Game* 283) – with Sansa's overstimulated gushing about gilded heroes, snowy cloaks, and magic armour. This sudden rupture in the tone of the narrative puts the reader on notice, *per* Booth, to observe Sansa's focalisation as ironic, to regard it as expository in tone as well as content. The shift makes Sansa a horse of a different colour, standing out among her focalising colleagues much as Jaime Lannister, as she sees him, does among his brothers in arms.

If Sansa's irony is methodologically and polemically conspicuous, however, it follows the same patterns as Arya's and Daenerys's. Her enchantment is there to be broken. She takes up her father's idealistic indictment of Westerosi chivalry. This means that this key barometer of public morality is read by someone exercising the two key demonstrated attributes of Mendlesohnian immersion: its capacity to pull the reader into the expository process by obliging them to follow lines of logical scrutiny, and the demystifying, deglamoursing hostility of such scrutiny to Romantic truths – as Clute would say, its propensity to create thinned worlds. As an immersive focaliser Sansa very methodically thins her rich medievalist world into a much darker vision. As such she builds a world focussed on the gap between her ideals and realities. A startling example of this comes when Meryn Trant fetches her to view her father's head on a spike. Only hours previously Joffrey, instructed by his mother that "it isn't fitting that a king should strike his wife" (*Game* 718–719) charges Ser Meryn with belting her on his behalf. Sansa thus considers him with a critical eye:

> "Are you refusing to come, my lady?" The look he gave her was without expression. He did not so much as glance at the bruise he had left her.
>
> He did not hate her, Sansa realised; neither did he love her. He felt nothing for her at all. She was only a...a *thing* to him [...]. She wanted to rage, to hurt him as he'd hurt her, to warn him that when she was queen she would have him exiled if he ever dared strike her again...but she remembered what the Hound had told her, so all she said was "I shall do whatever His Grace commands."
> "As I do," he replied.
> "Yes...but you are no true knight, Ser Meryn." (720)

Alesi (168) observes Sansa's cutting retort to Ramsay Bolton's concubine in the televisual episode "Unbent, Unbowed, Unbroken" as the culmination of the character's capacity for self-assertion. By this estimation, Martin's Sansa grows up much faster than Benioff and Weiss's. Trant was one of the heroes she gushed over at the tournament. But knights are not supposed to beat little girls bloody, she reasons, ergo Trant is not a true knight. She states the point baldly, displaying considerable pluck for an (this is worth emphasising) eleven-year-old girl already nursing a thick ear. Sansa is now establishing the critical distance her reportage of the tournament so ostentatiously lacked, gathering and correlating the data with which she shifts intellectual allegiance between two competing theoretical models of social morality. Those models are the ones described in chapter one; the first that vows, titles and chivalric grandeur are licenses, imparting inherent nobility, and the second that they are job descriptions, and that a person's character is best calibrated by the diligence with which they are dispatched. Sansa's critique of her ideals emerges as she examines a pattern of evidence; her puzzling-out of the matter obliges the reader to follow her logic and appreciate her position all the more intimately as a result.

If Sansa seems naive and romantic, then it is because her chivalric ideals, an enduring notion of what *should* be, remain a part of her frame of reference as she undertakes the process incumbent upon any immersive focaliser: the rational interrogation of *what is actually there.* Her longing for the verities of the songs renders her susceptible to the blandishments of the venal sot Dontos Hollard and thus throws her out of the Lannister frying-pan and into Petyr Baelish's fire. Her adolescent sexual thrill at contact with Loras Tyrell – "*He's touching me*, she thought, *He's holding my arm and touching me*" (*Storm* 1.77). – demonstrates her enduring idealism via the game of beds. But she quickly loses patience with Hollard's boozy over-familiarity (*Clash* 681) and assesses the court's reaction to her thrashing by Boros Blount in interesting terms:

> *Knights are sworn to defend the weak, protect women, and fight for the right, but none of them did a thing.* Only Ser Dontos had tried to help, and he was no longer a knight, no more than the Imp was, or the Hound...the Hound hated knights...*I hate them too,* Sansa thought. *They are no true knights, not one of them.* (*Clash* 444)

Note her ongoing use of the ideal of the "true" knight as a point of contrast for the appalling behaviour of factual knights. What is happening here is not a Candide-like insistence that her initial ideals must be accurate but a retention of them as a point of reference in a highly critical indictment of the state of Westerosi chivalry. This is in keeping with the operation of Mendlesohnian immersion demonstrated by the incacerated Jaime Lannister. She looks for true knights and cannot find them, because immersion deals not with truth but with rational, substantiated fact, ascertained by departing from, rather than cleaving to, ideals. Sansa develops this perspective far more quickly than is sometimes appreciated (Johnston 139). Her capacity to grasp the gap between what ideally should be there and what is there in fact emerges at the Tournament of the Hand, when she first meets Petyr Baelish and observes that "He had grey-green eyes that did not smile when his mouth did" (*Game* 288). She continues to note this attribute when living under his dubious protection at the Eyrie (*Feast* 374). Indeed, her capacity to spot his lies, far outstripping her sensible, perceptive mother's, is what makes Littlefinger's protection dubious. Sansa has never trusted this man. From a Mendlesohnian standpoint the maturation Alesi identifies begins very quickly indeed.

Sansa's retention of her idealism among the terms of reference for her deductions creates the problem that this medievalist problem novel addresses. By referring back to a hypothesis that she suffers bruises, taunts and groping to test, Sansa keeps her immersive rhetoric explicitly focussed on the gap between what is and what should be. Her immersive bain-marie runs at a consistently high temperature, making Martin's thinned world highly conspicuous as such. She therefore shows Martin not transcending or subverting the tropes of his chosen genre but using them to further his authorial aims. He wishes to depict a world defined by a problem, a society falling short of its own supposed motivating ideals. The notion of a world defined by the loss of former glories is a common enough theme in the fantasy tradition to have a name. Thinning is especially evident in Martin's work because he has, adroitly if not uniquely, adopted an approach to his world-building responsibilities that operates by depicting the rational process by which characters interpret the world around them. This shows the world directly through the focaliser's eyes, adding to the immediacy of their accounts and the intimacy of their resulting emotional responses – the reason, probably, for the vividness of scenes such as Sansa's beating by Boros Blount. The reader sees the problem as a problem because Martin constructs it by evoking the thought processes of a frustrated idealist.

This narrative strategy abets Martin's goals more generally, however, by encoding a demanding, interrogative scepticism directly into the reading process. Most of Martin's characters follow this strategy, but Sansa is a particularly striking example. Martin has created this character, endowed her with idealism, highlighted her with loud stylistic colours, and dunked her into a scalding immersive environment. Although it costs her father his head, she realises the folly of naïve faith and begins rationalising her situation just as Daenerys and Arya do. This makes Sansa, much like her diminutive husband, an idiosyncratically damning witness for the prosecution in Martin's indictment of Westeros. The idealistic point of departure for her immersive investigation focusses reader attention on the deficits of the Westerosi, demonstrating just how thinned this society has become. Sansa is, to extend Clute's metaphorical label for the device, the one who points out how much weight this world has lost.

So Sansa plays an especial role in Martin's construction of a world that can, and indeed must, be argued with, interrogated, and thinned out. Her brother and half-brother, interestingly, further this effect. Bran Stark and Jon Snow contruct their worlds and move their tales on different Mendlesohnian principles, and in their distinct ways add, in radically different ways, to the effect that Sansa, Daenerys and Arya create. As such Martin's involved patchwork of focalising techniques achieves literary effects not by contravening the commonplaces of fantasy but by using them to his advantage.

4 "Dead Men Come Hunting" – Intrusion and Recovery

Mendlesohnian immersion is where gritty fantasy gets much of its grit. "Gritty fantasy" is the term Helen Young applies to a recognisable trend in twenty-first century fantasy towards the use of low-mimetic diction and plot elements as reactions to the "inauthentic evocations of history" (63) offered by the "high fantasy" of the twentieth century (Tolkien's legendarium being the inevitable exemplar). She cites Martin as a major contributor to the trend, which by some obvious metrics seems to be fair comment. Rather than "dealing with matters affecting the destiny of worlds" as high fantasy does (Clute 466), gritty fantasy tends to focus on interrogating the difficulties of living in them. The dirt and violence that are so often foci of Martin's narrative discourse are clear examples of this in action. His greatest divorce from the destiny of worlds, however, is his approach to the expositional imperatives inherent in his chosen literary form. Fantasy worlds must be explained, and Martin explains much of his via a method that seems to deny the notion that the world could *have* a destiny. The rational interrogation required by immersive fantasy world-building creates a tangled mass of contingencies, not any essential meaning. The world is a subject of study, a network of elements and connections to be demystified; essential meanings and identities are repeatedly frustrated. Those who speak in absolutes are fools. Note how Joffrey's "screamed" insistence that Eddard Stark is lying when he denies the boy's place on the Iron Throne (*Game* 509–510) includes no refutation of the logical case Eddard has presented for his endorsement of Stannis. Joffrey's illusion that a mere contradiction of Eddard's analysis suffices to dismiss Stannis's claim is as silly as Eddard's assumption that the gold cloaks will necessarily back the rightful king. Martin's method of fantasy world-building works by stripping away illusion, interrogating ideology and exploding assumption. A puppy, it is said, is never quite as endearing after its owner takes it apart to see how it works.

Martin's cynicism is not ubiquitous, however. As shown in the first two chapters of this book, he manipulates the modality of his characters in order to provide some of them with considerable dignity. Eddard and Catelyn Stark, Barristan Selmy, Syrio Forel and Squire Dalbridge all enjoy this treatment. So too does Briene of Tarth, another character who, like those just mentioned, goes to considerable efforts to walk the medievalist walk rather than simply mouthing the right words. Brienne's mooning after the unattainable (and reputedly homosexual) Renly Baratheon lacks the ironic edge that Sansa Stark's naïve crush on Joffrey has. Her position in the game of beds is, like Barristan Selmy's, the entirely sympathetic one of someone unable to pursue an object of affection. Moreover Brienne is substantially free of the humanising dirt of Martin's world. Questing after Sansa, she rides around eastern Westeros for long enough to raise questions about how one changes a pantyshield in full armour. Martin provides no answer. Given his use of bodily fluids as an indicator of a person's modal stature, this editing of her focalisation is revealing. As well as dirt and sexuality, however, Martin uses expositional strategies, his approach to his responsibilities as a fantasist, to manipulate the reader's engagement with the narrative. Martin is *critiquing*, not dismissing, the aristocratic values his characters strive towards, demonstrating that greatness cannot simply be asserted, it must be demonstrated. The purpose of this chapter is to show how he uses Mendlesohn's world-building rhetorics to that end. Mendlesohn's system allows for fantasies to move from one rhetoric to another as the narrative proceeds. Chapter 3 mentioned two texts, *The Lord of the Rings* and Pullman's *Northern Lights*, which do precisely this. Although Martin's story is generally immersive, a handful of focalisers follow different Mendlesohnian strategies, serving as narratological outriggers of a sort. They do this by aping high fantasy in opposition to which Young places Martin's "gritty" work, engaging directly with the essences of his invented world. Rather than detracting from the thinning effects of his immersive narrative mainstream, these subplots throw that thinning into sharp relief by positioning the reader in much the same place, heterodiegetically, that Sansa Stark diegetically occupies, struck by how thin this world has become. This perspective furthers Martin's inquiry into the nature of human morality. It also precisely vindicates J.R.R. Tolkien in one of his opinions on the key functions of the fantasy genre; that fantasy provides a clear view of fundamental aspects of the human condition. Martin's wide-ranging approach to fantasy world-building show him utilising the imperatives of his genre as vehicles for his creative vision.

Bran Stark, for example, is undergoing a clear Mendlesohnian portal-quest. Such tales require the focaliser to take an attitude that is almost diametrically opposed to that required in an immersive fantasy. The portal-quester "leaves her familiar surroundings and passes through a portal into an unknown place" (Mendlesohn 1). This portal can be a literal one, moving characters from a world they know into a world they do not. The most famous of C.S. Lewis's Chronicles of Narnia names its portal, the wardrobe, in its title. Alternatively, the character can embark on a quest, moving geographically from a part of the world they know into one they do not, as in the case of *The Lord of the Rings*. Mendlesohn conflates these two forms in that both derive narrative impetus from the deference of the focaliser to a received explanation. In portal fantasies, the focalising character is by definition unfamiliar with what they find and must ken to the explanations of the natives – in Lewis's example, Tumnus, Mister and Mrs Beaver and Aslan himself. In quest fantasies, the world-building depends upon the protagonist accepting as a given the need for the quest to continue. If the object of quest itself is not to preserve the world (as it often is), then the journey inherent in the quest forms the narrative by which that world is constructed. Frodo Baggins leaves Bag End because he accepts Gandalf's analysis of his Ring. Both portal and quest fantasies therefore require an act of faith, a suspension of analysis and a belief that something that is told is inherently accurate – as indeed it may as well be. Where the immersive focaliser must be permanently inquisitive, constantly relating what they see to what they know, a portal-quester creates meaning by doing what he or she is told.

In Bran's case, the contrast is particularly clear in that he begins the tale as an industriously effective immersive focaliser. Martin delegates some important exposition to him in that capacity. It is he, for example, who introduces the protagonist-apparent:

> Bran's father sat solemnly on his horse, long brown hair stirring in the wind. His closely trimmed beard was shot with white, making him look older than his thirty-five years. He had a grim cast to his grey eyes this day, and he seemed not at all the man who would sit before the fire and talk softly of the age of heroes and the children of the forest. He had taken off Father's face, Bran thought, and donned the face of Lord Stark of Winterfell. (*Game* 12)

Bran describes Eddard Stark, not only in his capacity as a loving father but also as a stern, disciplined warrior-aristocrat, in a manner familiar from the previous chapter. He rationalises what he sees in relation to what he knows, noting a change (for the worse from his perspective; the world has fractionally thinned out). The passage also shows Bran introducing the children of the forest to the narrative discourse as an exercise in Mendlesohn's irony of mimesis. He describes Winterfell in a similar manner. He understands his home very well, explaining its size, age, aspect and idiosyncrasies to the reader via his familiarity with its lofts and ledges. That Winterfell has gargoyles (more common in church architecture than the medieval military engineering that Winterfell supposedly ensamples), for example, becomes apparent as readers observe that he *is accustomed* to swing between them on his climbing expeditions (*Game* 77). Bran's ascent of the First Keep therefore fits the definition of Mendlesohnian immersion. His actual *story*, however, begins with a sudden shunt into a new context. Tipped out a window by Jaime Lannister, Bran falls into a coma, in which he experiences dreams where he communes with the Three-Eyed Crow, eventually spreading his wings and flying. He has not passed through any literal, recognisable portal, nor has he yet embarked on a quest (indeed he will not do so until the conclusion of *A Clash of Kings*). Nevertheless, Bran has transcended what he understands to be possible; he is dependent on external explanations to make sense of what is going on around him. His fall marks the transition of his focalisation from immersive to portal-quest rhetoric.

The existence of a talking crow – one that, unlike Jeor Mormont's, actually holds conversations – is not what changes the rhetorical structure of Bran's subplot. Immersive focalisers can focalise the supernatural perfectly well; their doing so really fuels that particular narrative mechanism. Daenerys Targaryen explains dragonbone and its uses (*Game* 25; 30; 99) without breaking immersive stride. What makes Bran's story a portal-quest is the nature of his relationship with the Three-Eyed Crow. Bran is not an equal of this creature. He is a babe in the wood, as ignorant of the trans-portal world in which he finds himself as the reader is, denuded of any of the frames of reference that immersive focalisers bring to bear on that which passes before them. He cannot interpret the vision of the world he receives in his dream, or meaningfully act on it, in the way that he called upon his previous experience to make sense of his father's solemnity at the execution of Gared. In short, he no longer has any idea what is going on. As such he cannot actually act on his own initiative; his story can go nowhere until he follows the instructions of someone who understands what is happening:

> "What are you doing to me?" he asked the crow, tearfully.
>
> *Teaching you how to fly.*
> "I can't fly!"
> *You're flying right now.*
> "I'm *falling!*"
> *Every flight begins with a fall*, the crow said. *Look down.*
> "I'm afraid..."
> *LOOK DOWN!* (155–156)

Note that the Crow's speeches do not feature quotation marks. It is not speaking; its statements are matters of narrative truth rather than stated opinions. Bran's willingness to acquiesce to such imperatives sets the pace of his subplot once he wakes from his coma. He is by definition ignorant of the trans-portal world and its supernatural contents, and thus dependent on explanations from competent natives (Mendlesohn 5). Each significant movement in his narrative stems from him heeding the advice of somebody else. Osha warns him the giants and wights of his bedtime stories are all too real (*Game* 559–560); Jojen Reed explains he is a warg (*Clash* 472–473) and mandates a northward path after the sack of Winterfell (873); the mysterious Coldhands leads him from the Wall to the cave of the Three-Eyed Crow; the Crow himself trains him in magic. The fact that the "grey mists" (*Game* 154) that surround him in his dream clear to reveal a panoramic, prophetic view of Martin's world once he follows the Crow's advice demonstrates this point. Rather than continuing to explain things himself, therefore, after his fall Bran discovers Martin's written world by accepting the explanations of others.

When the portal-quest focaliser is deprived of fresh world-building discourse, their tale stalls. J.K. Rowling's *Harry Potter* cycle, cited by Mendlesohn as an "almost archetypical" (2) portal-quest, demonstrates the point. Harry's Uncle Vernon attempts to block his passage through the portal with his frantic elusions of his letter of acceptance from Hogwarts. In the brief period he succeeds (*Philosopher's Stone* 31–36), the story is stalled. The same happens to Bran. After learning everything Osha can teach him, he prowls Winterfell's godswood inside Summer, aware there is more to know but incapable of reaching it; "Beyond its sky-tall man-cliffs the true world was calling, and he knew he must answer or die" (*Clash* 72). A native of a cis-portal environment, he cannot predict the operation of the components of the trans-portal world – he is no more familiar with this warging business than the reader is – and thus cannot act within it without guidance. Harry Potter's guides break the deadlock by bombarding him with letters of acceptance (assertions of his wizardly status) until one gets through. Bran's guides must occasionally do the same:

> "Did you dream of a wolf?"
>
> He was making Bran angry. "I don't have to tell you my dreams. I'm the prince. I'm the Stark in Winterfell."
> "Was it Summer?"
> "You be quiet."
> "The night of the harvest feast, you dreamed you were Summer in the godswood, didn't you?"
> "Stop it!" Bran shouted. Summer slid towards the weirwood, his white teeth bared.
> Jojen Reed took no mind. "When I touched Summer, I felt you in him. Just as you are in him now."
> "You couldn't have. I was in bed. I was sleeping."
> "You were in the godswood, all in grey."
> "It was only a bad dream…"
> Jojen stood. "I felt you. I felt you fall. Is that what scares you, the falling?" (*Clash* 397)

Hoping against hope for a supernatural world, but flustered by Jojen's insistence on his precise position in it, Bran goes to the most credible arbiter of knowledge he knows and asks for clarification. When Maester

Luwin, his equivalent of Harry Potter's Uncle Vernon, dismisses Jojen's claims about the continued existence of magic, Bran is distraught:

> So long as there was magic, anything could happen. Ghosts could walk, trees could talk, and broken boys could grow up to be knights. "But there isn't," he said aloud in the darkness of his bed. "There's no magic, and the stories are just stories."
>
> And he would never walk, nor fly, nor be a knight. (402)

The bitter finality of his comments at the end of the chapter is, within his understanding of the situation, quite accurate. Like Harry Potter's, Bran's story cannot proceed until naysayers, sympathetic or otherwise, hold their peace. "Perhaps your maester is wrong" (401), says Meera Reed, gently introducing a point that Bran must accept before he can go any further. The portal-quest brooks no dissent. Focaliser and reader alike must accept explanations of the trans-portal world as inherently accurate. To spurn that explanation is to disengage with the only available method of making sense of the new environment, to divorce oneself from the text, and to paralyse the narrative; one may as well stop reading.

This leads to a particular relationship between the focaliser and the world. A given world-view is presented as inherently accurate, and must be accepted as such for the tale to continue. What this means is that portal-quest world almost inescapably have the essential meaning that immersive world seem to lack, a sense of "moral expectation" (Mendlesohn 5) suggesting that there is a way things *should* be, and that certain things must happen. Destiny and prophecy appear frequently in this type of fantasy, moving the plots of Rowling's *Harry Potter* cycle, the *Star Wars* films and Pullman's *His Dark Materials* trilogy. Mendlesohn traces the portal-quest form, and the jealous authority of its arbitrators, to Christian allegories such as that of Bunyan, influenced by the Augustinian notion of a central *sine qua non* of reality (18–19). Information about a portal-quest world is not only accurate, it is the universal truth of Augustinian monotheism, the measure of reality; characters become, in a sense, fully real by allying themselves with this truth. Bran Stark faces exactly this challenge. He must fly, or never wake from his coma; he must then find the Three-Eyed Crow and train for his predestined role training with a mentor who has magically observed him from infancy (*Dance* 206–207). The plot of a portal-quest fantasy is therefore a secondary source of dramatic tension; of greater significance is the question of how the focaliser will cope, intellectually, emotionally and morally, with the truth laid down for them. When, shivering and starving beyond the Wall, Jojen pronounces "We go with Bran's monster [Coldhands], or we die" (*Dance* 80), he is not simply referring to their precarious bodily situation. The world of wargs, prophets and nature spirits that Bran moves into is a test of character, a demanding, inscrutable quantity in relation to which his mettle, his capacity to cope with reality and thus become real himself, will be measured. To fail in this test is to disintegrate – that is, to reverse one's integration into the written world the author is shaping, which for a literary character is suicide.

Bran must therefore believe wholeheartedly in the very thing that his parents, sisters, crippler, cripper's deformed brother and crippler's incestuous lover repeatedly query and undermine with their immersive rhetoric: that there is indeed a fundamental ideological truth to the world. His lessons in Bloodraven's cave labour the eternal, unchanging nature of the trans-portal world. Throughout that chapter (*Dance* 521–536), time is kept by the incantatory movement of the moon from "a black hole in the sky" to "a crescent, thin and sharp as the blade of a knife" to "fat and full." Martin rarely uses such metrics, tending to prefer the rhythms of human activity. Note Arya's habit of keeping time in Gregor Clegane's slave train via the Mountain's routine of having someone tortured each day (*Clash* 375–376) or how Davos Seaworth, explicitly isolated from the diurnal cycle, counts his days in Dragonstone's dungeon via the work of his jailers (*Storm* 1.345–1.346). When discussing Bran's magical training, by contrast, Martin refers to the phases of the moon, a natural cycle. Bran's tuition is full of references to the eternal, essential stability of the magical world:

> "Truths the First Men knew, forgotten now in Winterfell...but not in the wet wild. We live closer to the green in our bogs and crannogs, and we remember. Earth and water, soil and stone, oaks and elms and willows, they were here before us all and will still remain when we are gone." (*Dance* 522)

> "Never fear the darkness, Bran." The lord's words were accompanied by a faint rustling of wood and leaf, a slight twisting of his head. "The strongest trees are rooted in the dark places of the earth. Darkness will be your cloak, your shield, your mother's milk. Darkness will make you strong." (523)

> "For men, time is a river. We are trapped in its flow, hurtling from past to present, always in the same direction. The lives of trees are different. They root and grow and die in one place, and that river does not move them. The oak is the acorn the acorn is the oak. And the weirwood...a thousand human years are a moment to a weirwood, and through such gates you and I may gaze into the past." (533)

The propensity for portal-quest worlds to be built via reported speech, leaning on the reader's implied faith that Martin's heterodiegetic voice is reporting these statements accurately (Mendlesohn 20), is very much in evidence here. More importantly, Bran's guides present the magical world as being as essential to Martin's written cosmos as its cycles and elements. The Three-Eyed Crow's observation that weirwoods are essentially immune to the ravages of time (*Dance* 533) illustrates the point. There are no contingencies to Bran's lessons, no actual explanations: merely the truth.

"This kind of fantasy," Mendelsohn states, "is essentially imperialist. Only the hero can change; fantasyland is orientalised into the 'unchanging past'" (9). Her choice of orientalism as a point of comparison is useful. Orientalism almost by definition strips the subject of intelligible internal factors, creating the "inscrutable orient" as a static, monolithic challenge to, and tool of self-definition for, the focaliser. The trans-portal world, created via the acceptance of the guide's accounts, becomes such a monolith, a static quantity that cannot be engaged with fully on its own terms, because it *offers* no terms; it cannot be questioned on any fundamental level. Instead, it is "moved through" (71), observed and utilised as challenge for the protagonist to rise to, focussing attention, for all of the wonders it may possess, on the focaliser. Actual engagement with the supernatural world is often slight. Mendlesohn (63–64) observes that for all the wizardry classes Harry Potter sits through, little real sense of magic as an academic discipline emerges from Rowling's novels. This is because Potter is not actually at Hogwarts to learn magic, but rather to learn that magic exists, and respond to the static, obdurate, unavoidable moral challenge it presents. The same is true of Bran. The central, overall narrative outcome of his fall, his dreams, his elusion of the treacherous Theon Greyjoy, his journey north and his training with Bloodraven is to reveal to the reader the true nature of the world. The question is not whether Bran will engage with the truth he finds – for he must do, since his doing so generates the narrative matter of his quest – but how he will respond and measure up to it.

Bran's subplot is edited into *A Song of Ice and Fire* by Martin's heterodiegetic narration. He is one of Martin's most isolated focalisers. The world, except Sam Tarly and Gilly, believes him dead, and his ability to keep abreast of the game of thrones rapidly diminishes as he journeys north, but the reader, observing Martin's shuffling-together of his subplots, actually knows all. While Martin plays extensively with what the reader does not know, therefore, he plays here with what they do appreciate. The weirwoods revered by Bran's father and respected by most other Westerosi (Joffrey may be a little shit, but he does not fell the Red Keep's godswood) are indeed magical. The result of this is the existence of a fundamental, essential direction to a world otherwise constructed in a manner that argues against any such. The little band journeying to Bloodraven's cave constitute an outrigger of sorts to an otherwise fundamentally wobbly narrative canoe, steadying it as it moves in a particular direction, but also implying that there is a particular favoured direction to go in. Martin's overall tale therefore becomes one of a large group of people who do not, by and large, grasp that they are going somewhere. The reader does. Portal-quests are convenient ways of establishing an ideological truth to the world, a mechanism that authors like Tolkien and Rowling have used to far subtler effect than is sometimes appreciated. Martin has bought into this technique rather more than some critics grasp; there is a natural order to his world.

Jon Snow constitutes another intriguing narrative outlier to Martin's preponderantly immersive rhetoric. Jon, and his narrative Man Friday Samwell Tarly, create their world via a third Mendlesohnian rhetoric, intrusion fantasy. Something new comes into Jon's world, and he and Sam must figure out exactly what it is and how to react. Like portal-quests, Mendlesohnian intrusion is based around a fundamental expansion of the focaliser's understanding of the world, a glimpse of what is really going on. Unlike the portal-quest, however, there is no guide, and definitive exposition is usually delayed (Mendlesohn 116). Rather than proceeding from the recognition of a fundamental truth, as Bran's story does, intrusion fantasy tells of someone being held back from such an epistemological bedrock, yet maintaining a firm belief in it. Practical demonstrations of truth, such as Bran's tuition in warging, are replaced by a visceral sense on the part of the focaliser that – to quote a famous televisual example of the species, *The X-Files* – the truth is out there. The pattern is prevalent in the early stages of alien-invasion fantasies such as *The War of the Worlds* or the film *Independence Day*, though the focus on the hauntingly suspected, rather than rationally established, means that intrusion fantasies tend to inhabit the darker end of the genre. Mendlesohn cites classic Gothic texts such as *The Castle of Otranto* as taproots of intrusion (121). Although Martin makes tangential use of some Gothic devices, as explained in Chapter 2, it may therefore be the subplot of the Night's Watch that bears the closest comparison to conventionally Gothic texts. That subplot, focalised primarily by Jon (Sam becomes a focaliser only in *A Storm of Swords* and begins *A Feast for Crows* by being packed off to Oldtown) is one of mounting suspicion, visceral faith and intellectual incredulity. It is therefore both very similar to Bran's story and wholly unlike it. It is similar in that it is abidingly concerned with a Mendlesohnian sub-surface that constitutes the essential truth of the world. Jon's story is unlike Bran's in that its truth is kept latent, repeatedly gestured towards rather than clearly laid out. He builds his world by striving towards a truth rather than acting on his reception of it.

Where Mendlesohn uses landscape painting as a simile to explain portal-quests (71), she likens intrusion fantasy to the building and releasing of tension in a musical composition (117). Intrusion fantasy is motivated by an escalating suspicion of something potent behind or beyond what the focaliser is seeing or hearing (127). The different ways in which Bran and Jon focalise the Haunted Forest demonstrate the point. Bran and his companions show a conspicuous interest in surfaces:

> Where the ice was flat and the ground was bumpy, the going was easy, but where the wind had pushed the snow up into ridges, sometimes it was hard to tell where the lake ended and the shore began. Even the trees were not as infallible a guide as they might have hoped, for there were wooded islands in the lake, and wide areas ashore where no trees grew. (*Dance* 73)

Scouting ahead of the band, Summer runs "Across the lake" and "over roots and rocks"; his paws break the crust of a snowdrift, but he races on regardless (74). Solid, dependable surfaces move Bran's story forward; anything doubtful, fragile or occluded merely holds the covers of the book apart. By comparison Jon experiences the forest as something he knows is auspicious, but cannot put his finger on:

> Jon had often hunted with his father and Jory and his brother Robb. He knew the wolfswood around Winterfell as well as any man. The haunted forest was much the same, and yet the feel of it was very different.
>
> Perhaps it was all in the knowing. They had ridden past the end of the world; somehow that changed everything. Every shadow seemed darker, every sound more ominous. The trees pressed close and shut out the light of the setting sun. A thin crust of snow cracked beneath the hooves of their horses, with a sound like breaking bones. When the wind set the leaves to rustling, it was like a chilly finger tracing a path up Jon's spine. The Wall was at their backs, and only the gods knew what lay ahead. (*Game* 503)

Note the contrast here with Bran's perception of the trees. He uses metaphor to describe them; they are not *like* guides, fallible or otherwise, but rather they *are* guides. Bran describes the trees, and everything else, as being something or not something; signification is valued, ambiguities useless. By comparison Jon, noticing how the shadows "seem" darker, how the forest "feels" different from those he knows, begins to think not in terms of metaphor, but of ominous similes – "a sound *like* breaking bones," "*like* a chilly finger tracing a path up Jon's spine." This bespeaks Jon drawing on past experience to articulate his mistrust what he sees. Within the weirwood grove, Jon appreciates the "black rot" beneath the scarlet leaf-litter. This is a rhetoric of inkling, intuition and unease, not specific information. The emphasis is on what is sensed as latent in the written world rather than what is made explicitly clear; "there is an assumption," Mendlesohn observes of intrusion fantasy, "that the visceral response is meaningful in itself" (138). This is, put very simply, why Jon Snow knows nothing. Comprehension is not his role. It is the immersive focaliser Arya's job to know things, and the portal-quester Bran's to learn them. Jon's job is to suspect, fear, and pursue the latent truth of his world, and only belatedly grasp it.

The latency in Jon's chapters becomes particularly apparent when their endings are compared, again, with Bran's. The young lad tends to sign off with a sense of a narrative being hemmed in or shut down. As Bran plummets from the tower window, the first-time reader must assume they will not see the poor lad again. Robb's tearful assertion that their family will be reunited (*Game* 241) smells of wishful thinking. Following Robb's departure Bran finds Winterfell "deserted and dead" (562). Confirmation of Eddard's death follows (715) as does Summer's sense of confinement in the Godswood and Maester Luwin's shattering denial of magic. By contrast Jon's focalised episodes often end on moments of high drama, begging questions that remain unanswered until the tale returns to him. After swearing their oath in the weirwood grove, Jon and his fellows are confronted with Jafer's severed hand (*Game* 504). Jon's next chapter ends with him praying that the revivified Othor will burn (*Game* 548), the one after that with Maester Aemon's ultimatum (640). Jon's narrative in the first volume climaxes with Jeor Mormont's announcement that the Watch will ride forth in search of answers to the questions raised by the appearance of the walking dead (759). This pattern continues later with reference to his emerging associations with Qhorin Halfhand (*Clash* 572), Rattleshirt (861), Mance Rayder (*Storm* 1.104) and Ygritte (1.219). In each case, Jon's chapters gesture towards the future, to forthcoming information and evolving plans. He is hardly unique in this – Martin is perhaps overfond of cliff-hangers – but it is a noticeable trend in this particular subplot. After the confrontation with Othor, the reader must wait almost a hundred pages to learn that wights burn and that Jon lives. This invests the intervening narrative with latent tension until Martin again turns his authorial gaze back to the Wall.

The result of this focus on a hidden, latent story going on behind what Jon can see is akin to crime fiction (Mendlesohn 142). In this sense, intrusion fantasy bears out the typology of detective fiction offered by Tzvetan Todorov in his essay of that title. Todorov argues that the detective novel is essentially an authorial arrangement of two stories, the first concerning an action (the crime) and the second the investigation of that action by somebody not involved in it (44–45). Eddard Stark's mission to King's Landing conveniently demonstrates this; Jon Arryn dies, and Eddard's story revolves around finding out why. Stark's role is not to do things but learn about things already done. The fact that his solution propagates further injustice rather than a reaffirmation of an established moral order probably contributes to the remarkable sense of grievance that Colishaw (66) credits the subplot with creating; successful detectives are supposed to be commended for their insight rather than executed for it. To remain focussed on Jon, however, the parallels with crime fiction mean that much of the Night's Watch subplot resembles television crime drama. Samwell's refutation of Jaremy Rykker's assessment of Othor's time of death (*Game* 536–537) closely recalls that of a police pathologist revealing decisive information to a detective. Later, at Whitetree, Jon and Dolorous Edd resemble gumshoes examining a crime scene:

> Dolorous Edd sniffed the air. "I smell dung."
>
> The smell was very faint. "Old dung," said Jon. The house felt as though it had been empty for some time. Kneeling, he searched through the straw with his hands to see if anything had been concealed beneath, then made a round of the walls. It did not take very long. "There's nothing here."
>
> Nothing was what he had expected; Whitetree was the fourth village they had passed, and it had been the same in all of them. The people were gone, vanished with their scant possessions and whatever animals they may have had. None of the villages showed any sign of having been attacked. They were simply...empty. "What do you think happened to them all?" Jon asked.
>
> "Something worse than we can imagine," suggested Dolorous Edd. "Well, *I* might be able to imagine it, but I'd sooner not. Bad enough to know you're going to come to some awful end without thinking about it aforetime." (*Clash* 187)

As on his trip to the weirwood grove, Jon struggles, and fails, to make sense of disquieting latent meaning. Edd's gallows humour elegantly underlines the sense of unease. Later, Jeor Mormont confers with an underworld informant, turning a blind eye to Craster's crimes against gods and women in order to abet a more pressing investigation. Qhorin Halfhand's talk of wildings who "lived long enough to be questioned" (567) brings to mind the stock character of the brutally uncompromising police officer roughing up criminal scum. Qhorin then sets up what amounts to an undercover operation against Mance Rayder. This requires a suspicious focaliser, one who believes they are not being told everything. Jon is such a character. Disappointed by Craster, a mere glowering bully rather than the demonic haemovore Old Nan promised ("Perhaps [Craster] had not heard the stories" [326]), he is nevertheless not relieved by the banality of his opposition. Rather he remains convinced that Craster is up to something – that the truth is out there. The only real difference between Jon and Agent Mulder of *The X-Files* is that many of Jon's colleagues share his concerns. The Night's Watch are making a collective attempt to make sense of something they dislike about a situation, to reject received explanations like Craster's and ponder what might be behind the trees. This separation from the truth is a direct violation of the imperatives of portal-quest fantasy, but the narrative engine of intrusion. The tale of the Night's Watch is principally concerned with their uneasy probing of a pre-existing, occluded story behind that which Craster tells them. "I know this wood as well as any man alive," states Dywin on the Fist of the First Men, "and I tell you, I wouldn't care to ride through it alone tonight. Can't you smell it?" (465) Like all good fictional policemen, Dywin has a hunch.

Just as Bran passes through the hands of a variety of guides on his portal-quest, Martin uses a variety of methods to maintain the sense of latent meaning in Jon's tale. One of the most straightforward is to isolate the protagonist in their knowledge. The focaliser of a portal-quest fantasy is locked into the magical community he or she encounters, forced to accept what they are told, if only because of their inability to offer credible rebuttal. By contrast, the suspicions of the intrusion fantasy protagonist locks them *out* of the inherently sceptical mundane society they once knew (Mendlesohn 136). *Pro forma*, few outside the Night's Watch share Jon's unease. Tyrion Lannister, a friend to the Watch whose judgement the reader has learned to trust, belittles Ser Alliser Thorne's assertion of the dead rising in the north:

> "Lord Baelish," Tyrion called down to Littlefinger, "buy our brave Ser Alliser a hundred spades to take back to the Wall with him."
>
> "Spades?" Ser Alliser narrowed his eyes suspiciously.
> "If you *bury* your dead, they won't come walking," Tyrion told him, and the court laughed openly. "Spades will end your troubles, with some strong backs to wield them." (*Clash* 367)

This episode preserves the intrusive-fantasy structure. A fictional society at large cannot be sensitive to the latent truth that such fantasies require. It is the job of the focaliser of an intrusion fantasy to notice things other people do not, which enter the narrative discourse as oddities few if any other people take seriously. The battle against scepticism is thus part of the structure of the form. Again, Agent Mulder of *The X-Files*, kicking against the scepticism of his superiors, is a good example. So too is David Levinson, the scientist trying to convince the president he has evidence of alien malevolence in the film *Independence Day*. The Night's Watch suffer the same fate. By having a column of 300 soldiers subscribe to the notion that the truth is out there, Martin is actually fairly generous in granting Jon fellow travellers. Nevertheless as they accept geographical isolation on their march north, the Watch also suffer epistemological marginalisation. Tyrion Lannister, so frequently a voice of reason in Martin's narrative, rubbishes their crisis. Jon Snow returns from his undercover mission only to find that his superiors scoff at his evidence and, in the best traditions of the television police procedural, throw their top man off the case. The world, at least temporarily, will not listen.

Another interesting method by which Martin feeds, escalates and elongates Jon's suspicions is the use of deuteragonists to encounter the terrible threat, in effect, on his behalf. Benioff and Weiss's Jon has, as of this writing, encountered wights so often that it is worth noting that Martin's version of the character falls into the snow at the end of *A Dance with Dragons* having not looked into blue eyes since he burned those belonging to Othor, fully four volumes previously. Jon does not observe or understand the threat; he merely meets people who have. The best example of this is the attack on the Fist of the First Men. As a demonstration that an army of the dead exists, this confrontation is more important to Martin's world-building than the Battle of Blackwater. Yet whereas the Baratheon attack on King's Landing is a major set piece played out over fifty contiguous pages (*Clash* 733–785), the attack on the Fist is diffusely (one might say barely) focalised. Jeor Mormont's lookouts blow thrice, signalling the nature of the foe, in the prologue to *A Storm of Swords* (1.16–1.17) Nothing more is heard of this until Jon, working his undercover mission, accompanies Mance Rayder to the Fist 200 pages later:

> Inside was more, and worse. Jon had never seen pink snow before. The wind gusted around him, pulling at his heavy sheepskin cloak. Ravens flapped from one dead horse to the next. *Are those wild ravens, or our own?* Jon could not tell. He wondered where poor Sam was now. And *what* he was. (1.215; emphasis Martin's)

This is another crime scene, like that in Whitetree. Something has happened here, some terrible escalation of a hidden threat, the precise narrative trajectory Mendlesohn identifies (116–117) as characteristic of intrusion fantasy. Any explanation or narration of what took place at the Fist must wait another twenty pages, until poor Sam is promoted to focaliser. Even then Sam focalises not the battle but the disarray of the retreat south. His focus on aural impressions of things he cannot see – "sometimes Sam heard shouts behind him, from the rear guard, and once an *awful* scream" (*Storm* 1.237) – maintains the focus on what is viscerally sensed rather than intellectually grasped. Again, the truth is out there, but it is not here. Even when Sam finally recalls what happened on the Fist itself, his focalisation holds the intrusion at a distance:

> "Here they come," he heard a brother say.
>
> "Notch," said Blane, and twenty black arrows were pulled from as many quivers, and notched to as many bowstrings.

> "Gods be good, there's hundreds," a voice said softly.
>
> "Draw," Blane said, and then, "hold." Sam could not see and did not want to see. The men of the Night's Watch stood behind their torches, waiting with arrows pulled back to their ears, as *something* came up that dark, slippery slope through the snow. "Hold," Blane said again, "hold, hold." And then, "Loose."
>
> The arrows whispered as they flew.
>
> A ragged cheer went up from the men along the ringwall, but it died quickly. "They're not stopping, m'lord," a man said to Blane, and another shouted, "*More*! Look there, coming from the trees," and yet another said, "Gods ha' mercy, they's crawling. They's almost here, *they's on us!*" (*Storm* 1.242–1.243)

Readers receive a depiction of the advancing dead via a deuteragonist's memory of *somebody else's* observations. Martin keeps them two degrees of narrative separation away from the wights. Jon, eventually hearing of Sam's experiences when they are reunited, is similarly insulated from the reality-rupturing foe that he, as Lord Commander of the first and possibly only line of defence, must eventually respond to. Rather than a climactic revelation the massacre at the Fist becomes, per Mendlesohn, a deep, strident note in the mood music of Jon's intrusion fantasy.

An illustrative point of comparison for Martin's strategy here is with "The Call of Cthulhu," H.P. Lovecraft's famous melding of pulp horror with the textual stratification of the Gothic tradition, noted by Mendlesohn (135) as an intrusion fantasy. Lovecraft's protagonist, Francis Wayland Thurston, never actually encounters the monster that redefines his life. Cthulhu's existence is revealed by Thurston's impulsive, worried correlation of police reports, press cuttings and conference proceedings. The smoking gun comes in the form of an eyewitness account of Cthulhu's abortive awakening written by a deuteragonist, Gustaf Johansen, composed at some point between the actual event and his murder by nefarious cultists and paraphrased into the narrative discourse by Thurston himself (191). Johansen has in a sense experienced the fully instantiated horror of Cthulhu on Thurston's behalf. With the tale presented as a manuscript found among Thurston's effects after his own death, the reader is held back from encountering Cthulhu through at least three layers of text: they read an executor's editing of Thurston's paraphrasing of Johansen's post-factum recollections of what he saw. It is as if Lovecraft, for all his adjectival excesses, is hiding his villain from the reader. In a sense he is. He records Thurston being frightened not by a monster but by the idea of a monster (Schultz 218). As Mendlesohn observes (135), this preserves the latency of the truth Thurston fears. Cthulhu has not acted in the story so much as put his capacity to act beyond any doubt. Lovecraft's narrative presentation cements the monster as a troubling presence in the mind, upsetting Thurston's view of the world via a glimpse of what is really going on behind the illusions of humanity. The intruders, the actors in the story, and in many respects its true villains, are the evil human acolytes who know of this quiescent peril.

This almost precisely mirrors how Jon experiences goings-on north of the Wall. The narrative engine is not revelation (as in a portal-quest) but the pursuit thereof, itself motivated by the abiding fear that there is something to be revealed. Jon is confronted with a breach of his understanding of the world in the revivified Othor, whose body, even before its eyes turn blue, bodes little good about the fate of his mysteriously absent Uncle Benjen. The parallel with Thurston's discovery of a Cthulhuoid artefact among his great-uncle's effects after the old man's suspicious death is weirdly precise. So too is Jon's neurotic involvement in a search for information about this. He puts aside the petty game of thrones to involve himself in the search for the meaning of this strange disruption (*Game* 759). This is a concession that the viscerally sensed Mendlesohnian substratum is a greater motivator than the intellectually comprehensible world to the south. He leaps at the chance to take the investigation further by associating himself with Qhorin Halfhand, who bluntly asserts that magic is afoot somewhere in the Frostfangs (*Clash* 571). As such he finds himself on the undercover mission Halfhand died to launch, behaving more and more like a wildling in order to operate on their level and get information out of them. This is a phase of engagement with the intrusion that Lovecraft's Thurston, warily interviewing those who have had dealings with the Cthulhu cult ("Cthulhu" 184–186), would recognise. Mendlesohn notes that the intrusion's forcing of itself into the world "is matched by a dragging of the protagonist into its range, or into the 'true story' of the world" (137) as the focaliser loses faith in the capacity of their own discourse community to analyse strange events and goes looking further afield for clues as to what is *really* going on.

In this effort, Jon demonstrates an escalating faith in the unseen, implied world. He sees no more of the living dead, merely scattered, disturbing hints of the dark, inhuman world beyond the Wall. These hints come from the wildlings who, unlike the Others themselves, repeatedly intrude upon Jon's world bearing frightening hints and evidence directly comparable to the "bits of hideous legend" ("Cthulhu" 182) that captured cultists reveal in Lovecraft's story. Gilly has looked into blue eyes, confirming her father's reputation for traffic with demons (*Clash* 336; 322). "Burn them," warns Ygritte with reference to her companions killed by Jon and Stonesnake, "or it might be you'll need them swords again" (671). Coming upon the aftermath at the Fist, Mance Rayder states baldly what Jon suspects – "When the dead walk, walls and stakes and swords mean nothing. You cannot fight the dead, Jon Snow. No man knows that half as well as me" (*Storm* 1.217). By the time Tormund Giantsbane discusses having to kill his son after "he rose pale with them blue eyes" (*Dance* 817) scepticism is no longer an option, and Jon understands Cotter Pyke's desperate pleas for help at Hardhome (910) only too well, just as Thurston comprehends the post-factum account of Cthulhu's awakening better than Johansen himself probably did. Yet, the latency is preserved. The Others and their revivified army in fact remain, as of the mutiny at Castle Black, the same sort of quiescent peril as Cthulhu.

The comparison with Lovecraft also demonstrates two important points of contact between intrusion fantasy and portal-quests. The first serves as an important point of contrast with the imperatives of Mendlesohnian immersion. Immersion, as noted in Chapter 3, thins the world via a series of rational appeals to contingencies and "the logic if decision chains" (Mendlesohn 66) rather than any organic truth. Portal-quests and intrusion fantasies both do the reverse, the former explicitly and the latter implicitly. Portal-quests require acquiescence to the pronouncements of the guide; Jojen Reed announces Bran is a greenseer, and the story stops until Bran accepts this and the reader implicitly does the same by continuing to read. The result is a magical world open to only a finite number (typically one) of moral interpretations. As J.R.R. Tolkien has proved, great and resonant moral subtlety can be achieved with the aid of such narrative presences, though not all authors seize that potential and even successful attempts at doing so are not always apparent at a first reading. The propensity of many readers to judge fantasy on the basis of a single reading of *The Lord of the Rings* probably accounts for the genre's alleged moral superficiality, in contrast to which Martin's work is often praised. Whether or not authors use the potential for moral experimentation that a fixed truth provides them, the point stands. Portal-quests are about the opposite of thinning, Clute's formalistic healing, the re-establishment of an unquestionable natural order, of how things ought to be, which requires the assumption that there in fact *is* a way things *ought* to be. Portal-quests are defined by an abstract presence in the written world rather than an absence.

Intrusion fantasies do the same, albeit in a different way. They move forward by means of the focaliser's faith, contra to the scepticism of third parties, that something that *should not* be there *is*, in fact, present. Clute refers to this notion as "wrongness," arguing that the "central moments" of tales in which "the real world is impinged upon or violented" are those in which the story "somehow *does not add up*" (1,038). Francis Thurston, Lovecraft's unhappy focaliser, is an example; the world is perfectly fine until the presence therein of Cthulhu becomes apparent. Tellingly, Thurston repeatedly relates the Cthulhu-cult to a variety of outré ideas he is already very sceptically familiar with. A report of "A theosophist colony donning white robes en masse for some "glorious fulfilment" that never arrives" ("Cthulhu" 174) on the date of Cthulhu's abortive awakening suggests the adherents of that odd creed are, knowingly or otherwise, complicit in the cult. That report is among a bundle of newspaper clippings about voodoo orgies, twittering mystics and restless lunatics – the sorts of people that someone like Thurston would usually dismiss ipso facto – suggesting that the evidence of the cult was staring rational thinkers like himself in the face all the time. Thurston's ilk simply lacked the presence of mind to see them; Thurston himself develops this. A similar situation is apparent in *Independence Day*; the genocidal aliens visited Earth once before, on a scouting mission to Roswell, New Mexico in 1947. Earthlings who observed this were dismissed as cranks. Chimeras gradually coalesce into flesh and blood; nothings turn into somethings.

Martin provides a textbook case of this; indeed he labours the point. He has endowed Westerosi oral culture with enough folkloric silliness to make the most obvious examples, snarks and grumpkins (*Game* 120; *Storm* 2.130; 2.381) Mendlesohnian pointers, tips of an iceberg of tall tales. Tyrion Lannister talks of merlings in the bay at Lannisport (*Game* 202); Nimble Dick frightens Podrick Payne with tales of squishers, man-eating bogeymen peculiar to Crackclaw Point (*Feast* 319). The reader quickly develops the understanding that no thinking Westerosi take these stories seriously, and – since the process of reading a Mendlesohnian immersion is that of appreciating points of view – falls into the same habits themselves. The same is true of Old Nan's stories, first mentioned by Eddard Stark as nonsense to entertain children (*Game* 14). Those preposterous tales, however, appear to be fairly close to what Jon is thrown into in the Night's Watch. Babysitting Bran in Winterfell, Nan tells of a winter "cold and hard and endless beyond the memory of man."

> "In that darkness, the Others came for the first time," she said as her needles went *click click click*. "They were cold things, dead things, that hated iron and fire and the touch of the sun, and every creature with hot blood in its veins. They swept over holdfasts and cities and kingdoms, felled heroes and armies by the score, riding their pale horses and leading hosts of the slain. All the swords of men could not stay their advance, and even maidens and suckling babes found no pity in them. They hunted the maids through the frozen forests, and fed their dead servants on the flesh of human children." (233)

She goes on to tell of a "last hero" who sought out the children of the forest to forestall this dreadful harrowing of the world – to provide what Clute would call healing. Bran, in due course, will embark on precisely the same (portal-)quest, just as Jon, participating in Jeor Mormont's contemporaneous Great Ranging, begins to establish an inkling of what is intruding into his story. That Jon knows nothing is less of an indictment of his intellect or life experience than an unavoidable consequence of the nature of what he is focalising. Intrusion fantasies are so often dark and difficult because they are tales of people coping with epistemological growing pains as they deal with a presence in their heaven and earth that their philosophy very explicitly did not dream of. Jon Snow may know nothing, but standing with Qhorin Halfhand reconsidering things that "belonged in Old Nan's stories, not in the world he had lived in all his life" (*Clash* 695), he actually fulfils his job in the narrative exceedingly well.

Thus where focalisers like Sansa and Catelyn dissect the puppy with their immersive rhetoric, Bran and Jon, in their distinctive ways, feed it. Bran's story constructs a supernatural world out of his and his reader's faith in received explanation, which in an immersive fantasy would likely mark him as an *alazon*. The truth established in Jon's world is implicit rather than explicit, but just as real and just as contrasting with the world built by the distaff Starks. Immersive focalisation builds the world by thinning it down to its facts, by taking note of what ought to be there and is not; focalisation of intrusion fantasy revolves around a gradual recognition of something that ought not to be there. These two half-brothers focalise a faith in the sort of essential, inarguable presence in the narrative that Martin's other focalisers sceptically analyse.

The second similarity between Bran and Jon's tales is that both half-brothers orientalise that presence, denuding it of its interior workings and engaging with it as a natural feature of the world rather than as something contingent upon anything else. Whether laid out in "overbright" (Mendlesohn 71) detail in Bran's portal-quest or festering as a resilient, escalating suspicion in Jon Snow's intrusion, the supernatural in these Mendlesohnian forms cannot be argued with or changed; it is presented as a part of the bedrock of the world. In Bran's case, this process has already been discussed. To approach the trans-portal world with any degree of scepticism paralyses his story. The protagonist and reader alike must adapt themselves to this imponderable presence or demonstrate their nugatory ineffectuality in the same way that the televisual Janos Slynt does ("No such things as giants. Stories for the children" ["The Watchers on the Wall"]) when Mance Rayder's army attacks the Wall.

Mendlesohn observes that intrusion narratives often paint the intruder in similar orientalist colours (148). H.P. Lovecraft demonstrates the point blatantly, even if the critic overlooks his attribution of Cthulhu-worship to non-white peoples. Inspector Legrasse of the New Orleans police provides Thurston's dossier with an eyewitness account of his answer to a complaint about something dreadful in the swamps:

> They said it had been there before D'Iberville, before La Salle, before the Indians, and before even the wholesome beasts and birds of the woods. It was nightmare itself, and to see it was to die. [...] Only poetry or madness could do justice to the noises heard by Legrasse's

> men as they ploughed on through the black morass toward the red glare and the muffled tom-toms. There are vocal qualities peculiar to men, and vocal qualities peculiar to beasts; and it is terrible to hear the one when the source should yield the other. Animal fury and orgiastic license here whipped themselves to daemoniac heights by howls and squawking ecstasies that tore and reverberated through those nighted woods like pestilential tempests from the gulfs of hell. (179)

Two points are worth observing here. The first is the imponderable antiquity of the monster the cultists are communing with, which predates both the white founders of Louisiana and the natives they displaced. It thus makes a mockery of any human claim to autochthony. The second is that those who commune with this entity are depicted as blurring the distinction between the human and animal kingdom. Colonialist discourse has a long and chequered history of depicting native peoples as part of the flora and fauna of their home environments, and as such part of the moral and utilitarian challenge of the colonial enterprise. Lovecraft obviously does something very similar. Cultists of Cthulhu know the *truth* their world partly because they are essentially akin to that world in a way that civilised men like Legrasse and Thurston are not. Magicians become comprehensively othered, challenges to which *normal* people must rise.

Jon Snow makes exactly the same discovery about Martin's wildlings. Qhorin and his troop are whittled down as they retreat from wildling witchcraft – Orrell's capacity to spy on them in animal form. Orrell has a particularly obvious link with the animal world, as does Varamyr Sixskins, "a small mouse of a man" for whom Jon reserves particular opprobrium – "the mere sight of the man had made him bristle" (*Storm* 1.208–1.209). But Martin's characterisation of the wildlings as akin to animals far overruns the obvious example of the skinchangers, of which Jon may be one himself (*Clash* 694). Jon is amazed at the customs of the people he rides with on his undercover mission:

> Small wonder that the Seven Kingdoms thought the free folk scarcely human. *They have no laws, no honor, not even simple decency. They steal endlessly from each other, breed like beasts, prefer rape to marriage, and fill the world with baseborn children.* (*Storm* 1.208)

Jon is not the only person who describes the wildlings as breeding like beasts. Varamyr uses his animal forms to stalk desirable human women; he has mated as a beast and even given birth as a she-wolf (*Dance* 6). Tormund Giantsbane is garrulously proud of having copulated with a bear (*Storm* 1.205) and liaised with a giantess, a member of a race the wildlings revere as part of the natural world (1.212–213) and equate with "the whales of the great grey sea" (1.203). Bearing in mind Martin's pervasive habit of using sexual behaviour to calibrate the nature of his characters, this pattern of describing wildlings "breeding like beasts" is highly significant. It cements Ygritte's people as fundamentally linked to the natural world they inhabit, part of the fauna of the Haunted Forest. It also demonstrates why Jon is so neurotic about maintaining his oath of celibacy after having taken the seemingly rather more drastic step of killing Qhorin. Sexual ceremony, a concern for formalised partnerships and substantiated parentage, is a human attribute; embracing the sexual license of the wildlings will make him truly one of these animalistic barbarians. Sexuality north of the Wall stands as an example of colonialist "representing the human in terms of natural species and natural phenomena" (Spurr 156), as a means of focalising them as the postcolonial other. Ygritte and Jon's assignation in the cave, as wholesome a depiction of cunnilingus as may exist in modern literature, contains echoes of this. Ygritte's disrobing in front of Jon, peeling off first her rabbitskin vest then her three woollen undershirts – "I want you should see me" (*Storm* 1.363) – closely parallels the semi-formalised unveiling of native maidens, closer to nature than their observers in their unabashed sexual eagerness, that colonialist writers often took pains to construct in their writings (Spurr 175–176). Ygritte's people – those who liaise with the latent supernatural truth lurking in the shadows of Jon's intrusion fantasy – are therefore highly orientalised. The magic they associate with follows suit. Ygritte's cultural knowledge is a part of the truth of the world, as natural, inarguable and devoid of interior workings as what Bran experiences in Bloodraven's cave. The wildlings and their non-human compatriots – alive and dead – are therefore, per the imperatives of colonialist writing, compartmentalised as tools of self-definition for the civilised humanity of which Jon Snow believes himself to be a part.

One might use this as a point of departure for an indictment of Martin's colonialist writing, though this seems a misreading of what is going on here. Carroll finds critical difficulties in Daenerys Targaryen teaching the Ghiscari the error of their ways (119–125), and also in the presentation of the children of the forest as "idealised and romanticised" (111). The former indictment may just stick. The Ghiscari, a social order of swarthy, oddly dressed, vacuously prideful slavemasters banging on about the antiquity and magnificence of their crumbling empire, constitute the sick man of Martin's written world, a close approximation of colonialist indictments of the Ottoman Empire. The children, however, have no particularly clear Earthly referent. As such Martin's writing about them is more directly comparable to Romanticism than orientalism. Makdisi notes the similarity between the experience of the Romantic sublime and that of orientalism, seeing them as the private and public expressions, respectively, of the same desire for the creation of "an individual phenomenological 'self' as against some profound force" (603). The value of the supernatural to Romantic authors is that by definition it resists rational analysis; it cannot be questioned. Some of the more overtly Romantic fantasists of the nineteenth century actually draw attention to the point. George MacDonald, in his tale "The Light Princess," directly addresses the reader to head off their question about how a witch can render the title character weightless – "If you ask me how this was effected, I answer – 'In the easiest way in the world. She had only to destroy gravitation'" (10). Because magic can do that, period. The fantastic therefore constitutes as "a discourse of the sublime in literature" (Sandner 27). It is a way of presenting readers with something impervious to intellectual analysis and thus throwing them back on the intuition of the imagination that the Romantics sought to enshrine as humanity's key instrument for the comprehension of the world (Abrams 28). The plan was that the reader, by accepting light princesses and magic mirrors in their fiction, would have their imaginative sluices opened, and thus re-engage with the world on an emotional and spiritual level (McGillis 202). Praising the power of the human mind to imagine as a route to communion with God, MacDonald felt this "the best thing you can do for your fellow, next to rousing his conscience" ("The Fantastic Imagination" 198). MacDonald, whose Christianity was a highly Romantic affair, cited this as his chief reason for writing. He has more claim than most to have instigated the modern fantasy tradition and stands as a crucial influence on Tolkien, among many others. Most fantasists since have, deliberately or otherwise, set up the supernatural as the radical other against which the protagonist may redefine themselves. To indict Martin for colonialist writing on this count seems a somewhat judgmental misreading. The presentation of the children of the forest is less likely to be a consequence of any such instinct on Martin's part than a continuation of the neo-Romantic tradition that modern fantasy constitutes.

Following Bran's passage through Thomas Weiskel's three-stage "structure of Romantic transcendence" (22) demonstrates the point. In the first stage of Weiskel's process, the protagonist understands the world, its contents, and their own position in relation to both; "no discrepancy interrupts representation, the smooth correspondence of inner and outer" (23). Bran, happily climbing in Winterfell before his encounter with Jaime Lannister, typifies the situation. The fact that his climbing expedition is reported via Mendlesohnian immersion, and thus in terms of what the focaliser already knows, demonstrates the point. Such epistemological stability does not last, however. In Weiskel's second stage, the protagonist encounters the Romantic sublime – that is, something that fundamentally upsets their understanding of the world via its inarguable, obdurate alienage. Bloodraven, speaking to Bran in his dream, demonstrates this well, particularly given his sustained assault on what the young Stark takes for granted:

> "Are you really a crow?" Bran asked.
>
> *Are you really falling?* the crow asked back.
> "It's just a dream," Bran said.
> *Is it?* asked the crow.
> "I'll wake up when I hit the ground," Bran told the bird.
> *You'll die when you hit the ground*, the crow said. It went back to eating corn.
>
> Bran looked down. He could see mountains now, their peaks white with snow, and the silver thread of rivers in dark woods. He closed his eyes and began to cry.
> *That won't do any good, the crow said. I told you, the answer is flying, not crying. How hard can it be? I'm doing it.* the crow took to the air and flapped around Bran's hand.
> "You have wings," Bran pointed out.
> *Maybe you do too.*
> Bran felt along his shoulders, groping for feathers.
> *There are different kinds of wings*, the crow said. (*Game* 155)

The Crow forces Bran to engage in fundamental revisions of everything he knows about the world and his place in it. The story is now about the extent to which young Stark has the emotional and spiritual wherewithal to cope in a word that contains "a text which exceeds comprehension, which seems to contain a residue of signifier which finds no reflected signified in our minds" (Weiskel 24) As stated earlier, his growth into that sort of status is retarded by scepticism, some of it his own, though his eventual decision to travel north is a decisive indication that he grasps his role in the story. From there he can get cracking on Weiskel's third stage of Romantic transcendence, in which "the mind recovers the balance of outer and inner by constituting a fresh relationship between itself and the object such that the very indeterminacy which erupted in phase two is taken as symbolising the mind's relation to the sublime order" (24). Bran begins his transition into the third stage with his meal of weirwood-seed paste in the cave (*Dance* 531–532), which prompts visions that link him with the ancient order he has rediscovered. The idea certainly can be criticised as colonialist, though the effect is more commensalistic than parasitic. Rather than being robbed of their resources, Bloodraven and the children lose nothing, and Bran gains, via an encounter with the Romantic sublime, a fundamental overhaul, for good or ill, of his view of and place in the world.

Jon Snow's procedure through Weiskel's model is more difficult to chart, partly because of the carefully maintained latency of his engagement with the supernatural. Retardation of his procedure through Weiskel's model in fact demonstrates how intrusion fantasies like *The Castle of Otranto* and *The X-Files* torture their focalisers. Insulated from the Others but firmly convinced of their existence, Jon is mired inordinately in Weiskel's second stage, denied a full, cathartic confrontation with this external quantity by which to launch the third, reactive phase. The grammar of Mendlesohnian intrusion creates Weiskel's "abridgement of the sublime moment so that we are confined to the second phase and await futilely the restorative action which never comes, except ironically" (26). Such irony comes in the personage of Ser Alliser Thorne, scoffing at the intelligence Jon brings back from his undercover mission – "The Horn of Winter? Were you commanded to count their snarks as well, Lord Snow?" (*Storm* 2.381) – and thus disengaging from the Mendlesohnian sub-surface Jon continues to dig for. As with Joffrey, his assumptions reveal a great deal about his character. The master-at-arms was directly involved in Jeor Mormont's attempt to secure more resources for the Watch by publicising the threat of the walking dead (*Clash* 367). Yet he ignores further intelligence on that situation because it comes from Lord Snow, against whom he is pursuing a petty personal vendetta (*Game* 183). Jon's (and the reader's) faith in the magical world as an occluded truth turns this blanket denial into the pronouncement of an *alazon*. Jon remains focussed on what can be learned from his encounters with Varamyr Sixskins and Mag the Mighty, but the latent nature of the supernatural denies him Weiskel's third stage. He is still in the second stage when the knives come out at Castle Black.

For Weiskel's process to function, there has to be an inexplicable, obdurate quantity in the narrative. The focaliser must encounter something sufficiently outside their frame of reference to be resistant to the rationalisation characteristic of Mendlesohnian immersion, and obdurate enough that it will not go away of its own accord. The former quality launches Weiskel's second stage; the latter prompts the search for the third. Jon Snow's intrusion fantasy creates such a quantity. Just as Bran's tale derives its narrative motility from his ability to start following instructions, Jon's moves in accordance with his willingness to remain convinced, against the advice of sceptics like Tyrion Lannister and Alliser Thorne, that the truth – not his own quirky interpretation of events, but the inarguable, enduring *truth* of the world – is out there. Being held back from such a truth creates no pain when said truth can be discounted as a mere analysable oddity, a state of affairs Lovecraft's Francis Thurston happily abides in before discovering Johansen's manuscript. If the intrusion is disproved, found to be a misapprehension, the tale stops dead. This robs the focaliser of anything to do. Much like the portal-quest form, Mendlesohnian intrusion inescapably revolves around the focaliser's ongoing engagement with a presence in the narrative, a positive quality, rather than the absence articulated by immersive fantasy. Jon knows nothing but feels a great deal; again, this is his job, and however much it irritates his girlfriend, he is very good at it. As such Jon, like Bran, creates an outrigger for Martin's narrative, something that steadies the narrative ship and helps it move in a particular direction, but also implies, almost inescapably, that there is a direction to move in.

This combination of Mendlesohnian rhetorics in the same text might be decried as a loss of focus. The creation of an unquestionable, Romantically sublime presence in two subplots while the other narrative strands consistently argue away from such notions could be seen as a failure to do what Martin appears to generally be doing – utilising the imperatives of the genre to serve his authorial aims. Yet, the frequency with which Martin's work is praised for its apparent moral agnosticism demonstrates Martin offers a resonant, penetrating critique of the unpredictability of human morality.

J.R.R. Tolkien would recognise – and celebrate – this apparent contradiction. The situation just described is an almost textbook case of a key element of Tolkien's endorsement of fantasy as a literary form. In his essay "On Fairy-Stories" (published 1947), he states that fantasy has a particular capacity to emphasise and foreground elements of reality by means of obvious, absolute contrast. He calls this capacity Recovery, a formalised re-contextualisation of very basic aspects of reality in relation to purpose-written points of contrast, making them stand out in ways that help the reader overcome the contempt born of familiarity:

> Fantasy is made out of the Primary World, but a good craftsman loves his material, and has a knowledge and feeling for clay, stone and wood which only the art of making can give. By the forging of Gram cold iron was revealed; by the making of Pegasus horses were enobled; in the Trees of the Sun and Moon root and stock, flower and fruit are manifested in glory.
>
> And actually fairy-stories deal largely, or (the better ones) mainly, with simple or fundamental things, untouched by Fantasy, but these simplicities are made all the more luminous by their setting. ("On Fairy-Stories" 147)

Gram, the broken sword of the *Volsungasaga*, is an apt example. When the hero Sigurd brings it down on the anvil on which it is re-forged, it cleaves the anvil in two (15), a supernatural exaggeration that reminds the reader of a very basic idea: iron is a heavy, solid substance that ingenuity can craft into tools that greatly enhance the strength of the human body. The suggestion that this very straightforward idea requires no such elaboration contains the seeds of its own invalidation. Tolkien argues that some ideas are so straightforward that humanity risks losing sight of them amid "the drab blur of triteness and familiarity" (146). The novelty of fantasy brings them back to the reader's attention, the supernatural accentuating the natural just as the colonialist exotic certifies the normal. Tolkien likens this to viewing reality through a freshly cleaned window. "It was in fairy-stories," he avers, "that I first divined the potency of the words, and the wonder of the things" ("On Fairy-Stories" 147).

Tolkienian Recovery is relevant to Martin's work in that the supernatural presence focalised by Bran and Jon stands as an obvious, inarguable, unhuman challenge to a society Martin characterises as profoundly lacking in moral wherewithal. To reiterate a point touched on in Chapter 1, the use of a supernatural evil looming over Westeros throws the "black mad folly" (*Clash* 872) of the game of thrones into high relief. Martin's tale may not be one of – to revisit Grossman's phrase – "pretty elves versus gnarly orcs," but it is one of a society tearing itself to pieces over pretty trifles while an altogether gnarly common enemy recrudesces beyond the ill-defended Wall. These creatures are an entirely alien quantity, devoid of the intricate interior workings with which Martin has endowed his human society. Whatever plans Martin may have for his forthcoming volumes, it is safe to assume that the Others will not be bought off like the Dothraki, hamstrung by financial difficulties like the Baratheons, or paralysed by infighting like the Night's Watch. The Others are the biting, interminable Westerosi winter incarnate, as devoid of human motivations as they are of mercy.

Martin has broken the generally immersive rhetoric of his tale in order to build this part of his written world. This aspect of the tale therefore takes shape in ways that force readers to accept and meditate upon an obdurate, unarguable, inhuman truth rather than assemble rational evidence into a report of a subjective point of view. The presence of Bran's, and especially Jon's, subplots therefore creates a moral yardstick by which the passions and follies Martin writes about in his southern stories can be measured. As Susan Vaught puts it, "Winter is coming, and with it a host of horrors, making the very survival of society dependent upon inhabitants cooperating and acting for the benefit of the whole instead of pursuing more selfish or individualistic aims" (105). In-country, Jeor Mormont makes the point more succinctly – "When dead men come hunting in the night, do you think it matters who sits on the Iron Throne?" (*Game* 758). The rulers of Westeros should obviously be putting aside their petty differences to coordinate the defence of the realm against this implacable, murderous, morally opaque common enemy. As Mormont's successor collapses into the snow at the end of *A Dance with Dragons*, however, they have failed to do so, instead allowing the game of thrones to continue on its divisive, destructive way. The tragic irony of Martin's tale therefore deepens and darkens in the context of the supernatural crisis beyond the Wall, the shortcomings of Westerosi society highlighted by the verities Martin encodes into Bran and Jon's focalisation. The Westerosi fail to engage with a threat which the reader has come to terms with via the reading processes demanded by Mendlesohnian portal-quests and intrusion fantasies, which enshrine their subjects as neo-Romanic truths. As such Martin focuses attention on the moral shortcomings of his characters, the fundamental human concerns that, per Tolkien, his fairy-story is about. He has therefore produced a particularly clear-cut case of Tolkienian Recovery – and a successful one, if the chorus of praise for his focus on moral ambiguity is anything to go by. Martin has, like most fantasists of substance, used the supernatural to deepen, rather than simplify, the moral focus of his narrative. The presence of the Others allows Westeros's lack of moral literacy to be measured in something akin to the literary equivalent of experimental conditions – a perfect, sterile context in which it can be analysed in abstract terms via the application of a dark, necrotic reagent.

Martin's iteration of Tolkienian Recovery effectively reiterates the diegetic effect of Sansa Stark's immersive focalisation at a heterodiegetic level. Sansa's focalisation, as noted in the previous chapter, is particularly resonant because she articulates the Clutean thinning characteristic of Mendlesohnian immersion in the context of a conscious opinion that the missing quantity – moral literacy – really ought to be there. That context focuses her attention on just how thin Westeros is. This is precisely what the reader experiences when examining King Joffrey's puerile sadism, Stannis Baratheon's grinding intransigence, Vargo Hoat's asinine bloodlust, Arya Stark's murderous vendettas and Petyr Baelish's willingness to throw Ayra's father under the Lannister bus. They can see everything, and they know that winter is indeed coming, on feet that do not "break the crust of the new-fallen snow" (*Storm* 1.251), in armour that is "proof against most ordinary blades" (*Feast* 91) and with weapons "sharper than any razor" (*Game* 9). As such their heterodiegetic perspective echoes Sansa's diegetic one. Approaching the immersive mainstream of Martin's narrative, they interrogate an absence in light of a contrasting presence. The reader is thus placed in the same position outside the text that Sansa occupies within it. Martin's depiction of the moral shortcomings of the Westerosi is as vivid as it is because the reader is learning about it on multiple mutually complementary levels at once.

Martin is therefore not subverting or denying the tropes of fantasy but using them to subtly powerful effect. The tale of an exhausted, etiolated world, a place somehow less magical than before, is all but fundamental to the modern genre. Martin's depiction of a word where the romanticised truth of a practically demonstrated aristocracy has died away, resulting in a collapse of the sort of faith required for a social order based on honour, oath and loyalty to function, is a classic example of Clute's concept of thinning. He has bolstered this impression by building the bulk of his world with Mendlesohn's immersive rhetoric, an expository method composed of rational demystifications. This places the reader in an inescapably sceptical, interrogative frame of reference, looking for evidence and never taking anything on trust. Martin then emphasises the resulting depiction of loss and thinning by using Mendlesohnian portal-quest and intrusive rhetoric to force the reader into an entirely different perspective on the magical world beyond the Wall as it begins to impinge upon his all-too-human political slugfest. The only way Bran Stark's portal-quest makes any sense is if the reader takes the existence and advice of Bran's guides as seriously as he does. Similarly, a reader who assumes that Jon Snow is worrying about nothing when he continues to seriously concern himself with the latent looming dread he first encounters in the Haunted Forest may as well stop reading. The Night's Watch subplot, like Bran's, is focussed on an unavoidable, obdurate presence in the narrative. These plots enshrine the supernatural as an essentially orientalised, Romanticist challenge to the focalisers. Rather than detracting from the sense of thinning created by the immersive focalising mainstream, these subplots, focussed on unavoidable *truth*, reveal just how much thinning Martin's world has *in fact* suffered. This is a clear case of Tolkienian Recovery, a diffusion of the contempt born of familiarity and a recovery of a clear picture of human attributes, positive or negative, that might be obscure in the absence of a clear, inarguable point of contrast. This narrative achieves perfect Tolkienian and Clutean affect by dint of judicious authorial choices of Mendlesohnian rhetoric. *A Song of Ice and Fire* could be used as a textbook example of some of the core features of modern fantasy literature in action.

5 "Remember That You Were Brothers" – Superstition and Cohesion

Arriving in Qarth, Daenerys Targaryen feels that "All the colors that had had been missing from Vaes Tolorro had found their way to Qarth; buildings crowded around her as fantastical as fever dreams in shades of rose, violet and umber" (*Clash* 384). Buildings do not move independently. This is a compositional flourish of Martin's, meant to underscore the novelty of the colours of Qarth to a focaliser who has just spent months squatting in a dusty ruin. One aspect of Qartheen society, however, is presented as quite genuinely magical. Among the delegation sent to meet Daenerys is the "great warlock" (183) Pyat Pree. "Come with me to the House of the Undying," he suggests, "and you shall drink of truth and wisdom" (385). His compatriots dismiss this purported wizard as a charlatan. "Pyat Pree has blue lips" observes Xaro Xhoan Daxos,

> "and it is truly said that blue lips speak only lies. Heed the wisdom of one who loves you. Warlocks are bitter creatures who eat dust and drink of shadows. They will give you nought. They have nought to give." (525)

Xaro's professed love is mere rhetoric. He wants Daenerys for her dragons and plans to exploit Qarth's marriage customs in order to acquire one (528). It would hardly be surprising if he were to lie to denigrate potential rivals for her attention. His scepticism has some corroboration, however, and from an unlikely source:

> "One time" Sam confided, his voice dropping from a whisper, "two men came to the castle, warlocks from Qarth with white skin and blue lips. They slaughtered a bull aurochs and made me bathe in the hot blood, but it didn't make me brave as they'd promised. I got sick and retched. Father had them scourged." (*Game* 260)

Randyll Tarly was prepared to try a magical solution to a perceived problem. The ritual was deemed a failure. Yet the queasy weakling fished out of the bloodbath later becomes Sam the Slayer, killing one of the Others beyond the Wall (*Storm* 1.252–1.253). Was this a long-delayed result of this ritual – a confirmation of Eddard Stark's sagacious observation that one can only be brave when one is afraid – or merely an act of hysterical desperation? It is very difficult to tell what, if anything, the warlocks have achieved here. As is often the case in Martin's world magic is an unknown quantity, a matter of experimentation and superstition among the characters and conjecture and tension among readers.

Jesse Scoble contrasts Martin's approach with that of "traditional fantasy," in which the authoritative nature of magic can become "ubiquitous and predictable" (124). One of the hallmarks of genre fantasy is that "magic works or misunderstood science is so sophisticated that it doubles for magic" (Grant 396). Martin certainly presents some of his magic this way. The reader must accept Bran's communion with Bloodraven and Sam's confrontation with the Other as indisputable for their tales to make any sense. By contrast Sam's experience with the warlocks is a matter of uncertainty. Readers of *A Song of Ice and Fire* often find themselves unsure if what they have read is a report of magic, trickery, or credulity. Brian Cowlishaw uses the point as a striking example of Martin's bent for frustrating reader expectation, observing that the order of maesters in particular "don't get it [...] Much of what the maesters know is wrong; much that is essential to know, the deny, ignore, or mistake as a tale for children" (62). This may be giving the maesters too little credit. Luwin's conservative dismissal of magic (*Game* 561) is undeniably ironic, but he does not speak for his order. Pycelle cautions Cersei Lannister away from magic not because it is fruitless but because it is dangerous (*Feast* 613). Archmaester Marwyn's (attested [*Game* 648]) fieldwork with warlocks and shadowbinders has convinced him that such caution is foolish in itself (*Feast* 774–775). This is interesting given the care Martin takes to build the credibility of the maesters in most other respects. Luwin's history lesson for Bran Stark (*Game* 713–714) overstates the thinning of the world, but is later corroborated, in its essentials, from the horse's mouth (*Dance* 527). Tyrion Lannister owes his life to the accumulated medical knowledge of the Citadel (*Clash* 846). So too, probably, does Jaime; for all of Qyburn's dismissals of the maesters, someone taught him to effectively clean out a suppurating injury (*Storm* 1.423–1.425). But this credibility underlines the general uncertainty. Credible arbiters of knowledge cannot agree on what magic, if any, is real.

Cowlishaw's broader point that Martin makes a game of reader expectation is unquestionably valid. Scoble's suggestion that Martin's extension of this game to his presentation of magic differentiates him from the bulk of modern fantasists also makes sense. Yet by doing so, Martin perpetuates a presentation of literary thaumaturgy that is by some measures more traditional than that of genre fantasy, which only really coalesced as a recognisable form in the 1960s and 1970s (James 72–73; Williamson 186). Martin is, to a striking extent, reiterating the fantastic as defined by Tzvetan Todorov. The purpose of this chapter is to explore the literary effects arising from the ways in which Martin's work reiterates Todorov's schema. Such a reading may be mildly controversial. Once praised for his insight on the matter (Armitt 6–7; Cornwall 3; Jackson 5), Todorov has been questioned by more recent critics, who suggest his theoretical system has "a greater prominence than its relevance warrants" (Attebery 2012 89). I have made such statements myself in the past and do not retract them here, but I would submit that *A Song of Ice and Fire* is something of a special case. Martin's work, forcing the reader to hesitate over what magical forces actually exist in his world, provides an interesting candidate for Todorovian analysis.

In *The Fantastic: A Structural Approach to a Literary Genre*, Todorov suggests the fantastic depends upon "hesitation" (31), an uncertainty on the part of readers and characters alike over whether untoward events in a narrative have rational or supernatural explanations. Thus, the fantastic is that period in a tale between something going bump in the night and anybody discerning what caused the noise. Hesitation cannot arise out of symbolism, metaphor or other compositional flourishes such as Daenerys's appraisal of Qartheen architecture; it can only emerge from reports of actual narrative events (33). It is a mode of epistemological instability; in the absence of conclusive explanations of exactly what the written world does or does not contain, readers are uncertain not just of what to think, but *how* to think. It is an inherently "evanescent" (42) mode, as characters and reader alike are always interrogating it in a search for resolutions to that tension. Most authors will eventually reward the reader by explaining the strange events, resolving the fantastic into one of two "adjacent" genres, the uncanny (if events were merely the result of a counterintuitive oddity) or the marvellous (if the supernatural is confirmed). Texts in which hesitation is resolved are termed either fantastic-uncanny or fantastic-marvellous, intermediary stations in a tripartite division between the uncanny, the fantastic and the marvellous. The Todorovian fantastic in its pure state, leaving the reader confused as they set down the book, is actually quite rare.

The problem with this definition is that most modern fantasy falls into Todorov's marvellous mode. Much of his book examines a small corpus of mostly European texts written between the Romantic era and the advent of twentieth-century psychoanalysis (158–160), offering only passing discussion of the marvellous. Martin's depiction of a world of unfamiliar geography, invented history and characters belonging to fictional nations and ethnicities, presented without explanation or apology, is what Todorov calls it the "exotic marvellous," in which "supernatural events are reported without being presented as such." (55) He presents such situations as examples of what he is *not* looking at. The acceptance of his model has caused problems. It leads to such critical oddities as Christine Brooke-Rose's dismissal of *The Lord of the Rings* as "pure marvellous, since no surprise is created by the magical elements" (235) and therefore not really fantasy at all. In strict Todorovian terms this is fair comment – or nearly so; like Martin's invented world Middle-earth is actually exotic-marvellous – though this demonstrates how far adrift Todorov's model is from the modern genre. Johnathan Langford (51–52) suggests Todorov has damaged modern fantasy's critical credibility by directing scholarly attention towards earlier forms of the literary supernatural. I agree, but this does not mean the Todorovian model is useless. Within his exotic-marvellous world, Martin presents different subplots occupying different points along Todorov's spectrum from the uncanny to the marvellous.

Much of his story, for example, is profoundly uncanny. Todorov formulates the uncanny as concerned with "events which may be readily accounted for by the laws of reason, but which are, in one way or another, incredible, extraordinary, shocking, singular, disturbing or unexpected" (46). Defined with reference to Freud and "uniquely linked to the sentiments of the characters" (47) it serves the central authorial purpose of provoking fear within the text, and discomfort and perhaps offense outside it. This definition fits horror literature and "dissolves away into the general field of literature" (46) encompassing most narratives of transgression – violence, spite, sexual misconduct and other malfeasance. Nabokov's *Lolita* is a straightforward example. Martin's narrative includes several characters – Vargo Hoat, Ramsay Bolton, Euron Greyjoy, perhaps Patchface – who serve primarily to provoke the uncanny, thriving and revelling in Martin's tragedy of manners. The fact that Arya Stark encounters paedophiles as frequently as she appears to do (*Clash* 498; *Feast* 576; *Game* 695) also demonstrates the notion. Arya herself, with her infamous list, embodies the mode. Had the superstitious (*Clash* 609) Hot Pie focalised the death of Chiswyck, the result might have been a fine example of the Todorovian fantastic, with an explanation of the Ghost in Harrenhal delayed or possibly withheld altogether. As Martin actually writes it, the reader knows precisely what is going on and is left with the unsettling idea of a ten-year-old child gloating to herself about causing an extrajudicial killing (425). A ghost would have been a comparative relief. Much of the controversy that surrounds Martin stems from his use of this mode. Todorov therefore provides a formal diagnosis for the criticism of the sex and violence in *Game of Thrones*. Those who indict Benioff and Weiss typically do so for a perceived overreliance on the uncanny.

Within this overall climate, Todorov's other modes episodically appear. Mance Rayder's search for the Horn of Joramun is an example of the Todorovian fantastic-uncanny, in which rumours of the supernatural eventually yield to mimetic explanations. Chastened by his encounter with a wight, Jeor Mormont takes the threat of some sorcerous weapon in the Frostfangs at least broadly seriously; he "must know" what Rayder is doing (*Clash* 571). Qhorin Halfhand promptly lays down his life in pursuit of that information. Jon Snow, the protagonist of a Mendlesohnian intrusion fantasy, is hotwired to believe Ygritte when she tells him Mance was looking for the horn (*Storm* 1.413). He thus believes Mance when he presents the warhorn in his tent as the fabled artefact (2.444–2.446). A reliably attested weapon that can blow down the Wall then sits in the background of Martin's tale for over 1,000 pages. Then Melisandre burns it (*Dance* 156). Martin's description of the conflicting light sources in that scene make it hard to tell if the glowing runes on the burning artefact amount to anything. Several hundred more pages elapse before Tormund Giantsbane informs Jon that he has been had;

> We found it in a giant's grave, and no man o' us had ever seen a horn so big. That must have been why Mance got the notion to tell you it were Joramun's. He wanted you crows to think he had it in his power to blow your bloody Wall down about your knees. But we never found the true horn, not for all our digging. (905)

Jon doubts Tormund's dismissal. If Giantsbane is lying, however, Martin has presented three layers of conflicting information (Ygritte, Mance, Tormund) about this horn. Unless this is a quadruple bluff, the narrative of the Night's Watch has maintained the Todorovian fantastic for nearly 2,000 pages before resolving into the uncanny with the revelation of Mance's duplicity.

Some of Martin's subplots incorporate the pure Todorovian fantastic. One example is Varys's tale of how he was mutilated. He tells Tyrion Lannister of his castration by a sorcerer seeking a severed phallus for a strange and – to hear Varys tell it (*Clash* 584) – successful attempt at theurgy. He offers the story as an explanation for his antipathy for Stannis Baratheon, a man literally in bed with a sorceress. What he does not offer, however, is shred of evidence for the tale. Readers therefore have no idea if they have heard a genuine account of magic, the confused memories of a drugged child or the fabrications of a practiced deceiver. As Todorov observes of fantastic events (113–114), physical action and the reportage thereof have become confused, and readers rush to settle the confusion by picking over Varys's story. Martin even takes care to muddy the waters as the reader tries to figure out who is misbehaving here:

> When he was done, they rode in silence for a time. Finally Tyrion said, "A harrowing tale. I'm sorry."
>
> The eunuch sighed. "You are sorry, but you do not believe me. No, my lord, no need to apologise. I was drugged and in pain and it was a very long time ago and far across the sea. No doubt I dreamed that voice. I've told myself as much a thousand times." (*Clash* 585)

This might be a moment of pathos, an insight into the isolation of a man accustomed to scepticism about his tale of abuse. But then, this man lies for a living. Why would he be admitting this particular story seems ridiculous except to build sympathy and throw listeners off his deeper schemes? Come to think of it, what proof has he ever offered that is even a eunuch? This episode demonstrates the accusitory nature of the Todorovian fantastic, which essentially revolves around the presence of an explanation for an event (Varys's castration) that accuses someone (the Myrish sorcerer) of not just behaving badly (uncannily) but impossibly (marvellously). Martin is good at harnessing this effect, as will be discussed shortly; of immediate note is the fact that he has inserted both natural and supernatural explanations into the narrative discourse surrounding a particular event and invited the reader to take both fairly seriously.

Daenerys Targaryen's experience in the House of the Undying, meanwhile, demonstrates the fantastic-marvellous. This is an altogether strange episode, perhaps Martin's most sustained depiction of magic in the narrative to that point. "Perhaps" is the operative word, however. Daenerys's adventure begins with Pyat Pree administering a dose of shade-of-the-evening, the warlock's mysterious tonic. As Daenerys explores the maze a reader could be forgiven for construing her visions as symptoms of a fast-acting hallucinogen. When she is accosted by the Undying, "a mouth descended on one eye, licking, sucking, *biting*" (*Clash* 638) yet she emerges from the house with her eye uninjured. There is no witness to attest that she was actually bitten at all. Most of her visions draw on either her previous experiences or the stories she heard from her hectoring brother. Viserys left Daenerys prone to vivid nightmares (*Game* 95–96); she has seen her guardian grotesquely killed, eaten a heart, suffered a traumatic miscarriage and been party to dramatic killings herself. Pyat Pree claims shade-of-the-evening will "unstop your ears and dissolve the caul from your eyes, so you may hear and see the truths that will be laid before you" (*Clash* 630), but there are people on Earth who make similar claims for actual intoxicants that can impair judgement, skew spatial and temporal perceptions and stir up disconcerting memories. Without agonising over how realistic a depiction of psychoactive drugs this may be, the episode closely parallels Todorov's reading of the literary drug experience. "The physical world and the spiritual world interpenetrate" (118), propagating uncertainty over whether stimuli are external or internal. Unlike his televisual counterpart, furthermore ("The Ghost of Harrenhal"), Martin's Pree offers no demonstration of his powers. All the warlocks seem to do is "read their crumbling scrolls, drink shade-of-the-evening until it turns their lips blue, and hint at dread powers" (*Clash* 385) – and get thrown out of Horn Hill, battered and bleeding, after their ritual emboldening of Sam Tarly fails. Is Daenerys exploring the headquarters of a magical order, or the Essosi equivalent of an opium den full of sickly addicts claiming – as addicts sadly sometimes do – that their affliction furthers their art?

As Jorah Mormont calms his disorientated queen, that question remains quite valid. Daenerys later expresses contempt for these people – "if a warlock's spell could kill me, I would be dead by now" (*Dance* 246). This point makes sense; they conspicuously outsource their retaliation to a well-spoken but mundane cutthroat (*Clash* 795). Xaro Xhoan Daxos certainly sees the warlocks as pathetic addicts. While his intentions towards Daenerys are cynical his scepticism appears genuine. Visiting her in Meereen he makes no mention of the portents with which he ran her out of his mansion, noting only that "the Undying are all dead" (*Dance* 239). It seems he does not take phantom tortoises (*Clash* 787) particularly seriously after all. Only as time vindicates the "sights and sounds of days to come" (*Clash* 630) Daenerys saw does the reader get any solid confirmation that magic has taken place. She has clearly seen, for example, a portent of the Red Wedding in the form of the wolf-headed king murdered at his cups (631–632), and slaves do indeed touch her and call her *mother* (*Storm* 2.19). While the question of what went awry at Horn Hill remains open, these points gradually become too convincing to admit scepticism; the warlocks are clearly onto something, even if they are not everything they claim. Martin creates an ambiguity over the nature of reality in his invented world, then gradually resolves it in favour of a supernatural explanation, the essence of Todorov's fantastic-marvellous mode.

At the far end of the Todorovian schema from the uncanny is the pure marvellous, in which untoward events simply fail to conform to the laws of nature defined by the narrative discourse. This calls for the characters to reassess what in their written world is going on, to wonder, and often to fear. The attack on the Fist of the First Men is a prime example. It is interesting that nobody questions the third blast from the lookout's horn, as Sam does the second (*Storm* 1.16). A second blast *can* be questioned; to be taken unawares by wildlings is frightening but explicable. The implications of the third blast are not. "They never blow three," observes Sam. "Not for hundreds and thousands of years. Three means…" (1.17). His intellectual response falters, replaced by Chett's very visceral one (hysterical urination). The Others represent an unapologetic, unambiguous breakage of the character's understanding of their universe.

The taxonomy therefore fits. Martin may offer an ornate example of the sort of exotic-marvellous milieus Todorov deliberately ignores, but the manner in which he presents the supernatural elements of that world demonstrate frequent, wide-ranging use of the modes Todorov does discuss. He punctuates an uncanny narrative with numerous isolated examples of the Todorovian fantastic and its adjacent modes the fantastic-uncanny and the fantastic-marvellous, with an overarching incident of the pure marvellous lurking beyond the Wall. This systematisation is not an end in itself but a framework for further analysis. What follows is a consideration of the ways Martin uses these tropes to lend moral and narrative shape to his tale.

Martin's use of the uncanny reveals a definite preoccupation. It serves to differentiate his invented world morally and intellectually from that of the reader, making it a place of pain, absurdity and injustice. The career of one ancillary character illustrates the point. When Eddard Stark's broken leg prevents him from leading the campaign to bring Gregor Clegane to justice, a substitute quickly volunteers:

> "*Lord Eddard*!" The shout came from the west side of the hall as a handsome stripling of a boy strode forth boldly. Out of his armour, Ser Loras Tyrell looked even younger than his sixteen years. He wore pale-blue silk, his belt a linked chain of golden roses, the sigil of his House. "I beg you the honor of acting in your place. Give this task to me, my lord, and I swear I shall not fail you." (*Game* 453)

The emphasis here on this "stripling's" youth subtly underlines the ridiculousness of Martin's invented culture: a sixteen-year-old seriously volunteers for a seek-and-destroy mission, something he has been training for since childhood. The consequences of this culture of violence surface two volumes later when Loras recalls killing Robar Royce in the Stormlands campaign (*Storm* 1.79). Royce was present at Eddard's court, and trusted with an important mission (*Game* 452). Yet, the demands of medievalist loyalties and methodologies cost him his life in combat against someone with whom he once happily sparred (288). Loras, Sansa notes, takes no pleasure in this. His misfortunes continue as he bravely and fittingly volunteers to retake Dragonstone for the Lannisters. He is promptly rewarded with a quarrel to the shoulder, another to the thigh, a mace to the ribs, and a bucket of boiling oil down his back (*Feast* 599–600). For behaving exactly as someone in his medievalist position is expected to, Loras Tyrell is matter-of-factly destroyed.

Chapter 2 noted that Martin's medievalism bore similarities to that of the classical Gothic authors of the 1700s. Products of the eighteenth-century Enlightenment, the Gothic authors sought to entrench their modernity by contrasting it with the supposed horrors of the Middle Ages (Botting 4). As such their medievalist worlds became a grandly unjust, irrational, vanished regime, written into existence with the specific intention of offending modern sensibilities. The Inquisitor of Matthew Lewis's *The Monk*, ripping out Ambrosio's fingernails (362) is an example, his lack of individual identity anticipating Martin's Tickler. Both are animate job descriptions rather than characters, existing solely as symbols of a barbarous imagined past. That is to say that the classical Gothic tradition employs the medievalist past as the natural habitat of the Todorovian uncanny. The unmaking of Loras Tyrell is an example of this trend. Boiling oil is a paradigmatically medieval weapon, categorisable alongside thumbscrews, iron maidens and arranged marriages as emblematic of the hyperviolence of unsympathetic medievalism. Its use to kill this poor kid ("*Dying is not dead!*" shrieks his sister [*Feast* 600] but good luck ever getting him back on a horse) underlines the extent to which the suffering in Martin's tale stems from its medievalist setting. Martin's Middle Ages are not meant to be accurate. They are meant to reiterate the Gothic trope of putting a medievalist regime on trial by emphasising its uncanniness.

Chapter 2 also examined Martin's use of sex to keep readers orientated in that environment. That device is necessary because Martin cannot make the moral standing of his characters obvious by having them actively eschew the medievalist traits of their world. As such the reader meets Eddard Stark, the putative hero of the tale, forcing his seven-year-old son to watch as he conducts a ritualistic beheading (*Game* 12). "The shock effect of the scene is clear," note Jensen and Qvistgaard; "the viewer understands that Westeros is harsh, cruel and unforgiving; very different from our modern, protective societies" (138). Eddard cannot be seen to flout the uncanny regime he serves without a significant degradation of reader engagement in the story. Nor can his son:

> The axe crashed down. Heavy and well-honed, it killed at a single blow, but it took three to sever the man's head from his body, and by the time it was done both living and dead were drenched in blood. Robb flung the poleaxe down in disgust, and turned wordless to the heart tree. He stood shaking with his hands half-clenched and the rain running down his cheeks. (*Storm* 1.282)

Robb commits a deeply uncanny act, a public beheading (using a poleaxe, another emblematically medieval weapon), in accordance with the demands of the medievalist regime. Martin cannot credibly make him less violent than his foes. This creates a difficult problem; if everyone must be equally violent, how can the violent acts of one character be deemed more frightening – more uncanny – than those of another? How can Martin convince his readers to convincingly inveigh upon certain characters at certain times? One way, discussed earlier, is the game of beds. Another way, which Martin uses very effectively, is to harness the rhetorical structure of the Todorovian fantastic.

That structure always begins with an accusation. Characters may investigate a bump in the night without countenancing a supernatural cause. Roose Bolton demonstrates the point. Eerily soft-spoken, he unnerves Robb Stark (*Game* 585) and is later revealed as an enabler (*Clash* 801) and practitioner (*Dance* 499–500) of rape. But nobody actually suggests he has anything to do with demons. As such he instantiates the Todorovian uncanny, not the fantastic. By comparison Gendry accuses

Qyburn of performing "black magic" (*Clash* 802). This accusation shifts the disbarred maester from the uncanny into the fantastic. Qyburn is now not only inhumane but also potentially inhuman; the reader is grappling not with value judgements about what people should be doing – the engine of the uncanny – but with the possibility that his capabilities overstep what they *can* do. Unpleasant as it is to admit, it is within the powers of a human being to desecrate a corpse as the Freys do Robb Stark's. It is however beyond human means to restore a corpse to life, as Qyburn appears to have done when he introduces Cersei to Ser Robert Strong. *Game of Thrones* has confirmed Kevan Lannister's suspicion (*Dance* 1,106) that Strong is the revivified Gregor Clegane (Sandor recognises him) and readers awaiting *The Winds of Winter* have produced a notable shortage of competing theories. Qyburn's similarity to Shelley's Frankenstein is broader than his ability to reanimate the dead. Like Frankenstein he is a seeker of forbidden lore, a Romantic aspirant to fantastic-marvellous abilities beyond the ken of man. That status can only be reached via an accusation, from within the text, of dealings with the forbidden. "Language alone," Todorov says, "enables us to conceive what is always absent; the supernatural" (82).

Todorov abstracts such accusations as an attempt to compensate for "deficient causality" by proposing "an *imaginary causality* for what might just as well be called chance, fortune or accident" (110). Apparently random event events are attributed to occluded, superhuman causes as the narrator attempts to impose "pan-determinism" on uncanny events (110–111). The Qohorik armourer Tobho Mott straightforwardly demonstrates this. Among his skills, he promises, are the spells required to work Valyrian steel. When the blades he fashions for Tywin Lannister come out the wrong colour, his excuse is interesting. He speculates on the imponderable properties ascribed to this rare and precious substance. "Valyrian steel is stubborn," he explains. "These old swords remember, it is said, and they do not change easily" (*Storm* 1.435). Mott therefore attributes the flawed outcome of a demanding commission to occluded, superhuman causes. Tywin, a man particular about ornamentation (he wants rubies set in the scabbards because "garnets lack the fire" [1.434]), takes what he can get from this unseen world. Via such discussion, Martin creates the notion that Valyrian steel is magical.

This happens frequently in Martin's narrative, simply because his characters are so incorrigibly superstitious. Discounting the prologue and events stemming from Daenerys's last-minute decision to trust Mirri Maz Durr, supernatural events in *A Game of Thrones* are limited to Bran Stark's two dreams of the Three-Eyed Crow and Jon Snow's confrontation with the reanimated Othor. Along with those, however, Martin's first volume includes references to omens (95), theurgy (686–687), divine retribution (487), apotropaic runes (285), vengeful ghosts (577), haunted ruins (136), cursed islands (492), fabulous beasts in faraway lands (228), fertility charms (568), and the resurrection of dead heroes (556). Martin only gradually addresses this imbalance between speculation about magic and instances of it. Hot Pie believes in ghosts (*Clash* 609). Polliver entertains even odder possibilities:

> "The northern girl. Winterfell's daughter. We heard she killed the king with a spell, and afterward changed into a wolf with big leather wings like a bat, and flew out a tower window. But she left the dwarf behind and Cersei means to have his head." (*Storm* 2.455)

That particular tale is, the reader knows, nonsense. It serves as a Mendlesohnian pointer demonstrating that the Westerosi rumourmill takes such suggestions broadly seriously; Polliver presents it as hearsay ("We heard..."), but does not dismiss it on those grounds. Such credulity is not confined to the smallfolk. Arya Stark credits the possibility of wizardry (*Game* 337) and only discounts Polliver's story because Sansa, last time she checked, has no such powers. Her mother accuses Varys of gaining his intelligence via "some dark art" (194). Victarion Greyjoy belts Ralf the Limper for speculating that their mission to Essos is cursed (*Dance* 863) but privately wonders at the improvidence of the Drowned God (864–865), privileging one pan-determinism over another. Magic may be "rare and ephemeral" (Jones 108) in Martin's world, but his characters spend a great deal of energy attempting to contact, interpret, invoke or counteract unseen forces – that is, to compensate for deficient causalities by attempting to manipulate occluded, pan-deterministic ones.

As Tobin Siebers observes, the term *superstitious* means to be paralysed with fear; "the superstitious person is the one who hesitates" (34). This is an uncomfortable situation to be in, and one which people tend to instinctively try to break out of by force. When the Night's Watch come across the undecayed corpses of their missing rangers their immediate response is to inveigh upon these affronts to necrology: "'*Burn them*,' someone whispered. One of the rangers; Jon could not have said who. 'Yes, burn them,' a second voice urged" (*Game* 537–538). Something has upset their understanding of the world; physical erasure thereof will allow them to put this unsettling glitch behind them. Note how the calumnies voiced against Daenerys Targaryen by Wise Masters of Slaver's Bay swiftly escalate from gossip about promiscuity into accusations of succubus-like witchcraft, stealing the souls of men via intercourse (*Dance* 335). Haldon Halfmaester dismisses these as slander, though in doing so he identifies a key point about superstition. In his commentary on the Todorovian schema, Siebers suggests that superstitious discourse is an essentially invective, exclusionary enterprise. Speculation about supernatural agency invites observers to "differentiate one element in a conflict by representing it as exterior or alien" (40). He offers the "witch's marks" identified in early modern witch-hunts as examples of this rhetoric in action. By offering a pan-deterministic re-interpretation of a pre-existing accident of dermatology, a witch-hunter could indict his quarry as operating outside the understood limits of human ability, and therefore unworthy of a place in human society. A mob therefore quickly forms. Note that this is precisely the process described above with regard to Qyburn's career. Siebers suggests that the post-Enlightenment fantastic literature Todorov focuses on "reenacts the logic of superstition in aesthetic form" (56), achieving literary affect by reproducing this anthropological reality within the confines of a text.

Siebers observes this process in James's *The Turn of the Screw*, noted by Todorov (43) as an exemplary fantastic tale. James's governess "has the bad habit of suspecting evil of everyone," says Siebers, eventually identifying the apparent innocence of the children as a cover for their traffic with demons – that is, as a witch's mark (53). Siebers notes that the tale only makes sense if the reader adopts the same accusatory, exclusionary approach to proceedings. The death of Miles demands one of three responses. The reader may assume that Quint's shade scared the boy to death, justify his murder as the neutralisation of a demonic medium or condemn the governess as psychotic. The first two interpretations admit the existence of ghosts, forcing the tale into Todorov's fantastic-marvellous mode. The third makes the tale uncanny; the focaliser is dangerously insane (55). Someone – Quint, Miles or the governess – must end up in the epistemological doghouse. This, according to Siebers, explains the resonance of the story, which "derives its immense power from its ability to represent the governess's accusatory nature with such clarity, while continuing to invite the reader to make the same types of accusations" (54). A sufficiently clever author can therefore aestheticise the witch-hunting impulse to create resonant characters and situations.

Some of Martin's characters seem to appreciate this themselves. Varys is a case in point. As noted above, his tale of mutilation immediately creates a sort of medievalist black helicopter story. In trying to iron out a point of discoursal uncertainty, the reader immediately becomes open to the possibility that this man's admission that the story makes no sense is a layer of deception. Note the parallel with James's governess and her suspicion that Miles is putting on his angelic act to cover for his supposed diabolism. In considering Varys, as Siebers predicts, the reader begins to see evil everywhere. The Spider may be telling the truth, in which case there is or was a man in Myr who successfully communed with otherworldly entities – who was, in cold fact, a witch to be excluded from human society. If the young actor was confused and no voice came from the flames, this hardly reflects any better on his tormenter, who practiced the uncanny in an attempt to *become* a witch. Conversely, Varys may be lying in order to further some undisclosed agenda. In that case he perjures himself and has further questions to answer about what he is up to. *Somebody* is misbehaving here. Exactly who is less important than the demonstration of the emotive effect of the Todorovian fantastic: a pan-deterministic attempt to compensate for a deficit of interpretive discourse creates epistemological tension that cannot be resolved without someone being ejected from the spectrum of acceptable human behaviour. Some of Martin's characters deliberately court this kind of reputation. "A sorceress who can inspire such dread in grown men is not to be despised" (*Clash* 147), opines Stannis Baratheon, planning to use Melisandre as a psychological weapon. Another example is Wisdom Hallyne, the spokesman for the guild of alchemists. He and his colleagues receive the full bite of Tyrion Lannister's scepticism:

> They called each other *wisdom* as well, which Tyrion found almost as annoying as their custom of hinting at the vast secret stores of knowledge that they wanted him to think they possessed. Once theirs had been a powerful guild, but in recent centuries the maesters of the Citadel had supplanted the alchemists almost everywhere. Now only a few of the older order remained, and they no longer even pretended to transmute metals. (280)

Tyrion believes Hallyne's spells are "clever tricks" (282). The reader might well agree. Wildfire, the guild's only marketable product, would be easy enough to manufacture in reality. Larrington notes its similarity to historical Greek fire (117–118) and if the guild happens to have discovered anything akin to boric acid (used by Earthly pyrotechnicians to turn flames green), the substance is nothing magical. In a classic example of how only diegetic accusation can create the Todorovian fantastic, only Hallyne's claims of spellcraft make him appear to be anything more than an entrepreneur with a trade secret. But Hallyne wants a reputation for "dread secrets" (*Clash* 283) and puts those claims about, whether they are real or not. Wanting to be feared, the pyromancers affect a discourse of the Todorovian fantastic, sparking the witch-hunt logic identified by Siebers.

Martin occasionally displays the same sort of guile in allowing such discourse into his narrative, creating the aestheticised witch-hunts Siebers describes. One example is his presentation of Aeron Greyjoy. Very much a background detail in *A Clash of Kings* – one his nephew does not seem to take particularly seriously (159) – Aeron is reintroduced in *A Feast for Crows* very bluntly; "The prophet was drowning men on Great Wyk when they came to tell him the king was dead."

> The first three men had offered their lives to the Drowned God fearlessly, but the fourth was weak in his faith and began to struggle as his lungs cried out for air. Standing waist-deep in the surf, Aeron seized the naked boy by the shoulders and pushed his head back down as he tried to snatch a breath. "Have courage," he said. (18)

Thus begins Martin's explanation of the initiation ceremony of the Drowned Men, which Aeron focalises as entirely normal – a perfect example, if the pun may be excused, of Mendlesohnian immersion. It would also neatly demonstrate the Todorovian uncanny were it not for the way Aeron focalises events. The boy, Emmond, loses consciousness and is carried to shore, where "Norjen worked his arms while Rus knelt astride him, pumping on his chest" (*Feast* 19) before Aeron revives him via the kiss of life. Readers will identify this as a crude form of cardiopulmonary resuscitation, but the Damphair does not see it the same way as the maesters do their rough but rational grasp of pharmacology. Like Tobho Mott, the Drowned Men attribute Aeron's skill and Emmond's restoration to an occluded cause, seeing them as demonstrations of "the Drowned God's favour".

This activates the Todorovian fantastic, and with it the epistemological exclusionism Siebers identifies. Aeron, a focaliser, has his unguarded thoughts and feelings exposed to reader examination, and cannot be the sort of charlatan Tyrion Lannister believes Wisdom Hallyne to be. His faith is genuine. The fact that he has never lost a supplicant in fifteen years of performing this ritual is, furthermore, distinctly eerie. Television hospital dramas have exaggerated the efficacy of CPR; if the Drowned God is *not* interceding, Aeron must be *very* skilled at the procedure. The object here is not to settle the ambiguity but to note that neither interpretation clears him of the double-bind described by Siebers. If the Drowned God returned Emmond, then Aeron, particularly skilled at invoking that favour, is a genuine thaumaturge. The brutality of his ritual (which anyone could be capable of) is less dehumanising than his ability to direct the favour of god to practicable effect (which nobody is capable of). Conversely, if Aeron is mistaken, his actions become those of a dangerous lunatic tramping around the Iron Islands asphyxiating and resuscitating people, only avoiding killing anyone by dumb luck. The Todorovian fantastic introduces a narrative tension that the reader cannot resolve without ejecting Aeron from acceptable human frames of reference.

This has interesting consequences for Martin's depiction of the Ironborn, a culture whose values Aeron charges himself with upholding. Martin takes care to depict that culture negatively. They are subject to an intensification of his strategies for building an unsympathetic picture of greater Westeros. Their nicknames – Dagmer Cleftjaw, Ralf the Limper, Wulfe One-Ear – bespeak a culture of rampant, debilitating violence. Spectators at the Tournament of the Hand enjoy violence as entertainment, but at least gasp and weep at bad falls and accidental deaths (*Game* 286–287). By contrast, the Ironborn have their finger dance, the losers of which receive scant sympathy from onlookers; "A roar of laughter went up when one of Eldred's fingers landed in Ralf the Limper's wine cup" (*Feast* 291). Victarion Greyjoy dismisses Maester Kerwin's complaint of rape as evidence of an effeminate inability to defend himself

(*Dance* 870). Victarion's insensitivity is symptomatic of his people's position in the game of beds, as discussed in Chapter 2. The Iron Islands are a primitive, inhumane lost world, lagging behind even the militaristic patriarchy of mainland Westeros in cultural development. The islander's aspiration to freedom is not the idealism of Ygritte (*Storm* 1.93) or the humanitarianism of Volantis's Widow of the Waterfront (*Dance* 433). They want to establish a violent, misogynistic tyranny "everywhere the sound of waves [is] heard" (*Feast* 20). As constructed by the immersive assumptions of Balon, Theon and Victarion Greyjoy, Ironborn culture is singularly shocking and disturbing – adjectives Todorov uses to describe "the uncanny in the pure state." (46)

The focalisation of Aeron Greyjoy raises the ante. Tied directly to the ethnic identity of the Ironborn, faith in the Drowned God colours the actions of his followers more so than either the old gods or the new of the mainland. Emmond is the fourth man Aeron drowned that morning, and the only one who had second thoughts. Though a mollified alternative apparently exists (*Feast* 20), these people are happy to breathe water for their god, and to trust a hardliner like Aeron to help them do so. Since it is unclear whether Aeron is a thaumaturge or an unhinged fanatic, the reader's interrogation of his culture shifts into the epistemological sphere. The behaviour of the Ironborn is no longer merely inhumane – as Dothraki rape culture is, for example – but potentially inhuman. The accusatory nature of Martin's narrative choices means Theon's people must be either partnered with a pan-deterministic agency who demands human sacrifice, or sufficiently convinced of such a partnership that they conduct such rituals almost absent-mindedly (*Clash* 652). The Faith of the Seven has its own disgraces, but like Roose Bolton, it remains an example of Martin's gothic medievalist uncanny. The Drowned Men are fantastic, and thus, per Siebers, invite urgent, rigorous, accusatory reader attention. Aeron's focalisation of his culture turns Martin's readers from a jury tutting over negative character witnesses into a mob sharpening its pitchforks.

Martin employs this effect just as the Ironborn are coming into their own. They are little more than a Mendlesohnian pointer in *A Game of Thrones*, with Theon Greyjoy demonstrating that Eddard Stark's story is taking place in a broader universe. The Ironborn subplot in *A Clash of Kings* is still focussed almost entirely on Theon, serving mostly to demonstrate the Islands have bred one overconfident nitwit. A synopsis of *A Storm of Swords* could justifiably omit the Ironborn altogether. These pirates only begin to make good on their fearsome self-images with the coronation of Euron Greyjoy in *A Feast for Crows*. That volume opens with a depiction of the Drowned Men that activates the accusatory logic identified by Siebers. Martin confronts the reader with the epistemological crisis of the Drowned God at the exact moment his worshippers acquire the wherewithal to become a serious threat.

There are other instances of Martin waiting until auspicious points in his narrative to utilise this function of the Todorovian fantastic. Like the Ironborn, Cersei Lannister is never a particularly sympathetic character. Her incest, discovered within the first hundred pages of the story, places her directly into the Todorovian uncanny, a status she shows no great interest in changing. Some of her crimes, such as her lack of sympathy for rape victims, have already been mentioned. This may not completely dispel reader sympathy for her as she reveals that the dysfunction in her marriage extended to sexual assault (*Feast* 543) but as noted earlier her complaints are about insults to her own dignity, real or imagined, not anybody else's. Her claims of maternal piety (*Game* 469) follow the same pattern. Readers who are parents might briefly applaud her assertive management of Tommen's pouting demand to sit on the Iron Throne, though surely not the spiteful self-aggrandisement – "*If Margaery Tyrell thinks to cheat me of my hour in the sun, she had bloody well think again*" (*Feast* 386–387) – from whence it springs. Note furthermore how she regards celebration of Tommen's boyish achievements as a tedious obligation; she "had little choice but to don a smile and go to see her son" (391) joust with his glamorous brother-in-law. When Tommen opposes her casual threats of savage medievalist violence, she responds by forcing him into complicity with such acts himself (607). She claims great love for Myrcella as well, but offers no demonstration of the sort of parental affection Catelyn Stark shows when recalling how she "often sent away her maid so [she] could brush [Sansa's] hair myself" (*Clash* 710). Catelyn's memory is wistful partly because such bonds are necessarily fleeting. Children grow up; Sansa will "grow into a woman far more beautiful than I ever was," and be married off. Her budding sexuality, directed first at Joffrey and then at Loras Tyrell, shows that process is underway. Catelyn accepts this. Cersei by contrast avariciously seeks to shield Tommen from influence by Margaery Tyrell, interfering in what ought to be, at least by Westerosi standards, his entirely normal sexual development. Her peculiarly eroticised memories of Joffrey's "lovely lips" (*Dance* 998) are worth recalling here. Sexually or otherwise, she wants these children for herself. Cersei's Todorovian uncanniness deepens as she reveals that she is a controlling, selfish parent.

As this point becomes apparent in *A Feast for Crows*, however, Cersei's subplot shifts into the fantastic by revealing the prophecy of Maggy the Frog. It is difficult to tell, in that volume, if Maggy actually had any precognitive gifts. Prognostication by tasting the subject's blood is an Essosi practice (*Feast* 577), but that does not mean it actually works. Cersei certainly married a king with a roving eye, but the Westerosi sexual double standard being what it is, that is hardly a striking enough prediction to merit a magical explanation. No younger queen has yet cast Cersei down. Tyrion is not responsible for Joffrey's death; as the Imp flees Westeros Tommen and Myrcella are still alive. Regardless of subsequent revelations, there is a large chunk of Martin's narrative in which Maggy's prophecy might well amount to a series of unspectacularly lucky, uncannily mean-spirited guesses. That said, the possibility of magic is imputed into the discourse surrounding her pronouncements. Like Wisdom Hallyne and Damphair, Maggy presents herself as interacting with an unseen world, and by doing so catalyses the Todorovian fantastic.

Cersei's conviction that Maggy was onto something leads her to behave in particular ways. She views Pycelle's caution over prophecy as evidence of his ineffectuality (*Feast* 613). Equating the *valonqar* with Tyrion, she leaps to the conclusion that he killed Joffrey (*Storm* 2.258), a flimsy accusation capitalised upon by a judge with a vested interest in ridding himself of the Imp. Her appraisal of Margaery Tyrells's appearance (*Feast* 201) is not just an indication of neurotic vanity but an attempt to determine if her good-daughter is the queen foretold to replace her. She is behaving in exactly the same way Siebers (53) identified in the governess in *The Turn of the Screw*, re-interpreting pre-existing character traits as signs of collusion with malevolent unseen forces. Children are dying as a result. Cersei pardons those who present the severed heads of children as Tyrion's ("the last had simply been an ugly child" [*Feast* 268]) lest punishing them dissuade others from hunting her nemesis. She also recalls how Melara Heatherspoon, the only other witness to Maggy's prophecy, "screamed and shouted" (661) in the well in which she drowned after arguing over how to deal with the incident. Cersei therefore witnessed Melara's death but did not summon help. The reader already knows that she tortured the newborn Tyrion (*Storm* 1.526) and began her affair with Jaime at a prepubescent age (1.286) – uncanny indeed. With the knowledge that much of her behaviour, notably her enmity for her little brother, was motivated by her superstitions, however, she begins to attract the indictment Siebers identifies in the Todorovian fantastic.

This indictment goes beyond her credulously amoral abuse of power. Cersei actively tries to claim Maggy's purported power for herself. This is where her partnership with Qyburn comes in. Qyburn leaps at a chance to live up to his reputation for unsavoury competence:

> "The *maegi* knew how many children I would have, and she knew of Robert's bastards. Years before he'd sired even the first of them, she knew. She promised me I should be queen, but said another queen would come..." *Younger and more beautiful, she said.* "...another queen, who would take from me all I loved."
>
> "And you wish to forestall this prophecy?"
> *More than anything*, she thought. "*Can* it be forestalled?"
> "Oh, yes. Never doubt that." (*Feast* 614–615)

Here, Qyburn is doing more than enabling an uncanny folly that will see Margaery traumatised and both Osney Kettleblack (740–741) and the Blue Bard (656–659) pointlessly tortured. By enlisting expert help in trying to forestall a prophecy Cersei is effectively attempting to predict her own future, to cashier Maggy just as she seeks to sideline Tommen and rule in his place. She is practicing what Jesse Scoble, the student of genre fantasy, would recognise as a counterspell, a mechanistic attempt to counteract the unseen causality she believes is ordering her life by substituting one of her own. She hopes in practical terms to become a witch herself, to usurp Maggy's apparently privileged position in relation to the unseen world determining her fate.

Siebers would recognise this trajectory. In *The Turn of the Screw*, he notes, is that the governess gradually becomes associated with the supernatural herself. At the climax of the fourth chapter, she sees Quint at the window, experiences "a sudden vibration of courage" and rushes out to confront him, only to find him gone; Mrs Grose, now in the dining room, sees the governess "as I had seen my own visitant; she pulled up short as I had done; I gave her something of the shock that I had received" (142–143). "From this moment forward," Siebers observes, "the governess is presented increasingly in uncanny terms. The awe of superstition associated with the apparition contaminates the young woman" (52–53). In her attempt to find out what is going on she becomes, in a sense, what she fears. The same thing happens to Cersei. Attempting to forestall magic, she allies herself with it and enables it via her partnership with Qyburn. Her patronage allows his uncanny experiments in the black cells, which leave Falyse Stokeworth alive but "perhaps not entirely ... comfortable" (*Feast* 613) and which are propelled into the Todorovian fantastic by his aforementioned reputation for black magic. Cersei's collusion with Qyburn places her in exactly the same position as the witch she sought to defeat. She is therefore both behaving like James's governess and giving readers cause to behave similarly towards her. The interpretation of Maggy's predictions is fertile ground for fan speculation, but Cersei's neurotic participation in that speculation is a more important element of the story. Her unhinged preoccupation with policing the witch's marks she sees around her becomes a mark of her own.

The reader learns nothing of Maggy's prophecy until *A Feast for Crows*. Cersei apparently never told her (supposedly) beloved Jaime of it. Had she done so, it would presumably be a factor in his reflections on the "half-mad witch-woman from the east" (*Feast* 750). The story only comes to light when Martin appoints the Queen Regent as a focaliser, which he does (as noted earlier) to provide her with the modal rope with which she hangs herself. Much of that length takes the form of her rampant, destructive superstition. Todorovian analysis reveals how self-defeating her efforts to fight the unseen world are. It has already been noted how Martin uses the ironic mode to emphasise that this self-styled political genius is an incompetent tyro and employs his customary pattern of sexual discourse to encourage an impression of her as an unstable narcissist. He could have done both in a mimetic novel, but having chosen to incorporate supernatural elements into his narrative, he employs them to raise the stakes of his indictment. As he did with the Ironborn, Martin uses the Todorovian fantastic to launch an aestheticised witch-hunt against Cersei at the precise moment that such invective would best serve his objectives.

Involvement with the supernatural does not tarnish the reputations of Bran Stark or Thoros of Myr. Both these characters are thaumaturges, yet neither attracts the opprobrium identified with relation to Damphair and Cersei. This is because of the lack of ambiguity in their involvement with the supernatural. The sort of exclusionary judgement Siebers describes results from Todorovian hesitation, of which there is precious little in Bran's story. That subplot in fact demonstrates why the Todorovian fantastic is typically of scant value as a theoretical model of modern fantasy. Bran's Mendlesohnian portal-quest hinges on the acceptance of supernatural explanations. Nothing can actually happen to him until he accepts his magical destiny. Portal-quests thus involve a leap from the uncanny (weirdly vivid dreams) to the marvellous, with none of the Todorovian hesitation that provokes the witch-hunts Siebers describes. Therefore Todorov's ideas are of little help in assessing such texts. It is also why Bran's siblings, seemingly developing similar abilities (*Clash* 693–694; *Dance* 703), also avoid Siebers's double-bind. Wargs are a neglected but clearly extant part of Martin's exotic-marvellous world. Bran, Arya and Jon represent a statistical oddity – three siblings all exhibiting a trait supposedly confined to one thousandth of the population (*Dance* 525) – rather than a destabilisation of the reader's understanding of how this world works.

The chief tension related to Bran is not whether he can do magic but what he will do with it. When superhuman power is part of a fictional world it very quickly becomes a moral litmus test for the characters. Plato uses this literary device in *Republic*. The story of the Ring of Gyges is marvellous, not fantastic. Gyges discovers a ring that makes him invisible, not one that might do so if certain aspects of the discourse are accepted as more credible than others. He adjusts the ring, vanishes, and becomes a test case for the moral consequences of power (2.359–2.360). The modern fantasy tradition recapitulates this closely in the form of Tolkienian Recovery; the reader finds out what a character is really made of when the author places them in a supernatural context. Bran Stark faces exactly this test. Martin offers Varamyr Sixskins as an example of how bad a warg can go. It will be up to Bran to discipline himself in light of such possibilities. His behaviour is already suspect. Varamyr lists three crimes a warg can commit – mate as an animal, eat people, and ("the worst abomination of all") possess a human being (*Dance* 2). Bran has already committed the last two and enjoyed them very much. He is of the informed opinion that "no meat ever tasted half as good" as human flesh (78) and violently dehumanises Hodor, likening him to "a dog who has had all the fight whipped out of him" via repeated possessions (528). The reader thus observes his promises to release Hodor with suspicion – not the exclusionary mentality with which they approach Aeron Greyjoy, but a keen awareness that Bran, like Gyges, possesses a power nobody can prevent him from abusing. Bran's marvels put him on a moral watch-list, but not an epistemological one.

There is, similarly, scant ambiguity about Thoros's awakening power. Hearsay about Ser Beric Dondarrion repeatedly penetrates the fog of the War of Five Kings (*Clash* 416; *Game* 582; *Storm* 1.299). Most of these instances, however, incorporate no superstitious discourse, failing to catalyse the Todorovian fantastic. One exception is the innkeeper's explanation of the lightning lord to Jaime Lannister:

> "They call him that 'cause he strikes so sudden, like lightening from a clear sky. It's said he cannot die."
>
> *They all die when you shove a sword through them*, Jaime thought. "Does Thoros of Myr still ride with him?"
> "Aye, the red wizard. I've heard tell he has strange powers."
> *Well, he had the power to match Robert Baratheon drink for drink, and there were few enough who could say that.* Jaime had once heard Thoros tell the king he became a red priest because the robes hid the winestains so well. Robert had laughed so hard he spit ale all over Cersei's silken mantle. (*Storm* 1.150)

This tale clearly incorporates superstitious speculation. Yet the reader is encouraged to discredit her account, for the same reason they dismiss Polliver's story about Sansa Stark's supposed lycanthropy; more reliable testimony exists. Martin has belaboured Beric's distinctive lightning-bolt sigil (*Game* 270; 285), discrediting Sharna's claims about the origins of his nickname. Jaime, being personally acquainted with Thoros's bibulous worldliness, is a more reliable character witness. The innkeeper's tale is therefore not as strong a Todorovian catalyst as Maggy's prophecy. Then, within ten pages of his eventual reappearance, Beric is killed and resurrected (*Storm* 1.464–1.473). Thoros explains the theurgy by which he accomplishes this the next time the pair are seen (1.536–1.537). Readers instantly go from believing Jaime to grasping what the innkeeper was carping about. This flips the irony on its head (the innkeeper was right, Jaime wrong) but it does so immediately, with no period of Todorovian hesitation.

Rather than an epistemological audit, Thoros faces a moral one – one he is faring rather better in than Bran. His resurrection of Beric allows the lightning lord to continue his mission to protect the innocent from banditry. The fact that Beric gave Sandor Clegane a trial is observed by Gendry (*Storm* 1.539), impressing the Brotherhood's moral authority on the reader. Thoros lives to regret transferring Beric's life to Lady Stoneheart, however:

> "Justice." Thoros smiled wanly. "I remember justice. It had a pleasant taste. Justice was what we were about when Beric led us, or so we told ourselves. We were king's men, knights, and heroes ... but some knights are dark and full of terror, my lady. War makes monsters of us all. (*Feast* 721)

It falls to the red wizard, as he comes to terms with his new ability, to observe "wanly" that Lady Stoneheart is turning a reasoned police action into exactly the orgy of vengeance her late husband feared (*Game* 453–454). He is no longer the wine-stained "madman" who approached imprudently sanctioned violence as a form of recreation (*Clash* 142; *Game* 306–307). Thoros's newfound abilities have prompted a profound moral awakening. As Tolkien observes ("On Fairy-Stories" 147), a reader gets the true measure of a literary creation when it is placed in relation to magic.

Melisandre of Asshai provides a particularly interesting example of this. In Todorovian terms, Melisandre is fantastic-marvellous. It is worth going into some detail on her magical exploits since her effects in the narrative consistently bear out Todorov's observations about the creation and function of the literary supernatural. In doing so, she demonstrates a little-noted point of contact between Todorov's ideas and Tolkien's.

Melisandre demonstrates the Todorvian fantastic from the moment she is first mentioned. "Stannis is building ships," Tywin Lannister complains. "Stannis is hiring sellswords, Stannis is bringing a shadowbinder from Asshai. What does it mean? Is any of it true?" (*Game* 743) This complaint postdates several Mendelsohnian pointers establishing Asshai as a focus of superstitious awe. Illyrio Mopatis sourced dragon eggs there (99). Others speak of moonsingers and bloodmages (648; 686), evocative portmanteaus that demand application to absent referents. Jorah Mormont tells his *khaleesi* the city lies near "oceans of ghost grass, taller than a man on horseback with stalks as pale as milkglass. It murders all other grass and glows in the dark with the spirits of the damned" (219). The suggestion that a plant can commit murder is the sort of compositional flourish that Todorov (32) explicitly excludes from the fantastic. Mormont's suggestion that "the spirits of the damned" inhabit ghost grass, however, directly invokes eschatological superstition, catalysing the fantastic. Nobody corrects him. Asshai inspires no cynicism; Tyrion Lannister never speculates about its unsanitary pigeons, drainage system, or debts to the Iron Bank. It is more a story to the Westerosi than a place; denizens and phenomena from it, like this "shadowbinder" Tywin complains of, intrude upon Westeros's immersive reality in as alien a manner as the foes Jon Snow faces. In Frye's terms, that story is modally romantic, defined by supernaturalism that places it one step above the high-mimetic glamour to which characters like Tywin aspire. In Todorov's terms, it is fantastic, with Jorah instinctively appealing to occluded causalities to compensate for deficient interpretive discourse. Martin hammers home this status by providing an example of the process in reverse. Mirri Maz Durr has been there, but knows Westeros only in terms of stories about a land "where men are iron and dragons rule" (*Game* 648). The reader recognises these as misinterpretations of stories about knights and heraldry; are the Westerosi interpreting what they have heard of Asshai correctly? Such questions give rise to the Todorovian fantastic. Anything from there is thus immediately suspect, prompting the invective identified by Siebers. Melisandre's home is a discursive abscess, an unsightly absence of sound narrative tissue discharging a sort of epistemological pus that must be drained before readers are comfortable looking at the picture Martin paints of his world.

That ambiguity shifts firmly towards certainty in the introduction to *A Clash of Kings*. Maester Cressen has observed this interloper, decided that she is uncanny rather than marvellous, and taken it upon himself to silence this dangerous idiot before her "madness" (4) – not magic – spreads beyond Dragonstone. He therefore retrieves his vial of the strangler, reiterating for the reader's benefit the convoluted method by which apothecaries manufacture this poison. This stuff is more akin to milk-of-the-poppy than shade-of-the-evening. Some of its ingredients (lime wash, sugar water) are named and it bears the Citadel's seal of rationalist approval (18–19). It is then shown to work as advertised. Cressen chokes to death while Melisandre, having consumed a larger dose, looks down on him with pity. Though he dies "denying her power, denying her magic, denying her god" (26), Cressen in fact methodically demonstrates that Asshai has produced at least one genuine thaumaturge. The Todorovian fantastic-marvellous is afoot on Dragonstone.

This would be why the invective potential Siebers identifies in the Todorovian fantastic never quite takes effect with regard to Melisandre. She is judged not via Siebers's epistemological interrogation but in Tolkien's moral one. This being the case, it becomes highly conspicuous that she performs some of her magic by siphoning energy from men via sex. Visiting Davos Seaworth in gaol, she offers him "pleasure such as you have never known, and with your life-fire I could make…" (*Storm* 1.347). This confirms the nature of her relationship with the sexually repressed (*Clash* 16; *Game* 265) Stannis, who ages prematurely under her caresses (*Storm* 1.491). Frankel objects to Melisandre's sex life from a feminist standpoint, describing it as "a parody of religious and political power rather than an embodiment of it" (2014 136), and noting that Melisandre's male counterpart, Thoros, works his wonders with his smallclothes on. Another Red Priest, Moqorro, warns Victarion Greyjoy of "terrible pain, such as you have never known" (*Dance* 875) before magically healing his festering hand, the direct opposite of what Melisandre offers Davos. R'hllor's clergy is gender-integrated, but his male and female devotees practice sharply differentiated forms of magic. Melisandre's use of sex magic identifies her squarely as a succubus, the female counterpart of the Romantic incubus (Ashley 904). A straightforward (if, it has been noted, slightly implausible [Punter 69]) example of the form is Matilda, a demon who takes the form of a beautiful woman in order to seduce Ambrosio in Lewis's *The Monk* (375). Martin therefore uses the game of beds to thrust Melisandre's moral fibre very squarely in the reader's face. Magically taking years off a lover's life in order to enable fratricide is a hideous act. Having female red priests work such magic while having the men perform an almost parental (*Storm* 1.536) lying on of hands may well be a dent in Martin's feminist credibility. Davos spurns Melisandre for her actions – "May the Seven protect me" (*Storm* 1.347) – and the reader might well do the same.

Placing Melisandre as a succubus links her with a particular trend Todorov observes in the fictions he studies. Observing the prevalence of transgressive themes, particularly sexual ones, in the texts he deems fantastic, Todorov argues that the genre sprang in part from the need for authors to circumvent censorship, both institutional and internal, to give literary voices to forbidden ideas (158). It was easier to write a tale about a vampire, for example, than one about necrophilia (160–161). Martin might be said to do this, though among his lusty cast of characters his thaumaturges tend to be oddly sexless. Martin reveals nothing of Pyat Pree's physical desires, or Quaithe's; Thoros's libido (*Storm* 2.21) appears to have evaporated with his spiritual awakening. Wisdom Hallyne pursues institutional credibility rather than the opportunity to touch anyone with his "soft damp hands" (*Clash* 280). By contrast, sex offenders like Tywin Lannister, Ramsay Bolton, and Petyr Baelish, author of a weird mock-incestuous frisson with Alayne Stone ("that's worth another kiss now, don't you think?" [*Feast* 711]), are depressingly, uncannily human. Given the centrality of sex as a literary theme in these books, Martin, a twenty-first-century author, could be said to demonstrate Todorov's suggestion that the advent of psychoanalysis, which discusses desires openly, rendered the social purpose of the literary supernatural obsolete (159–160). Yet Melisandre is a latter-day succubus, standing out among her magical peers.

With this point in mind the exact complication provided by her solitary focalising chapter in *A Dance with Dragons* becomes clear. The chapter is revelatory, but it does not confirm her status as a thaumaturge; this was accomplished by Maester Cressen. What this chapter actually does is take a succubus and make her human, carefully nuancing her fiery zealotry. Like the faith of the Drowned God (*Feast* 299), private devotions to R'hllor involve *enthousiasmos*, inviting the god into oneself bodily. Melisandre does this, at a cost of pain, but the experience fails to erase her own identity:

> The fire was inside her, an agony, an ecstasy, filling her, searing her, transforming her. Shimmers of heat traced patterns on her skin, as insistent as a lover's hand. Strange voices called to her from days long passed. "Melony," she heard a woman cry. A man's voice called "Lot Seven." She was weeping, and her tears were flame. And still she drank it in. (*Dance* 475)

Here, in a moment of self-abnegation before a god, Melisandre is moved to tears by a private memory. Exactly who Melony may be (Melisandre's true identity or that of a loved one) is unstated. Nevertheless, this is the first instance of anybody from Asshai having any sort of private life, any personal agenda beyond their public role as a representative of a weird foreign regime of inhumane habits and inuhman power. Quaithe never speaks of her private life in the manner that, for example, Thoros of Myr does. She remains an Asshai'i equivalent of what Kraznys mo Nakloz wishes Daenerys to think Stalwart Shield is, or what Viserys Targaryen imagines himself to be; a living symbol of a regime. To Daenerys, and to an extent the reader, she exemplifies transgression, irrationality and Gothicism, the weird, proscribed mysteries of the barely-real place that is Asshai. Melisandre takes care to maintain that pretence herself, employing pyrotechnic powders to keep up appearances among the heathen (*Dance* 479), just as Wisdom Hallyne may be doing, but like Stalwart Shield she reveals her human identity. This succubus has a soul.

She then promptly starts acting like it. She keeps Devan Seaworth as a manservant to keep him from the dangers of Stannnis's northern campaign, an act of mercy to his father, who she feels has suffered enough bereavement (*Dance* 476). She rescues Mance Rayder from the flames and dispatches him to rescue the girl she believes to be Arya Stark. Melisandre's magic is therefore instrumental in the deliverance of Jeyne Poole and Theon Greyjoy. In the space of a chapter, this character goes from representing one weird, fantastic, faceless regime (Asshai) to rescuing people from the uncanny, dehumanising violence of another (the Boltons). Bearing in mind Martin's habit of depicting certain characters as representing medievalism and others simply coping with its depredations, this throws Melisandre into the same light that Robb Stark and Jeyne Westerling once enjoyed.

Melisandre's shadow assassins are of particular Todorovian interest. These dramatic incidences of the pure marvellous serve as demonstrations of Todorov's thesis on the literary function of the supernatural.

One of the central provisos of Todorov's model is that a text must be a narrative – that is, a report of events – since none of his effects can spring from mere compositional flourish; something must actually be happening (33). At its simplest, Todorov argues, a narrative follows characters from one status to another by way of a period of dynamism (162–163). In order to maintain coherence, however, the characterisations, conditions and thematic considerations of the initial status must impose themselves on the period of instability. These can, by force of logic, halt the transition, crystalising a point of instability as a new status or "median disequilibrium" that cannot be resolved without compromising the integrity of the tale (164–165). The mythical King Acrisius of Argos, imprisoning his daughter Danae to prevent her conceiving the grandson he believes will kill him, is an example (Apollodorus 2.4.1). Danae's imprisonment is a logical development of a story about a jealous king. She will only be released if Acrisius repents his abuse of his authority, which turns the story into very different one, that of a tyrant renouncing his tyranny. Zeus, appearing to Danae to impregnate her, restores narrative fluidity (Acrisius releases Danae, whose imprisonment is now pointless) without compromising the tale's capacity as a meditation on kingly avarice. The god also ensures the imprisonment served a narrative purpose, the conception of Perseus, who will eventually kill his grandfather and (at least notionally) end the abuses of masculine authority that run through Argive legendry (2.4.4). The *deus ex machina* may have a bad name, but superhuman intervention can actually move a story along in a way that preserves, rather than detracts from its thematic integrity.

Melisandre's profane child demonstrates the point by resolving the deadlock between the two surviving Baratheon brothers. It is interesting to reflect on the extent to which the War of Five Kings is a Baratheon affair. For all of Robb Stark's precocious gumption, his campaign has little strategic impact, failing to prevent Tywin Lannister from riding to his grandson's aid against an opponent Joffrey honestly believes is his uncle. Renly is not wholly convinced by the tales of Lannister incest, and thus counts Joffrey as a nephew (*Clash* 435). The Greyjoys are, as noted earlier, still a sideshow. Reminders are frequent that the conflict in the Stormlands is one of bitter familial dysfunction. "Why did the gods inflict me with *brothers*?" (13) splits Stannis. Renly later remarks that Stannis "was never the most cherished of brothers" (435). These two march first against each other, and neither attends their parley in good faith. Catelyn's frustration, expressed in terms of parental discipline – "If you were sons of mine, I would bang your heads together and lock you in a bedchamber until you remembered that you were brothers!" (431) – reminds the reader of the relationship these two have put aside to pursue the game of thrones. This uncanny lust for power is one of the central themes of Martin's tale, and here it creates a median disequilibrium.

These two brothers cannot establish any common ground without compromising their common intransigence, and with it the integrity of the story.

For one brother to achieve a conventional victory over the other would also damage that integrity. A victory for Stannis would reduce Renly to a link in what Mendlesohn calls a "bracelet fantasy" (29), an adventure dropped into a tale simply to pad out an underweight narrative. The Baratheon fleet would sail into the trap that awaits them on the Blackwater; Allard Seaworth would die, the Imp would lose his nose and the Hound would desert, just as published. Renly would have been a mere obstacle for Stannis to overcome, doing nothing to move the story forward. A victory for Renly would be even less productive, as he himself intimates:

> "Tell me, what right did my brother Robert ever have to the Iron Throne?" He did not wait for an answer. "Oh, there was talk of the blood ties between Baratheon and Targaryen, of weddings a hundred years past, of second sons and elder daughters. None but the maesters care about any of it. Robert won the throne with his warhammer." He swept a hand across the campfires that burned from horizon to horizon. "Well, there is my claim, as good as Robert's ever was." (*Clash* 319)

Renly may have a point here, but his plan will not accomplish anything. Pundits from Castle Black (90) to Highgarden (*Storm* 1.81) dismiss him as a stuffed shirt. His plans for kingship amount to preening; "The crown will suit me, as in never suited Robert and would not suit Stannis" (*Clash* 435). To have him take King's Landing would return the story to the situation Eddard Stark encountered upon arriving in the capital. The throne would be occupied by a fickle hedonist who pursued power because he could rather than because he had any idea what it really is. This would do little to build the sort of political stability Westeros bleeds for the lack of. A victory for Renly would return to the story to a Todorovian initial equilibrium (164) rather than a move it towards any final one. The entirety of *A Game of Thrones* would become a link in a Mendlesonian bracelet. A human resolution to the conflict in the Stormlands would either reduce the campaign to a gratuitous distraction or create a complete narrative u-turn.

Melisandre's magic solves this problem. The shadow demon dissolves the blockage without turning the campaign into a speedbump for Stannis or a story about how a wise councillor (Catelyn) can convince feuding brothers to listen to reason – an occurrence that would completely alter *A Song of Ice and Fire's* abiding focus on the evil that men do. Stannis's solution in fact demonstrates how intransigently divorced from conventional notions of familial harmony he is. That he continues to work with the person who foretold his brother's death (*Clash* 557) accentuates rather that compromises the character trait that creates the disequilibrium. It also prevents Renly from devolving into a narrative distraction. It is hard to imagine the course of subsequent events if Renly had died by human means. Brienne of Tarth would have been killed or captured after a military defeat, or else gone over to Stannis as the Florents do. If Stannis had sent a human assassin, then Brienne, capable of moving "faster than Catelyn would have believed" (456), would have thwarted them. Even if someone had managed to get a knife into Renly, Brienne would have the apprehended murderer (or their body) and Catelyn Stark's testimony to prove her innocence. Either way she would never have had to flee Renly's camp and thus never entered Catelyn's service. In that case, Jaime Lannister might never have experienced the moral awakening that begins with his travels with Brienne, who would not subsequently have been sent questing after Sansa Stark, and thus never met Lady Stoneheart. He would have kept both hands, and perhaps even answered his sister's call for rescue. With one thrust of a "blade that was not there" (455), therefore, Martin cracks a Todorovian disequilibrium and launches subsequent experiments in the literary depiction of moral fluidity. A tale about a terrible bloody mess can move forward without the terror and bloodiness of that mess being diminished by anyone acquiescing to Catelyn's plea that they act their age.

Renly's brittle claim to the throne is worth dwelling on as it demonstrates one of the central problems Martin writes about. There is no intrinsically rightful monarch of Westeros. Martin's characteristic use of Mendlesohnian immersive rhetoric denies the essential meanings and destinies upon which monarchy rests. That expositional methodology encourages the contrary impression that civil authority, like everything else, stems not from organic order but from a series of contingencies, contrivances and conveniences (Bould and Vint 109). The coronation of Renly, First of His Name, would prove this. The reader has heard him damn himself out of his own mouth with his statement that his army will secure him the throne, whether it belongs to him or not. Robert demonstrated this precedent in his rebellion, and by *A Clash of Kings* – as his televisual equivalent observes ("The Wolf and the Lion") – everyone with enough cash is following his example. As realistic as this may or may not be, it will not serve in the creation of an actual story. It prohibits a Todorovian final equilibrium, a sense that anything has actually changed or been accomplished. Fiction differs from verity in that readers expect a plot to be closed; they rightly assume they will be able to close the book with some sense of a problem having been meaningfully addressed. Such a story is beyond the methodologies at the disposal of Martin's characters. Benioff and Weiss's Daenerys Targaryen gestures towards this problem with his metaphor of an ever-revolving wheel with one dynasty after another on top and the others crushed underneath it

("Hardhome"). Daenerys plans to "break the wheel," but her choice of a metaphor of violence shows that all she can actually do is perpetuate a problem.

Martin might give some narrative shape to this effulgence of uncanny distemper by having some power bloc establish a degree of moral authority and gradually educate the others. But this would have the same result as Catelyn Stark bringing the battling Baratheon brothers to some agreement. The thematic integrity of the tale would suffer as Martin compromised his characterisations, putting limits on vaulting ambition and ingrained grievance in order to maintain narrative motility. The story would also become one of competing factions heeding wise council, which would inescapably put Martin's stamp of authorial approval on one human approach to a human political issue. This is not the story Martin is clearly trying to write. But in the absence of any human solution the game of thrones also lacks any conceivable final equilibrium. Daenerys's wheel cannot be stopped or broken. Whoever drops their buttocks onto the Iron Throne at the end of *A Dream of Spring* and says "Well, thank the Warrior/R'hllor/Joramun/the Many-Faced God we sorted that out" will be answered by the reader echoing the cynicism of Yoren – "That's no law, just a sword" (*Clash* 81) – while some of their courtiers privately conclude Yoren's point – "Happens I got one too." The game of thrones is one grand median disequilibrium, one that the characters, and more importantly the author, cannot effectively get out of the way they got into it.

Supernatural intervention is the solution. Martin's story features and overarching common enemy, one so inhuman that they are actually called the Others. As noted earlier, these creatures do not feel lust, greed, pride or any of the human emotions whose consequences Martin depicts so uncannily. Comprehensively orientalised as an external, monolithic challenge to the human characters, they operate outside of the game of thrones and, left unchecked, will break Daenerys's wheel with fatal, all-consuming thoroughness. What Melisandre's shadow assassins do for the Stormlands campaign, the Others do for the broader problem that petty quarrel instantiates. They impart narrative shape to the tale by providing an obdurate, looming endgame for the conflict. Martin could probably keep a strictly human game of thrones running for as long as he felt like writing about it. But the result would be as gratuitous as *Game of Thrones* is occasionally accused of being, a meaningless cycle of violence, misogyny and malfeasance probably met with waning reader interest as Martin struggled for new synonyms for "Red" and "Wedding". The death of Ser Arys Oakheart, for example, would be largely devoid of narrative meaning because the conflict in which he dies would lack any thematically tenable conclusion. The likelihood of a supernatural disaster, however, imparts meaning to the death. As animate winter returns from the storied past to destroy all creatures with hot blood in their veins, the death of Arys needlessly deprives Westeros of a clearly capable, conscientious, doughty warrior, a figure with the exact skills, values and temperament they will soon be in dire need of. With an externally-mandated final equilibrium on the horizon, deaths such as Arys's go from being examples of a substantially meaningless literary theme ("In *Game of Thrones* lots of people die") to actual plot points, incidents that might well have some bearing on where this is all going. The monsters lend shape, weight and context to Martin's human themes.

Note, crucially, that this is precisely the opposite effect that the *deus ex machina* proverbially produces. Abrams and Harpham note the pejorative use of the phrase to refer to "any forced or improbable device [...] by which a hard-pressed author resolves a plot" (76–77). The result of such writing is often the alienation of the reader from the story stemming from a sense that nothing before the final chapter actually mattered, that the themes and characterisations evident in the story have not come to anything. Such criticism is undoubtedly valid in many cases. It would probably have been valid of Martin if he had omitted the Night's Watch's subplot from the story or sprung the Others on the reader in *A Dream of Spring*. He has not done this, however. Fantasy requires world-building, and Martin has, as noted in Chapters 3 and 4, responded to that imperative to good effect. The Others appear in the prologue of his first volume and gradually infect the narrative via the creeping, visceral dread of Mendlesohnian intrusion. This lends narrative shape to Martin's otherwise unresolvable succession of amputations, assassinations and assignations. This is how Martin makes the cold-bloodedness of characters like Alliser Thorne, Arya Stark and Theon Greyjoy seem so vivid; what makes the destruction of fair-minded characters like Jeor Mormont, Catelyn Stark and Loras Tyrell seem like actual losses. Martin has found – or rather, effectively employed – a way to invest his tale of unyielding malfeasance with weight, to make each misdeed meaningful, without compromising his themes in order to maintain narrative flux. These characters can sin or be sinned against to their author's heart's content without the engaged reader developing the sense that they are observing anything gratuitous. These things *do* matter; these losses *do* amount to something, this story *is* going somewhere, and Martin has not had to dilute any of his characters for that progress to occur.

The parallel with Tolkienian Recovery is worth making it explicit because it complements a point made at the conclusion of the previous chapter. Martin's marvellous provides a barometer for Westeros's climate of the Todorovian uncanny. The inhuman, imponderable threat of the Others creates what Tolkien ("On Fairy-Stories" 146) cites as the central purpose of the literary supernatural: a controlled context in which human attributes, in this case the moral shortcomings of the Westerosi, become particularly apparent. In the context of that "looming catastrophe" (Garcia and Antonsson x) the follies of the game of thrones actually mean something, which means that the reader focuses all the more on them. With events such as the magical outcome of the Stormlands campaign, Martin also allows those follies to abide in clear, refined forms, unalloyed by the demands of narrative motility, on what might be described as a tactical as well as a strategic level. The game of thrones can move forward without anybody necessarily growing a brain or a social conscience. Rather than rendering its constituent moral and fraternal compromises meaningless, this focusses the reader's attention upon them by allowing them to persist unadulterated. Stannis's Cain-like fratricide also serves the purpose of integrating Renly into the tale properly, rather than as a link in a Mendlesohnian bracelet. Stories such as that of Cain and Abel, or Acrisius and Danae, and indeed *The Song of Ice and Fire* abide in the cultural imagination as compelling depictions of human emotions at work. While Todorov and Tolkien disagree with each other on some key issues, their respective approaches to the fundamentally, unambiguously magical actually display an interesting point of convergent evolution. The purpose of the supernatural is to refresh and restore the reader's perception of humanity.

Martin therefore makes constructive use of the three key stations of the Todorovian schema of the literary supernatural. His is a tale of the uncanny, of the evil that men do, set in an emblematically medieval exotic-marvellous world. Much of the impact of his tale derives from its Gothicised uncanniness, the irrational violence of Martin's unsympathetic medievalism. This cannot be compromised to establish reader sympathy for anybody, however. When the time comes to press the reader's nose to the perfidy of a particular character or group, therefore, Martin activates the interrogative capacity that Siebers identifies as consequent of the Todorovian fantastic. Per Siebers, Aeron Greyjoy and Cersei Lannister become loci of genuine fear, standing out amidst their uncanny medievalist colleagues via their transition from inhumane to potentially inhuman behaviour. Other characters practice unambiguous magic, the Todorovian marvellous, but in doing so they too impart moral and narrative shape to the tale. The moral shape comes from the inherent challenge of superhuman power; characters like Bran and Melisandre face the same moral judgement as Gyges. The narrative shape from the way the supernatural can dissolve the impasses caused by Martin's characterisations, allowing a story to proceed without the author having to dilute his characters to maintain flux. The result is a sprawling tale of man's inhumanity to man in which Martin calls down the judgement of his readers on particular characters at opportune times, and still coheres and moves in discernable directions, its numerous subplots functioning as part of a whole, even after the roguery of his characters should have caused it to come to bits or grind to a halt thousands of pages ago.

Once again, Martin gets the imperatives and patterns of the form working to serve his creativity rather than constrain it. His story is unusual not in that he is breaking the rules, but in that his sprawling narrative has room to demonstrate so many of those rules working at once. As with his use of Mendlesohnian rhetorics, the aggregate of his Todorovian approaches lends shape and force to narrative and character. The labyrinthine moral ambiguity of Martin's characters in no way detracts from this point. The natural state of humanity is moral ambiguity, and the literary supernatural provides a set of laboratory conditions in which that quality can be analysed. Martin's magic – actual, supposed or feigned – is there to focus attention on the human kernels of the story. This is what fantasy does, and why Martin is so good at it.

6 "But Here You Are" – Magic and Healing

In the seventh season of *Game of Thrones*, Tyrion Lannister hatches a plot to convince his sister of the looming threat beyond the Wall. At his instigation, a resurrected Jon Snow assembles a team of Westerosi adventurers so reminiscent of *The Seven Samurai* that one must assume screenwriter Dave Hill drew inspiration, at least second-hand, from Kurosawa's film ("an almost inescapable model for any group of volunteers who fight for the good" [Clute 853]). Jon leads his team beyond the Wall to capture a still-animate wight. Succeeding in this, they lock their captive in a crate and bring it to a parley in the Dragonpit. There Sandor Clegane (resurrected like Jon, and part of his team) releases the wight, which rushes homicidally at Cersei, held off her by a chain. Jon then dispatches the monster with dragonglass. The demonstration has, seemingly, the desired effect; a fragile, ostensible entente is formed between the living against the dead. Cersei later confesses to Tyrion that the moment she saw the creature everything "disappeared down its black throat" ("Eastwatch"; "Beyond the Wall"; "The Dragon and the Wolf").

Cersei here explicitly addresses the essential matter of modern fantasy literature: the real confronted by the unreal. This is an important point that the genre's detractors often overlook. There is, in fact, no such thing as a story *about* dragons, or wizards, or aliens, or zombies. Such phenomena do not exist, and an author cannot discuss them without contextualising them in relation to that which does. The use of the awkward term *still-animate* to describe Jon Snow's captive illustrates the point. Martin's wights are not alive, but nor do they exhibit the permanent corporeal torpor that is the essential feature of death. The English language has no term precisely describing the vital status of these monsters, except perhaps *undead*, which is conspicuous by its absence from Martin's discourse. Even if that term were used, however, it illustrates the core difficulty rather than dispelling it. The non-existent can only be described in terms of how it differs from the extant. The terms *supernatural* and *non-existent* also demonstrate the conundrum, describing the narrative presence to which they are adjected only by contrasting them with the other entities with which they share the written world. Stories that emerge from such contrasts are not about the supernatural but about how the natural responds to and interacts with it. By describing the non-existent a storyteller inescapably recontextualises the existent, pushing the engaged reader to revisit and reconsider matters they may otherwise overlook. Such Tolkienian Recovery is evident throughout the modern fantasy tradition. Anne Rice's *Interview with the Vampire*, for example, is not about vampires. It is about a *person* who *becomes* a vampire, and contemplates how this altered state of being influences his perceptions of human ideas such as morality, gender and fertility. The tale that Rice's might be most intuitively compared to, *Dracula*, is not about a vampire either, but rather a vampire hunt, a battle to re-establish normality – and thus lionise a given set of circumstances as normal. The core issue in any fantasy is how human beings react when a throat – sometimes black, sometimes not – opens and swallows their pre-existing view of the world.

The purpose of this chapter is to examine some of the ways in which the characters in *A Song of Ice and Fire* react to this moment. Whether or not Cersei herself is ever confronted with a wight in Martin's novels, many of his characters have the experience she describes, a breakage of what they understand to be possible, and their reactions vary widely. The categorisation of these responses via the taxonomy that emerges out of David Sandner's examination of eighteenth-century critiques of the fantastic reveals themes in Martin's deployment of the device that bear direct comparison with those of other fantasists. These parallels reveal that Martin is demonstrating another of the great themes of fantasy, Clute's concept of formalised healing, and with it the overall neo-Romantic program of the modern fantasy tradition. With that, further parallels with the Tolkienian concept of Recovery become apparent.

In *Critical Discourses on the Fantastic 1712–1831*, David Sandner observes the focus of theories of the literary supernatural on the moment of breakage. The revelation of the Todorovian marvellous (such as Melisandre's shadow assassin) is a crisis point in a narrative. It irrevocably shapes the subsequent progress of the tale, in a manner largely dependent upon the character's reaction to it. The same is true, Sandner observes, of the Tolkienian model, which is largely dependent on *eucatastrophe*, the "sudden joyous turn" ("On Fairy-Stories" 153), the snatching of victory from the jaws of defeat which Tolkien suggests is near-pivotal to a successful fairy-story. Tolkien formalises such endings as Consolation, placing them alongside Recovery as key features of fantasy. For such an ending to have any particular emotional effect, however, it must be difficult, incomplete, dearly won or at least unexpected; to be at all joyous, the turn must indeed be a turn. The distinct possibility, even likelihood, of a *dyscatastrophe*, an outcome of "sorrow or failure" (153), is therefore built into the Tolkienian model. The central strategic crisis facing Westeros is Martin's tale is a perfect example. The death of Ser Weymar Royce and his men introduces the possibility of a "looming catastrophe" (Garcia and Antonsson x) into the narrative. As noted in Chapter 5, this possibility creates the central tension of Martin's plot – will the Westerosi be able to put aside their petty fratricidal conflict and mount an effective defence against this *dyscatastrophe*? Sandner observes that in both the Todorovian and Tolkienian models, therefore, the supernatural inaugurates a period of crisis and tension that will completely shape the emotional course and impact of the tale (21–22). He extends the comparison to Weiskel's tripartite model of the Romantic sublime; characters confronted with the supernatural go from a settled understanding of the world into a period of instability, which gives way to a renewed understanding of the world and their place in it. The advent of the supernatural in both Tolkien's and Todorov's schemas inaugurates Weiskel's second phase, necessitating a search for the third, and with it the tension-causing possibility of how, if at all, that phase will be found. Sander therefore focuses his analysis on the effects authors pursue as they direct the "tremendous energy" (164) unleashed in that period of uncertainty.

He offers a quadripartite schema of possible responses to "the anxiety of the sublime moment" (164), the moment in which one enters Weiskel's second phase by supernatural means. These four responses are organised on two axes, open/closed and positive/negative. Two are "open," accepting the supernatural as an abiding feature of the observer's world. Two are "closed," endeavouring to restore the world to some semblance of its former state. Two of his responses are "positive," provoking an increase in ontological stature and emotional health for the observer; two are "negative," provoking the opposite. These four responses, between them, therefore include every possible combination of two polarities:

- Possession is closed and negative. The observer succeeds in getting the genie back into the bottle, an exercise engaged in out of an attempt to retrench the closest thing to a *status quo ante* as can be achieved. That status is therefore endorsed as correct.
- Domestication is closed and positive. The observer succeeds in getting the supernatural under control, working for them, and by doing so "tends to affirm and elevate the self" by extending the power of the pre-sublime self.
- Fragmentation is open and negative. The observer wishes to control the supernatural, but somehow fails to do so, leaving them contending with an ongoing relationship they did not want with forces they cannot control.
- Dispossession is open and positive. Rather than trying to control the supernatural, the observer accepts it as emblematic of an enriched universe, and in doing so experiences a renewed connection to that universe (165–169).

As with Mendlesohn's taxonomy, many fantasy tales demonstrate more than one of these responses, but the large majority of reactions to the supernatural do chronicle one or another of these categories. In most tales of supernatural horror, for example, the sublime moment is a problem the characters must attempt to contain – that is, close. The heroes of *Dracula* do so successfully, making theirs a tale of possession; Francis Thurston of Lovecraft's "The Call of Cthulhu" fails and thus suffers fragmentation. By contrast T.H. White's *The Sword in the Stone* is a tale of dispossession, with the Wart subjecting himself to Merlyn's tutelage and thus achieving virtual apotheosis as the rightful king. As in the case of the Mendlesohnian rhetorics and Todorovian modes, *A Song of Ice and Fire* includes instances of various Sandnerian responses.

Previous chapters observed that Mendlesohnian intrusion fantasies tend to occupy the darker end of the genre. The gradual escalation of unease is one of the defining features of horror cinema, and Mendlesohn, tracing the form to eighteenth-century Gothic texts (121), demonstrates its precursor on the printed page. Unease is not a straightforwardly enjoyable emotion, however. One of the central purposes of horror fiction is to aestheticise that experience in the safety of a text and – all being well – portray the expulsion, containment or destruction of its cause and the restoration of something resembling a *status quo ante*. This is possession, Sandner's negative and closed response. It is negative because it is born of fear; closed because humanity manages to end the sublime moment in a way that reaffirms human conceits. The result is an ideological conservatism, a rehearsal of the notion that people (as defined by the focaliser) can take threats to their perception and control of the world in hand; "the self is reclaimed; and the old order of things is confirmed or re-established" (Sandner 165). Supernatural horror challenges human conceits in order to road-test and reaffirm them.

One well-known story that neatly demonstrates this is *Dracula*. Mendlesohn discusses Stoker's novel as an intrusion fantasy, and the emotional response of the male characters to the intrusion is one of distinctly unmanly hysteria. Jonathan Harker faints at the discovery he is the prisoner of a vampire (63), Van Helsing scarcely contains his dismay as his plans are undone (140; 148–149) and Arthur Holmwood sobs "like a wearied child" at the fate of his beloved Lucy (236). Meanwhile, the women are not behaving in particularly womanly ways either. Mina Harker displays a calculating scientific intellect explicitly diagnosed as masculine (240), while the vampiric Lucy draws sustenance from children rather than vice versa (219). The supernatural threat is undercutting the gender roles that the characters are preoccupied with preserving (Craft 98; Roth 39). Preserve them they do, however. By way of a combination of self-mastery and scientific knowledge they rally their resources, expel the threat from England, hunt it to ground, and expunge it. Orthodoxies are neurotically re-established; the dead rest, England is saved, men are men, women are wives and mothers. Though there are readings which query the extent to which Stoker actually succeeds in this, his novel is a famous example of a narrative that utilises the supernatural in order to test and demonstrate the fitness of a given perception the world.

Samwell Tarly clearly demonstrates this pattern in Martin's tale. His martial incompetence very quickly attracts accusations of unmanliness. "What sort of *man* would proclaim himself a coward?" (*Game* 255; emphasis added) wonder his fellow recruits. Alliser Thorne refers to Sam as Jon Snow's "lady love" (253) the moment Jon sticks up for him; when Jon arranges for the other trainees to go easy on him, Alliser "called them cravens and women and worse" (262). Back home Sam was "dressed in his mother's clothing and paraded through the bailey to shame him into valor" (260). He flees from the Fist of the First Men along with the other Watchmen and spends much of the retreat back to Craster's Keep hysterical with fear. Yet in the final analysis, Sam is capable of some very manly behaviour. When one of the Others catches up with him – the first time these creatures have been seen since the prologue of Martin's first volume – he overcomes his fear and stabs the monster. Sam finds further courage when he and Gilly are cornered by wights in Whitetree. He initially backs away from the monster, "snivelling" and wetting himself. When the wight turns to regard Gilly and her baby, however, "there was no time to think or pray or be afraid;" Sam springs on the monster, shattering his dragonglass dagger on its armour and wrestling it into the fire (*Storm* 2.74–2.76). Sam, Gilly and the baby slept comfortably in front of that fire (2.73), which is set in the abandoned longhall of Whitetree. This is a man defending his adopted hearth, home, woman and child. Like Stoker's heroes Sam is, in the clutch, capable of precisely the paradigmatically male behaviour he previously seemed incapable of.

Like that of Stoker's heroes, the masculinity Sam eventually lives up to is a social construction. *Dracula* was written during the agitation campaigns of first-wave feminism, in relation to which Stoker saw fit to take a determinedly reactionary position (Glover 106). In his novel, he presents Victorian gender roles as essential, disrupted by the supernatural but eventually retrenched as the male characters increasingly take Sandnerian possession of the threat, and with it, themselves. The supernatural proves the natural rule by demonstrating it actually is a rule: this is what true masculinity looks like. Sam does the same thing at Whitetree. His idea of bravery is focalised very much in terms of the prevailing medievalist ideology of Westeros:

> *Do it now. Stop crying and fight, you baby. Fight, craven.* It was his father he heard, it was Alliser Thorne, it was his brother Dickon and the boy Rast. *Craven, craven, craven.* He giggled hysterically,

> wondering if they would make a wight of him, a huge fat white wight always tripping over his own dead feet. *Do it, Sam.* Was that Jon, now? Jon was dead. *You can do it, Sam, just do it.* (*Storm* 1.252)

Then he just does it. What slays the monster is Sam's ability to finally respond to his father's hectoring, Thorne's bullying and, decisively, Jon Snow's positive re-enforcement. Jon, despite being excluded from conventional Westerosi power structures, is among their most consistent defenders. He diplomatically concedes his bastardry at his first appearance (*Game* 17), takes the Watch very seriously (119), undertakes an ostensible suicide mission for it (*Clash* 850) and remains gnawed by guilt for breaking its laws, even under orders (*Storm* 1.358). Here his encouragement prompts Sam to adopt, belatedly but effectively, the martial fortitude expected of (but as Sam himself has proved, not essential to) Westerosi men of a certain station. The self-possession Sam takes from his possessive response to the anxiety of the sublime moment is a reversion to, and aggrandisement of, the social orthodoxies of the written world. Like Stoker's novel, Martin's uses possessive responses to the supernatural to lionise rather than challenge a constructed social order. As such, he perpetuates the social conservatism characteristic of horror literature.

This theme transcends Sam himself. He defeats one wight by living up to his medievalist oath, then follows Gilly outside to find her menaced by a crowd of them, including bodies that once answered to Chett, Lark and Softfoot (2.76) – the conspirators on the Fist, whose affirmation of their oath is very explicitly depicted as disingenuous (1.14). Sam and Gilly escape this necrotic horde thanks to the mysterious Coldhands, who is later revealed to be dead himself (*Dance* 79), but who has somehow contrived not to let that state get in the way of his duties as a Watchman. He addresses Sam as a brother (*Storm* 2.77) and extracts an oath of secrecy from him on the basis of that relationship (2.473). He also redeems the honour of the Watch by killing the mutineers at Craster's Keep, providing retribution for their breakage of the laws of guest-right. Whoever or whatever Coldhands is, his actions are motivated by loyalties, not just to the human world, but to the practices and institutions it claims to treasure as essential – but which are, as Terry Pratchett observes in *Hogfather*, actually entirely abstract.

The social conservatism evident in Sam's plotline should not be taken as an indication that Martin is uncritically lionising medievalist masculinity as Stoker appears to have attempted with regard to the self-image of the male Victorian. He is not. Catelyn Stark's prayer for her blood-splattered son after Robb executes Rickard Karstark – "*Gods forgive him; he is only a boy, and he had no other choice*" (*Storm* 1.282) – is sharply ironic. Robb *did* have a choice; he is allowing his actions to be dictated by the reflexively violent conventions of the medievalist regime to which he is subject (but of which, as demonstrated in Chapter 2, not essentially a part). What Martin certainly is doing here, however, is staunching an institutional wound. As Tyrion Lannister points out to Jon Snow, the Night's Watch is something of a joke in the Seven Kingdoms, and rightly enough so. Castle Black is a thinly glamorised prison colony. Among its wardens, Jeor Mormont is the only uncompromised figure; Benjen Stark is missing in action; Maester Aemon blind and not long for this world; Donal Noye shorthanded; Alisser Thorne a hectoring bully; Bowen Marsh a toothless bureaucrat, Janos Slynt a prize ass in every respect. Their inmates are no better, as Chett, Softfoot and Ryles demonstrate. In Braavos, Daeron requires scant inducement to desert, as heedless of the oath as the conspirators on the Fist (*Feast* 436). This pack of thieves, rapists and blowhards, united by a mere oath (the precise social convention the Westerosi have such trouble honouring), is all that stands between Westeros and the living dead.

Jeor Mormont's Great Ranging, however, has revealed what the Night's Watch is actually supposed to be. Their millennia-long winnowing-down to the surly skeleton crew Jon Snow encounters is a prize example of the Clutean thinning that Martin's world has undergone, but that winnowing proceeded, almost by definition, from a state of strength. Mormont grasps the point as the survivors of the Ranging regroup at Craster's Keep:

> "*We never knew!* But we must have known once. The Night's Watch has forgotten its true purpose, Tarly. You don't build a wall seven hundred feet high to stop savages in skins from stealing women. The Wall was made *to guard the realms of men*...and not against other men, which is all the wildlings are when you come right down to it. Too many years, Tarly, too many hundreds and thousands of years. We lost sight of the true enemy." (*Storm* 1.451)

This is a moment of what Clute calls "recognition," the moment when "the light dawns, and the labyrinth becomes a path" (804) as the characters grasp what their role in the story actually is. Clute cites recognition as a key structural feature in modern fantasy, the moment at which characters realise that the thinned stature of their world is fundamentally wrong and figure out how to forestall or reverse it. Mormont, arming his men with what dragonglass they have to hand (*Storm* 1.449) begins this process, though he is killed before he can embark on a broader reforms. His death may well be an example of how Clutean recognition "is frequently a late, and hurried note" (Mendlesohn 116) in intrusion fantasies such as that of the Night's Watch. Nevertheless it is there. The Watch is a fraternity of monster-hunters armed with magical weapons, united in their lifelong oath to man an ensorcelled redoubt against a blood-curdling foe, comparable to the Gondorian Rangers of *The Lord of the Rings* – they have merely been thinned out.

After recognition, says Clute, comes healing, the formalistic rectification of thinning (458). Fantasy narratives are characteristically, says Clute, "fables of recovery [...] the happy endings of much fantasy derive from the notion that this is a *restoration*, that before the written story started there was a diminishment" (942). Sam's acts of possession in the Haunted Forest and at Whitetree begin that restoration. A member of the Watch stands against the ancient foe his order was formed to oppose and defeats it with fire, a weapon with which he has ceremonially equated himself (*Game* 504). He thus becomes, quite precisely, what a Watchman is *supposed* to be. As noted earlier, fantasy often establishes aristocracies, not to promote such government in reality (a misinterpretation sometimes offered by commentators such as de Camp [133]) but to examine, in the literary laboratory conditions allowed by the supernatural, exactly what the "best" human qualities that an aristocracy supposedly possess might be. One of the most popular ways of turning that investigation into a story is by showing an aristocratic tradition or institution drifting from its ideals and thinned down by sloth, neglect or enemy action, rediscovering itself in the game-changing stress of Sandner's sublime moment. Martin's tale exemplifies this. The key virtue he lionises is not lineage, breeding or gender conformity, but fidelity. Placed against his true enemy – its truth enshrined by the reading process of Mendlesohnian intrusion – Sam *does what he promised to do, decisively motivated by reference to those depending upon him to do so*, snapping the Watch back to a semblance of its former self. The social truth, the natural state of affairs, that Martin heals his world back towards is the idea that, once again, the martial order of Westeros is a job description rather than a license, and that those accorded power and privilege therein are obligated to wield that power for the good of their society. The petty tyranny of Craster and the oafish response of the mutineers who kill him are two of countless examples of Martin lavishing attention on characters failing in this regard, and hardly the work of an author blindly promoting any sort of organic aristocracy. Rather, Martin is considering whether the values that such a social order supposedly embodies really amount to anything. He uses the pressure of the sublime moment to offer a competing illustration of virtue. Inconstancy, an inability to keep promises or remain mindful of what they are for, is the great ill plaguing Westeros, the most obvious human consequence of its thinning. Sam the Slayer is the tonic.

The healing Sam begins is already underway at Craster's Keep. "An aurochs is a fierce strong beast," Grenn observes, reflecting on his demeaning nickname, "and I *am* big, and getting bigger" (*Storm* 1.448). Note that Grenn achieves that insight *after* he sees Sam kill the Other. He allows the reader to entertain a similar optimistic reassessment of the situation. This rediscovery of what the Watch ought to be is a classic example of the true nature of a human or human institution becoming apparent under supernatural pressure. That is to say that Clutean healing is directly comparable to Tolkienian Recovery, the literary placement the real in contrast to literary artefacts that exist solely as illustrative points of contrast to the essential qualities of the former. Sam's native courage becomes apparent not against wildlings or bullies but Others, things contrasted by their very name with humanity. This importantly allows the reader to optimistically suppose that his colleagues might do the same. Clute (458) directly equates healing with the Tolkienian eucatastrophe, the "sudden joyous turn" that leads to Consolation, the formalised happy ending Tolkien regards as necessary for a structurally complete fantasy ("On Fairy-Stories" 153). Sam allows the possibility of this. Grenn's renewed self-confidence in the wake of his sublime moment reveals at least one of his compatriots has Recovered something of himself; that all is not lost.

Sandner's schema allows for people to end the sublime moment by harnessing the magic rather than destroying it. Such a harness ends the sublime moment by rendering it subject to human control, demonstrating that humans can make sense of Weiskel's notionally unreadable sign on some practicable level. Sandner refers to this process as domestication. Attebery's maxim that "When you put a unicorn in a garden, the unicorn gains solidity and the garden gains enchantment" (1982 3) – a rehearsal of Tolkienian Recovery – can be extended to demonstrate the principle. Put a saddle on the unicorn, and the two-way flow of affect immediately shifts in favour of the ostler. Tales of people using magic to better their lot are common in folklore; the tale of Alaeddin is an example. These tales are, in Sandner's terms, still closed, because the sublime moment has been brought under control, but they are positive, because the power of the supernatural now works for the natural. Rather than the police action of possession, domestication seeks to siphon the power of the supernatural to human ends.

One example of Sandnerian domestication is Tolkien's Saruman the White. This categorisation may seem unusual given that Saruman is a wizard, and indeed one of the Istari, angel-like beings dispatched into Middle-earth "to move Elves and Men and all living things of good will to valiant deeds" (*Silmarillion* 360). Saruman never learned magic as Bran Stark does, nor was he born to it; in a sense he *is* magic. Even so he experiences, from his perspective, a Mendlesohnian intrusion, one that gains traction on whatever part of his imponderable Tolkienian anatomy is home to the human emotions and neuroses he unmistakably exhibits. Ring-lore, the secret of the magic rings that set the tone of the latter stages of Tolkien's legendarium, is not Saruman's by simple right of being a wizard, even a celestially authorised one. "The Wise were troubled" (362) by the Ring's potential recrudescence, nagged by the visceral fear (vid. Mendlesohnian intrusion) that Sauron may regain and use it. Saruman's personal response differs, however. He studies Ring-lore, and by doing so becomes enamoured of its possibilities – "Too long he had studied the ways of Sauron in hope to defeat him, and now he envied him as a rival rather than hated his works" (362). Saruman has decided that the best response to the sublime moment is to get a saddle on it; he believes, as his colleagues do not, that the Ring can be controlled. He is "not [...] yielding to a cause greater than himself, but trying to impose himself on the cause" (Flieger 2002 158). Gandalf and Frodo by contrast yield to a greater cause, the destruction of the Ring, and are never the same again; their sublime encounters are open. Gandalf becomes the White rather than the Grey; Frodo can find no peace in Middle-earth and must eventually leave. Saruman seeks to end his sublime moment by bending it to a pre-existing agenda.

Several of Martin's characters behave similarly, and it is interesting to note they are among his least sympathetic creations. Stannis Baratheon, pondering the possibility that Melisandre "*can* do more" (*Clash* 147) than just scare people with her Asshai'i reputation, is a clear example. Single-minded in his ambition to exert the royal authority he firmly believes he has, Stannis nevertheless lacks practicable support from human sources, and thus turns to the inhuman. To Stannis magic is a means to an end, which explains his remarkable lack of respect for Melisandre when they discuss his leech-burning ritual:

> "You swore it would work." The king looked angry.
>
> "It will...and it will not."
> "Which?"
> "Both."
> "Speak sense to me, woman."
> "When the fires speak more plainly, so shall I." (*Storm* 1.501)

He later warns Melisandre she will "die by inches if you lie" (2.292) in the matter of Edric Storm. Largely disinterested in becoming the fiery messiah Melisandre believes he is, he remains impassioned about becoming an earthly king (1.496). He wants answers – the correct answers – from his god, rather than apotheosis, and he wants them now. Here, Donal Noye's assessment of Stannis becomes valuable; "pure iron, black and hard and strong, yes, but brittle, the way iron gets. He'll break before he bends." (*Clash* 90). The mineral metaphor closely echoes the Ent Treebeard's assessment of Saruman: "He has a mind of metal and wheels; and he does not care for growing things, except as far as they serve him for the moment" (*Towers* 76). Rather than seeing the supernatural as an imponderable sign of a larger and deeper universe, these two characters see it as a mechanism. Stannis's leech-burning ritual is an example of this mindset in action, being a seemingly very cynical industrialisation of Melisandre's statement that the blood of kings holds magical power. If this is the case, Stannis appears to have decided, then Edric Storm can become a sort of thaumaturgical milk cow. It is therefore unsurprising that Melisandre, a genuinely devout follower of R'hllor, regards this initiative dubiously. Capable of genuine prognostication, she is open to what R'hllor teaches her, aware of the dangers of "seeing what [she wishes] to see instead of what the Lord of Light had sent" (*Dance* 474) and content with the idea that her god works in mysterious ways. Stannis has no such reverence. He places himself above the magic, and indeed above his professed god, viewing R'hllor more as an absentee member of his council, there to give advice and render leal service though a red-cloaked medium, than as a deity. Unable to domesticate humanity, Stannis seeks to domesticate god.

Cersei Lannister does something very similar. Qyburn is to her what Stannis wants Melisandre to be to him: a problem-solving mechanism. He initially earns her favour by presenting a far-fetched explanation for the presence of Shae in her father's bed on the night of his death. The Queen Regent "seized on the suggestion eagerly" (*Feast* 58) – as well she might – since it allows her to maintain the consoling conceit that "*my lord father* [observe the use of an aristocratic title in her interior monologue] *had no use for whores*" (57). Qyburn thereafter neatly disposes of the stricken Gregor Clegane (125–126), solving the issue of his screaming, which has been keeping Cersei awake at night (125). He later proposes a solution to Cersei's fear that the Night's Watch have lost their traditional impartiality by electing Jon Snow (279–280), and rids her, swiftly and without apparent complication, of the traitorous Senelle (397) and the inconvenient Falyse Stokeworth (547). Note how each of Qyburn's solutions allows Cersei to abide undisturbed in her self-image.

This is most clearly demonstrated by Ser Robert Strong, the end result of Qyburn's experiments. Though not tested in battle before the end of *A Dance with Dragons*, he gives every indication of being a vector of loyal, fearsome coercive force (*Dance* 1,106). Cersei can thus seemingly use the Westerosi custom of trial by combat to establish a legal fiction of innocence. She and Qyburn have, in effect, conspired in a resolution to a Todorovian median disequilibrium. For her rule to be as capricious and incompetent as it is, the Westerosi must recognise it as such and, given the established lack of respect they have for their institutions, depose her. Cersei attempts to use the supernatural to prevent that from happening. Compare this with Margaery Tyrell's charm offensives among the smallfolk or Daenerys Targaryen's honest attempts at a Meereenese reconstruction. Those women understand their public role requires something of them. Cersei does not grasp this, and as a result her murderous regime wobbles increasingly during *A Feast for Crows*, with her toppling arguably the climax of that volume. By *A Dance with Dragons*, Qyburn has arrived at a way to restore her to power. With her mighty, mute champion Cersei can, she hopes, continue as queen without actually developing any of the skills or support networks required by that office. If her plan works, she will use her restored office to continue her vendetta against Tyrion and the Tyrells. Qyburn and Cersei seek to employ the supernatural to further an existing personal policy – in Sandnerian terms, a domesticating response.

Victarion Greyjoy also illustrates this response. He is as devout a follower of the Drowned God as will be found within the Ironborn laity. He accepts Aeron's briny benediction with none of the scepticism their nephew displayed (*Feast* 289; cf. *Clash* 159), commends the men he kills to the Drowned God (*Feast* 483), and interprets nightmares as omens from his deity (*Dance* 867). His attitude towards other potential supernatural causalities is initially highly dismissive. He has his doubts about the dragon queen that Euron dispatches him to fetch from Essos – "like as not, the girl would prove to be some pock-faced slattern with teats slapping against her knees, her 'dragons' no more than tattooed lizards from the swamps of Sothoryos" (865–866). Nevertheless when the maesters of the green lands – figures he regards as wizardly (875) – prove incapable of treating his festering hand, he turns to the red priest Moqorro for healing. Moqorro's evident success mollifies Victarion's puritanism – "*The Crow's Eye keeps wizards, why shouldn't I?*" (964) – and the Iron Suitor gradually comes to place R'hllor alongside his own unforgiving dualistic god in this theurgy. His human sacrifices are now to "honor both the gods" (970). The apparent success of that theurgy leads him to show Moqorro Dragonbinder, the horn Euron entrusted him with, about which the Valyrophone priest reveals much. For all his scepticism about the dragon queen, Victarion is already planning to seize Daenerys as a salt wife, the better to spite his brother. Now, it is revealed that he possesses an artefact reputed to control dragons. Euron did not become the most feared pirate in the world without a measure of cunning; he must anticipate Victarion's treachery. What is important to note is that Victarion, won over to the idea of magic, immediately begins speculating on how he can use it to cashier his brother.

Stannis and Cersei have exactly the same desire. Stannis, reciting his *causus belli*, curtly dismisses the Lannister incest as a distraction amid the two and a half pages (*Clash* 13–15) he spends whinging about the favours Robert heaped upon Renly – "an old grievance, deeply felt, and never more so than now." Cersei suspends rule of law to encourage the search for Tyrion. These three characters are all bloody-mindedly assiduous – if not wholly competent – players of the game of thrones, shameless and unselfconscious propagators of the turmoil engulfing

Westeros. As white shadows stir beyond the Wall, they turn not just upon their fellow human beings but upon their own families. Stannis, admittedly, leads his army to the Wall in response to Jeor Mormont's plea for aid, but then promptly marches it south again, hoping to retake Winterfell. He spends more time pondering the wildlings and the Boltons than the Others, clearly hoping to gain Northern support by engineering a Stark restoration. He wants Jon Snow in Winterfell supporting the Baratheon claim to the throne, not on the Wall masterminding a defence against the living dead of which Mance Rayder speaks. Stannis is, briefly, in the right place, but he no more has his eye on the ball than Cersei or Victarion. Notably, all three are also damned via the game of beds; the cold fish Stannis is enthused by homicidal sex magic, Cersei lusts after her own reflection in Jaime, Lancel and possibly Joffrey; Victarion reinstitutes the Ironborn tradition of salt wives. Qyburn is similarly impugned via his insistence on women for his experiments (*Feast* 397), which bespeaks an unnatural interest in the female anatomy. To take matters further, Martin also strips all three, via their own focalisation, of the high mimesis propagated by Hume's fantasy of subtraction. Both Stannis and Cersei undercut their own fervently espoused royal dignity with lavatorial wisecracks (*Clash* 145–146; *Feast* 285), while Victarion is bombarded with monkey faeces on the Isle of Cedars (*Dance* 873), an indignity that few other fictional pirates endure from the monkeys and parrots on their shoulders. These themes demonstrate that Sandnerian domestication is, in Martin's narrative, a goal of unsympathetic *alazons*, those to be decried for causing the problem these novels examine.

This is an interesting parallel with Tolkien's depiction of domestication. Saruman is operating in direct contravention of a point the reader has already heard from Gandalf; the Ring cannot be controlled. As discussed in Chapter 1, Tolkien's work gains much of the moral sophistication and resonance it possesses from its depiction of people making unpredictable choices in light of the existence of something established (via the inviolable faith the reader must have in Gandalf as a portal-quest guide) to be morally corrosive. Saruman's deviation from this program is an example of that sophistication in action; his moral choices are entirely rational but also wholly destructive. The same could also be said of the actions of those in Martin's tale who respond to their sublime moments via Sandnerian domestication. Martin's world is not laid down on visible portal-quest bedrock, though the Night's Watch subplot is motivated by its focaliser's faith that the bedrock is there somewhere. That the Others are out there is established in the prologue of the first volume, and all the violence and turpitude of the succeeding game of thrones takes place in the context that the real enemy is coming from beyond the Wall. This is the Tolkienian Recovery that makes the game so vivid and resonant. As with Saruman's attempt to domesticate a threat rather than align himself dispossessively with the attempt to expunge it, the characters to whom Martin ascribes a domesticating response are those whose objectives and arguments run contra to the moral expectations of the fantasy universe. Just as Martin mirrors Stoker in his depiction of Sandnerian possession as an attempt to launch Clute's formalistic healing process, he mirrors Tolkien's depiction of domestication as the presumptuous act of a dangerous fool. Domestication is not necessarily villainous – Alaeddin loses little reader sympathy when he opines to his mother, in Richard Burton's translation, that his lamp "is now our means of livelihood and this it is shall enrich us" (758). But both these authors are deeply sceptical about the mechanisation of the supernatural, using it to provide Tolkienian Recovery of the lowest ebb of humanity.

Not all of Martin's characters exhibit the sorts of responses Sandner categorises as closed. There are also those for whom the advent of the supernatural leaves their view of the world irreversibly altered. These are Sandner's "open" responses, those of characters who willingly or otherwise accept the supernatural as an ongoing, uncontrollable presence in their world. As with the closed responses, one open response is negative and the other positive. Sandner terms the negative open response fragmentation. A character exhibiting fragmentation concedes the ongoing presence of the supernatural as a feature of the universe, but regards this as a negative development since it renders their previous perception of the world irrelevant. Pining for the certainties Weiskel's first stage, they are denied the remedial dialogue that might lead to the third, and are thus mired in the second, at the mercy of dictatorial supernatural forces. Fragmentation often follows a failed attempt at possession or domestication. Having failed to bring an unwanted quantity under one's control, "one does not possess the sublime but is possessed by it" (Sandner 168). The reader too is ontologically marooned in the second phase, to "await futilely the restorative reaction" – Clute's healing – "that never comes, except ironically," (Weiskel 26) left with the uncomfortable feeling of having witnessed something outside human control. Fragmentation represents the Tolkienian dyscatastrophe, the "black throat" down which the televisual Cersei's world disappears.

H.P. Lovecraft's tales repeatedly demonstrate fragmentation. Climactic psychological breakdowns are common in his work, much beloved of his numerous parodists. Perhaps the best example is found in "The Shadow Over Innsmouth," a tale in which a nameless focaliser (named in Lovecraft's published notes [251] as Robert Olmstead), touring New England for genealogical data, undertakes a side trip to the ill-reputed coastal town of Innsmouth. There he hears a rambling story from the nonagenarian village idiot Zadok Allen about how the decline of the town began when civic leader Obed Marsh prostituted the townspeople to a race of immortal fish-demons living in the harbour. The result, raves

Zadok, was a generation of insane half-breeds who will eventually transform into monsters themselves. The protagonist dismisses the tale as "mad and pitiful" (625), but he is accosted by locals in the town's hotel that night and flees, pursued by "a legion of croaking, baying entities of unknown source" (645). He initiates a police crackdown on Innsmouth that all but destroys the place, but later discovers a family connection to the village; he is descended from a daughter of Marsh; "Who – or *what* – then, was my great-great-grandmother?" (651). Olmstead develops the outward signs of the trans-species miscegenation and goes insane, his account of his hatred for Innsmouth dissolving into raving praises of the monsters. In Sandnerian terms, "The Shadow Over Innsmouth" tells of a sublime moment (the encounter with the monsters) leading to an attempt at possession (the police raids) which fails as the pre-existing, highly personal dimensions of the supernatural intrusion lead to a complete fragmentation of Olmstead's pre-existing view of the world and his place in it.

Among Martin's characters, Ser Davos Seaworth merits comparison with Lovecraft's focaliser. Davos steps forward as a focaliser as he grapples with the knowledge that his superiors are meddling with dangerous things. He is uncomfortable at the burning of the statues of the Seven on Dragonstone and knows Maester Cressen "*drank a cup of death to free Stannis from Melisandre, but somehow her god shielded her*" (*Clash* 133). The creation of Lightbringer, Stannis's purportedly magical sword, perturbs him, particularly once Salladhor Saan tells the story he has just seen supposedly re-enacted:

> *A true sword of fire, now, that would be a wonder to behold. Yet at such a cost...*When he thought of Nissa Nissa, it was his own Marya he pictured, a good-natured plump woman with sagging breasts and a kindly smile, the best woman in the world. He tried to picture himself driving a sword through her, and shuddered. *I am not made of the stuff of heroes*, he decided. If that was the price of a magic sword, it was more than he cared to pay. (142)

As well as establishing Davos's considerable stock in the game of beds, his loyalty to Marya indicates his reticence towards the sublime. Saan's tale of Azor Ahai tempering a blade in the blood of his wife is one of Sandnerian dispossessions, the putting aside of old loyalties and identities in pursuit of a relationship with magic. Azor's desire to be a hero in a magical world overpowers his desire to be a loyal husband. Davos mulls this over and decides that the price for sublime transcendence, for reaching Weiskel's third stage, is too high. He resolves to maintain a closed, possessive Sandnerian response to the supernatural.

He obeys the king's order to ferry Melisandre under Storm's End, however. She there gives birth to the shadow that kills Cortnay Penrose.

As this being towers over him, Davos's recourse is to religion – "*Gods preserve us*" (563). Like the ranger Will praying as Weymar Royce rises to kill him (*Game* 10), the Onion Knight admits this situation is beyond him. He struggled to make sense of Melisandre's ability to drink the concoction that killed Cressen, but logic completely fails him here. This is his sublime moment, and he does not like it.

Davos's displeasure stems from his state of "excessive intimacy" (Sandner 167) with the supernatural. This intimacy is happening on two levels. The more superficial is simply that Davos, like Lovecraft's focaliser, has more to do with magic than he wants. He is, in fact, performing it. "The flames do not lie, Davos," Stannis says; "*Yet they require me to make them true*," laments Davos inwardly (*Clash* 559). This process bears comparison to the accusatory logic of the Todorovian fantastic described in Chapter 5. Davos does not know precisely what Melisandre is planning, but he knows it will not be constrained by human ingenuity; a woman who can swallow poison and stay vertical could be capable of literally anything. His statement of possession after hearing the tale of Azor Ahai, furthermore, draws a very sharp, explicit line in the sand regarding what sees as acceptable behaviour. Now his reverence for Stannis forces him to cross that line and use his seamanship to contribute to the casting of a magic spell that is going to kill someone. This would be why he is so depressed and self-critical on the trip across Shipbreaker Bay; the sea, which he usually loves, "brought him no comfort" and he "never felt evil until tonight" (560). He is tarring himself, in his own estimation, with an association with inhuman power. The reader pities Davos because he is not the man he hoped to be.

This intimacy with the supernatural goes beyond Davos's disgust at what he is doing. As in the case of Lovecraft's focaliser, it cuts to the heart of what he *is* at all. Davos Seaworth is Stannis Baratheon's creature, in the nearly literal sense of having been created by his king. He is wholly cognisant of this:

> *Everything I am, I owe him.* Stannis had raised him to knighthood. He had given him a place of honor at his table, a war galley to sail in place of a smuggler's skiff. Dale and Allard captained galleys as well, Maric was oarmaster on the *Fury*, Matthos served his father on the *Black Bertha*, and the king had taken Devan as a royal squire. One day he would be knighted, and the two little lads as well. Marya was the mistress of a small keep on Cape Wrath, with servants who called her 'M'Lady' and Davos could hunt red deer in his own woods. All this he had of Stannis Baratheon, for the price of a few finger joints. *It was just, what he did to me. I had flouted the king's laws all my life. He has earned my loyalty.* (134–135)

There are three points of interest here. The first is Davos's repudiation of his smuggling. Stannis's mechanical corporal punishment was, he feels, just. Davos never claims to have been a "fucking legend" in the underworld, as the televisual Watchman Karl Tanner does ("Oathkeeper"). Nor does not feel any renewed confidence returning to his field of expertise as Ser Barristan Selmy does (*Dance* 1,030–1,031). Slipping through the blockade around Storm's End, he is "taught as a bowstring" (*Clash* 560), expressing no rueful fondness for this game of cat and mouse. When he dreams of abandoning aristocratic privilege, he wishes not to return to what he knows – as Robert Baratheon does (*Game* 300) – but to his wife (*Storm* 2.157; 2.290). This is in keeping with the second point, the emphasis on family. Davos is a husband and a father, not a master criminal. His crimes were those of necessity, committed to save his little lads from "begging for a copper" (*Clash* 147). Spotting an alternative during Robert's Rebellion, he loaded his skiff with onions, exercised his job skills, curried favour with a lord, and happily gave up smuggling, and some phalanges, for a life in Stannis's service. This leads to the third point. Davos is loyal to his king in a way few Westerosi are. Unlike most of Martin's other focalises, he never discusses either of his biological parents, here or anywhere else in the tale to date, cutting off Salladhor Saan when he raises the matter (*Storm* 1.141). Stannis, the bestower of lineage upon his sons, is the only earthly progenitor he thinks about.

What causes Davos's fragmentation is the discovery that magic has permeated the lineage in which he is so invested. "He knew that shadow" he observes of the entity to which Melisandre gives birth, "as he knew the man who'd cast it" (*Clash* 563). Melisandre later (*Storm* 1.347) confirms Davos's suspicion that she bore the shadow of the king in his little skiff. The shadow is a product of a generative process more akin to the biological one than that which created House Seaworth, something the king is taking an active role in, a bastard son. For Davos, this is a critical problem. He is invested in his family and in his loyalty to its progenitor; he also has a personal policy in place to shield himself *and his family* from the chaos of the imponderable world. That policy fails; the inhuman element now squirms maddeningly in his identity. This is the Onion Knight's fragmentation, his "return of the other which one uncomfortably discovers to be the self" (Sandner 167).

The parallels with the focaliser of "The Shadow Over Innsmouth" are close. Lovecraft's protagonist is drawn to Massachusetts on a genealogical expedition, searching for his roots (588). Discovering a magical atrocity, he calls in the police, apparently successfully (587). Returning to his research, however, he discovers that this act of possession was doomed from the start; he is one-sixteenth "blasphemous fish-frog" (646) himself. In both cases, the Todorovian uncanny (a weird seaport; a father-figure's odd counsellor) has blossomed into the fantastic-marvellous (Innsmouth sleeps with the fishes; Melisandre shrugs off poison) prompting an attempt at possession (the police raids; Davos's resolution concerning magic), which fails when suspicions about personal matters (Lovecraft's genealogist chases up information about a disreputable branch of his family [648–649]; Davos suspects he may have an evil stepmother [*Clash* 547]) are explosively confirmed. Both men find themselves polluted at source, the orthodoxies they sought to normalise via Sandnerian possession invalidated by sexual crimes that are not their own. As in Lovecraft's tale, the shadow falls over the focaliser; Davos is half-brother to a monster.

This, however, launches Davos's actual story. In a tale about flexible and conflicting loyalties, he presents rather inert prospect. Compare his preparedness, against his better judgement, to deliver Melisandre into Storm's End with Eddard Stark's refusal to enable a mere human assassin (*Game* 343). "Stannis is our rightful king," Davos warns Allard, "It is not for us to question him" (*Clash* 137). Statements of loyalty to Stannis, against threats of confinement (*Storm* 1.354), mutilation (1.496) and death (2.293) pepper his focalisation. If things were as simple as that Davos would never contradict his king, and his sole function would be as a pair of focalising eyes in his preferred camp. For Davos to do more, he must overcome the median disequilibrium created by his regard for Stannis. The solution is a battle for the soul of the king – not a tale of compromised loyalty but a struggle for what the object of Davos's fidelity is and may become. This quickly vindicates Clute's model of the operation of fantasy narrative. From Davos's first focalised chapter, Melisandre's influence on Stannis creates Clute's formalistic wrongness, as the death of Cressen "somehow *does not add up*" (Clute 1,038). A tale of wrongness can only move forward by reaching a moment of recognition, when focalisers establish what is wrong (804). This is what Davos experiences, explosively and graphically, under Storm's End. Thereafter, cursing himself for not acting sooner (*Storm* 1.73), Davos makes his attempt on Melisandre's life, rescues Edric Storm from sacrifice, and directs his king north. His sublime moment launches his narrative, allowing him to do more than simply report Stannis's activity to the reader.

Davos's acts are, admittedly, attempts at possession, and the deliverance of Edric appears to have been successful. The same, however, could be said of Lovecraft's hapless genealogist, if one ignores the fifth chapter of the novella. His excessive intimacy with the supernatural only becomes apparent after a year of "wholesome" (684) activity. Davos's problem arrives much earlier in his story, and at the conclusion of *A Dance with Dragons*, it remains unclear if he will ever be able to fully close the sublime moment that began under Storm's End. As with Lovecraft's focaliser, his problem begins back up the family tree. For Davos, therefore, any final Sandnerian possession will have to involve his only relevant progenitor repudiating Melisandre and her god and repenting the deaths his thaumaturgy has caused. This would be why Davos, despite claiming Stannis as his god (*Clash* 141), is actually preoccupied by religious orthodoxy, discussing the Seven almost every time he appears (*Clash* 133; 563; *Dance* 288; 446; *Storm* 1.72; 1.141; 1.347; 2.154; 2.289). His story is centrally concerned with bringing the king back into the protection of the pan-determinism to which Davos subscribes. This is going to be a problem. As noted in Chapter 5, Stannis's grinding intransigence has already been preserved (per Todorov) and foregrounded (per Tolkien) by two successive exercises in sex magic. Stannis can, however, be made to listen to reason; at Davos's instigation, he comes to the aid of the Night's Watch. Until Davos can repeat this act of persuasion, the parentally, filially and spiritually pious Onion Knight is compelled to accept his lot as the half-brother of a horror. Unlike Sam and Grenn, Davos's Sandnerian fulcrum revels not how to fix a problem, or even that there is a problem – that revelation came in the banquet hall on Dragonstone – but that the problem is far closer to him than he thought. Whether or not he can successfully counteract Sandner's excessive intimacy is a central point of narrative tension in his tale. If Davos fails, his fate is the indignity of subjection to dictatorial alien forces – Sandnerian fragmentation.

If a relationship with magic is so disastrous, and attempts to harness it amount to a form of authorial invective, who then would play wizard? Perhaps one less attached to their pre-sublime identity. The name of Sandner's last codified response, dispossession, refers to the responder's willingness to let such things go. Like fragmentation, dispossession is open, conceding the continuance of the sublime moment. Rather than subjection to the dictatorial supernatural forces at play in fragmentation, however, the dispossessive focaliser is granted the dignity of a redemptive partnership or dialogue with the supernatural. Where possession positions the supernatural as something to be fought, dispossession perceives it as a vector for personal growth. This expedites their passage to Weiskel's third stage, the reconstruction of the self in relation to the revelations of the sublime moment, a reconstruction that ends with the subject in a fundamentally greater stature than they enjoyed (or in many cases suffered) in Weiskel's first stage. This is not a free ride, however. It requires an admission of an inability to control the supernatural or limit the intimacy of the relationship with it. The former self and any of its attendant certainties, positive or negative, must be abandoned. This partnership with the unknowable, uncontrollable other requires a humility that not all literary characters have. Yet the rewards are great; "What is given from the self, what from the other, remains radically unknowable, but the experience offers a felt experience of sublime discovery and newness" (Sandner 169). Rather than terror, the affect is exhilaration, emotional and spiritual solace, and a discovery of one's true identity in partnership with a deepened and enriched universe.

One character who very straightforwardly displays this response is J.K. Rowling's Harry Potter. Harry's Sandnerian confrontation comes early in his story, when the half-giant Hagrid catches up with him and his frantically fugitive foster-parents:

> "You never told him? Never told him what was in the letter Dumbledore left fer him? I was there! I saw Dumbledore leave it, Dursley! An' you've kept it from him all these years?"
>
> "Kept *what* from me?" said Harry eagerly.
> "STOP! I FORBID YOU!" yelled Uncle Vernon in a panic.
> Aunt Petunia gave a gasp of horror.
> "Ah, go boil yer heads, both of yeh," said Hagrid. "Harry – yer a wizard."
> There was silence inside the hut. Only the sea and the whistling wind could be heard.
> "I'm a *what*?" gasped Harry. (*Philosopher's Stone* 42)

The Dursleys attempt a possessive response to the supernatural in order to maintain their control over what they see as normal. Unlike Stoker retrenching the gender binary of Victorian London, Rowling uses the response ironically, to lampoon their narrow-mindedness. This contrasts radically with Harry's response. The question closing the quotation above, in Sandner's terms the fulcrum of Rowling's entire narrative, is neither a denial nor a dismissal, but an engagement with the matter that Hagrid brings to light. As the narrative proceeds, Harry gradually reconstructs a greater identity, not by mastering magic but by wondering at it, appreciating it, and engaging with it. He moves up in the world, both literally (becoming a star player on his school's aerial football team) and figuratively, becoming more closely acquainted with the true nature of his world and presenting himself for the moral challenge of Tolkienian Recovery. This requires him to put aside any of Uncle Vernon's concerns for propriety, indeed to abandon his previous identity and society. Sandnerian dispossession bears comparison to the schoolbook definition of a chemical reaction; one cannot get the reagents back in their pre-existing forms. The wage of Harry's courage in making this irreversible leap into the unknown is his true identity, the one his uncle kept from him (44). He learns who his parents really were and takes his place within their society. By dispossessing the old Harry, he becomes the true Harry.

Bran Stark's decisions in the cave of the Three-Eyed Crow also demonstrate the point. Bran is undergoing a Mendlesohnian portal-quest, a fantasy form that has a distinct affinity for Sandnerian dispossession.

For the story to move, Bran must give over his old identity to embrace his role in the trans-portal world. That response requires considerable courage, which Bran has:

> Bran did not want to be married to a tree...but who else would wed a broken boy like him? *A thousand eyes, a hundred skins, wisdom deep as the roots of ancient trees. A greenseer.*
>
> He ate.
> It had a bitter taste, though not so bitter as acorn paste. The first spoonful was the hardest to get down. He almost retched it right back up. The second tasted better. The third was almost sweet. The rest he spooned up eagerly. Why had he thought that it was bitter? (*Dance* 532)

Bran's repast is the dispossessive response in microcosm. The trans-portal world offers great things but demands a dispossession of the cis-portal world in return. This requires courage, self-abnegation and, in many cases, pain. Bran's initial nausea as he eats is testimony to that, but the consequences of the meal are the reward for his courage. It is telling that Sandner differentiates dispossession from fragmentation by observing that "its 'open' movement is not falling but flying" (169). His dreams of a white cloak shattered, Bran will gain something greater – "you will fly" (*Dance* 207) – by allying himself to the possibilities of the trans-portal world, just as Harry Potter ends up playing Quidditch. Both boys come up in the world, literally and essentially, by letting go of their old identities. "Flying," observes the boy whose father once called him a squirrel (*Game* 76), "was even better than climbing" (*Dance* 524).

Dispossession does not require a portal-quest, however, and it is one of Martin's immersive focalisers who achieves that response in the most macrocosmically significant way. Daenerys Targaryen's sublime moment takes place at Khal Drogo's funeral. She puts aside her experiments with fire and heat and puts her entire existence on the line to test her hypothesis about the dragon eggs. This is clearly her intent as she orders her husband's pyre constructed; when Jorah Mormont fears she means to immolate herself in her grief she responds "I am not such a child as that, sweet ser" (*Game* 773). Her stepping into the inferno is not an act of suttee-like suicide, but it is a complete dismissal of her former self; if the experiment fails, she will obviously not survive. If it succeeds, she will be reborn as something completely different. If her willingness to enter the flames does not signal her confidence clearly enough, her thoughts as Jorah Mormont cries out to her make the matter explicit:

> *No*, she wanted to shout to him, *no, my good knight, do not fear for me. The fire is mine. I am Daenerys Stormborn, daughter of*

> *dragons, bride of dragons, mother of dragons, don't you see? Don't you SEE?* (779)

Mormont does not see, because he has not yet achieved the degree of insight (Clutean recognition) that Daenerys has. He does not understand the importance of the dragon eggs to Daenerys's true identity, seeing them only as handsome treasures. Nor does he realise that she must give up her old identity to embrace her true self. This is what her passage through the fire of Drogo's pyre is intended to accomplish; a one-way trip into a closer engagement with truth.

Daenerys emerges from this baptism of fire not only as the Unburnt but as the Mother of Dragons. Her enthusiastic use of this title, one implying familial seniority, might be taken as a form of Sandnerian domestication, placing herself above the dragons. This reading would be a mistake. "A dragon is no slave" (*Storm* 1.380) she reminds the covetous Kraznys mo Nakloz. She *seeks* to control them in Meereen when it becomes apparent they have been eating human children, but finds this emotionally harrowing as well as practically difficult; "What sort of mother lets her children rot in darkness?" (*Dance* 183) she asks herself, clearly pained to have imprisoned entities she sees as parts of her own identity; "*I am the blood of the dragon. If they are monsters then so am I*" (185). Dispossession is not meant to be easy. Daenerys's equation of her own identity with those of the dragons is a pattern of behaviour. When Irri brings her to orgasm in Astapor, "She screamed then. Or perhaps that was Drogon" (*Storm* 1.325). Her thoughts when Drogon reappears in Daznak's pit echo the point; "*He is fire made flesh*, she thought, *and so am I*." Reflecting on her flight from the pit, she recalls that "On Drogon's back she felt whole" (*Dance* 1,084). She has trouble distinguishing herself from her children, a symptom of dispossession "confounding the categories of self and other" (Sandner 169). This is wholly different from Stannis's marriage of convenience with R'hllor. Daenerys cannot get her old self back, and does not, for all the anxieties her dragons cause her, actually want it back. Here it becomes instructive to compare her relationship with Drogon to that of Catelyn Stark with Arya. Catelyn finds her child "a trial" (*Clash* 710), impossible to manage, a horror, a headache and an affront to propriety, but accepts her as a part of her own identity that she is incomplete without. She dreads Arya's faults, but cannot cope without her; getting her back from the Lannisters is a higher priority than the high-mimetic concern of revenge for her widowhood (429). Daenerys clearly feels the same way about her three children. Parenthood is, after all, a dispossessive state, an abandonment of an old identity for a new one predicated on an association with an outside party one cannot wholly control and plans not to outlive. This is the state that Daenerys's maternal title refers to. Her experience of being borne aloft by Drogon is one of barely contained emotion:

> "*Higher!*" Her other hand clutched at his scales, her fingers scrabbling for purchase. Drogon's wide black wings beat the air. Dany could feel the heat of him between her thighs. Her heart felt as if it were about to burst. *Yes*, she thought, *yes, now, do it, do it, take me, take me, FLY!*" (*Dance* 814)

Like Harry Potter and Bran Stark, Daenerys gives herself wholly to her relationship with the supernatural and ends up airborne as a result. The ascent transcends the literal and becomes emotional and, perhaps, spiritual; "*If I fall and die, it will still have been worth it*" (1,087). These are not the thoughts of someone controlling the supernatural, as lesser folk attempt to do. She does not control Drogon on her return to the Dothraki Sea – "Neither whip nor words could turn Drogon if he did not wish to be turned" (*Dance* 1,084). Rather she keeps an eye out for him as he roams, the proud mother of an independent son rather than the owner of a fine horse. Her association with him is a partnership, a two-way flow of power and affect, rather than a domesticated dictatorship.

In that position, she has become in cold fact what her worthless brother so often claimed to be. She is now a true Targaryen, living the life that her ancestors denied themselves with their misguided attempt to domesticate the supernatural. The next time anybody sees Daenerys after her flight she is "beyond the social" (Gresham 151), a bald, animalistic figure in a faeces-stained tunic, but she has never been as powerful before. Khal Jhaqo finds her, not as the eccentric, pregnant widow as which he abandoned her (*Game* 733), but as a dragonrider, someone not simply possessed of a fearsome vector of coercive force, but in partnership with the sublime. She is mortal, but possessed of a power and an ability that exceeds that of her fellows in essence rather than degree. That is to say that she has entered Frye's romantic mode, achieving the sort of apotheosis the other participants in the game of thrones can only dream of. With the addition of this fundamental upward shift in her relationship with the world, low-mimetic intrusions upon her dignity are substantially repelled. A relationship with a dragon trumps an unwiped backside, not because Drogon will eat anyone who dares wrinkle their nose at his mother but because any dealings with her will involve the other party entering a sublime moment of their own. The absence that made Viserys's grandeur a delusion, Daenerys has turned into a presence. In accordance with her dispossessive response, that presence is part of her identity. Like Harry Potter and Bran Stark, Daenerys's willingness to be borne aloft has made her what she truly is.

Daenerys's dispossessive response is particularly interesting because it is contagious. This can be demonstrated by the behaviour of Jorah Mormont in the last chapter of Martin's first volume. Before Daenerys enters the pyre, he councils flight (773) and suggests she sell her dragon eggs to live like (not *as*) a queen (776). He changes his tune when the pyre gutters out, and he is not the only one to do so:

> Ser Jorah Mormont found her amidst the ashes, surrounded by blackened logs and bits of glowing ember and the burnt bones of man and woman and stallion. She was naked, covered with soot, her clothes turned to ash, her beautiful hair all crisped away...yet she was unhurt.
>
> The cream-and-gold dragon was suckling at her left breast, the green-and-bronze at the right. Her arms cradled them close. The black-and-scarlet beast was draped across her shoulders, its long sinuous neck coiled under her chin. When it saw Jorah, it raised its head and looked at him with eyes as red as coals.
>
> Wordless, the knight fell to his knees. The men of her *khas* came up behind him. Jhogo was the first to lay his *arakh* at her feet. "Blood of my blood," he murmured, pushing his face into the smoking earth. "Blood of my blood," she heard Aggo echo. "Blood of my blood," Rakharo shouted.
>
> And then came her handmaids, and then the others, all the Dothraki, men and women and children, and Dany had only to look at their eyes to know that they were hers now, today and tomorrow and forever, hers as they had never been Drogo's. (780)

This is a crucial point in Martin's story. The knees of his characters typically bend only after sharply utilitarian cost-benefit analyses. Roose Bolton, for example, kneels to the Lannisters because they offer him a better chance of victory than the Starks (*Clash* 804–805). Jorah Mormont knelt to Viserys Targaryen as part of his plan to return home. He wordlessly falls to his knees at the sight of the Unburnt and her children, transformative revelations that render such concerns irrelevant. Jorah's sublime moment among the ashes of the pyre prompts an unapologetically dispossessive response. His world is irreparably changed, his previous worldview gone, replaced by something greater, a powerful, palpable enrichment of the universe in relation to which he can reconstruct himself in greater stature than would ever have been possible otherwise. "Have you ever heard baby dragons singing?" the televisual Mormont asks Tyrion Lannister. "Hard to be a cynic after that" ("Unbent, Unbowed, Unbroken").

Here, Mormont directly addresses a point that various other characters make implicitly. The Dothraki follow strength and have an aggressively maintained sense of their individual dignity (*Game* 774). Jhogo pushes his face into the dirt because he has seen something wondrous, something that breaks his understanding of the world and trumps his human identity as a swaggering, misogynistic warrior. The same goes for Groleo, the Pentoshi sea-captain, and his crew, who travel from Qarth to Slaver's Bay with a cargo of greensick Dothraki – and three children whose mother will not allow them to be confined:

> Even Captain Groleo was glad of that, now. There had been one small fire, easily extinguished; against that, *Balerion* suddenly seemed to have fewer rats than she'd had before, when she sailed under the name *Saduleon*. And her crew, once as fearful as they were curious, had begun to take a queer fierce pride in "their" dragons. Every man of them, from captain to cook's boy, loved to watch the three fly. (*Storm* 1.107)

The crew see a particular value in the dragons, willing to compromise their safety (and rename their ship) for the honour of association with these creatures. They are not alone. In Astapor Barristan Selmy baulks at Daenerys's offer to trade a dragon for slaves (*Storm* 1.370), his profound faith in their unique value perhaps blinding this normally observant man to the fact his queen is bluffing. Like Groleo and Rakharo, Barristan the Bold rejects any rational reckoning of these creatures. Dragons are profoundly moving; even confirmation that they exist produces an emotional affect, and not a negative one. When Xhondo of the *Cinnamon Wind* says to Sam Tarly he "knows these dragons" (*Feast* 438), he smiles. Those who lack that confirmation tend to reach for it with whatever epistemological wherewithal they can muster. In Oldtown, the apprentice maester Mollander responds to scepticism about draconic tales from the East by insisting "All speak of *dragons*, and a beautiful young queen" (5). His colleague Roone is slightly more explicit in his desires. "I should like to see a dragon," he opines. "I should like that very much" (1).

Roone specifically articulates one of the key points about Martin's fantasy, the general sense among its inhabitants that their world *should* contain dragons, and the fact that it *does not* is somehow objectionable. Westeros, in sin and error pining, desperately wants these creatures back. By having the courage to enact the dispossessive ritual required to hatch dormant dragon eggs, Daenerys gives them back. She and her children instantiate one of the great trends in the modern fantasy tradition, the same one that Sam Tarly's possession made possible – the change from Clutean thinning to healing. The notion that Daenerys's dragons enact healing goes beyond the emotional affect displayed by Jorah and Groleo and yearned for by Mollander and Roone. Magical phenomena have proliferated since Khal Drogo's funeral. Tyrion Lannister has little time for Wisdom Hallyne's assertion that the spells necessary for the production of wildfire "seem to be working better than they were" (*Clash* 647). Readers properly informed about goings-on in Essos would be inattentive indeed not to attach great significance to Hallyne's institutional memory that "magic had begun to go out of the world the day the last dragon died" (648). If the clergy of R'hllor always had the power to resurrect the dead, they would presumably have made more of it in their missionary work, yet Thoros of Myr has resurrected Beric Dondarrion six times (*Storm* 1.536–1.537). His faith's customary funerary liturgy has clearly acquired some profound restorative effect. In Oldtown, Archmaester Marwyn's experiments with thaumaturgy have finally borne fruit. His obsidian candle is burning (*Feast* 773–774), an impossibility that has entered into the Citadel's institutional folklore as emblematic of the limits of human ingenuity (10–11). That ingenuity now has new limits. The reader has a solid indication of why. Speaking of another firemage in Qarth, the mysterious masked Quaithe tells Daenerys "his powers grow, *Khaleesi*. And you are the cause of it. [...] You are the Mother of Dragons, are you not?" (*Clash* 526–527). Daenerys's dragons have returned magic to Martin's world, enacting Clute's principle of healing.

This does not contradict the sense of thinning and loss that the earlier chapters of this book identified in Martin's tale. Rather, it positions that thinning as a necessary preliminary state for healing. As noted above with regard to Sam Tarly, the transition from a situation of wrongness or thinning to healing is almost the defining structural feature of modern fantasy (Clute 338–339). With Martin's narrative incomplete, tracing its precise passage through this transition would be speculative. The general shape, however, is evident as early as the concluding sentence of *A Game of Thrones*, when "for the first time in hundreds of years, the night came alive with the music of dragons." Daenerys and her children address a fundamental, palpable loss in the thinned world Martin builds during his first volume. In this they also address Martin's passage through the Tolkienian schema. Clute (458) directly equates his formalistic healing with the Tolkienian eucatastrophe or Consolation, the sudden joyous turn Tolkien regards as crucial to the success of a tale of fantasy. As noted above, the eucatastrophe is only joyous if it is sudden and, indeed, a turn ("On Fairy-Stories" 153). This possibility is what the filth, violence, institutional decay and moral apathy of the game of thrones creates. Johnston sees these factors as being crucial to the cultural and emotional impact of Martin's narrative. She argues that fantasy readers "have grown accustomed to grace, to the joyous turn no longer sudden but entirely expected" (141) and views the ostentatious unpleasantness of Martin's tale as his effort to whet reader appetites for Consolation. He is, Johnston suggests, building emotional tension, creating an impression that too much has been lost, that the thinning of his written world is too advanced, to admit anything other than a *dyscatastrophe*. With this, she suggests, he will restore a sense of occasion and importance to his eventual eucatastrophe. Speculation as to exactly how this will be accomplished seems fruitless, but Johnston's point is a solid one. Support for it is evident in the reputation Martin has for unflinching cynicism and innovative moral ambiguity. Critics like Grossman and Antonsson, applauding Martin for breaking the exact rules he is following to such good effect, have evidently become sufficiently blasé about the conventions of fantasy – or what they hold those conventions to be – that they fail to recognise particularly uncompromising examples of those conventions in action. For all its violence, turpitude, cynicism and filth, *A Song of Ice and Fire* absolutely contains an inkling of Tolkienian Consolation. Westeros hurts *so that* it can heal.

Not all characters who encounter the dragons take the sort of dispossessive approach characteristic of Daenerys and her followers. Those who do not are granted very short shrift, however. Xaro Xhoan Daxos is a merchant; he understands merchandise. His eyes do not glitter when he looks upon the dragons, therefore, but rather when the possibility emerges of gaining one by trade (*Clash* 789). This is Daenerys's conclusive indication that he is no ally. He seeks, as Jorah Mormont warned, to domesticate a dragon as a means of ruling Qarth. Kraznys mo Nakloz presumably has similar objectives in Slaver's Bay, and literally cries his eyes out as a result (*Storm* 1.380). Quentyn Martell's attempt to subdue Viserion and Rhaegal end equally badly (*Dance* 1,046). These men are incapable of allying themselves effectively with the program of healing Daenerys has begun. They are examples of the "Knight of Doleful Countenance," a stock character identified by Clute as originating with Cervantes and present in many narratives that, like Martin's, are based around an attempt to heal a wasteland. The knight, says Clute, essentially does not get it. He "has not only failed to pass through any knot of recognition into eucatastrophe, but [...] has set his face against attempting to do so" (544). Instead of getting with the healing program, such characters "retain an inveterate interest in the minutiae of science and in contriving aesthetic solutions to getting through the day." Tywin Lannister, snapping "dragons and krakens do not interest me," while ensuring the knees of deserters are broken (*Storm* 1.263) is an example. So too is Hizdahr zo Loraq, nagging Barristan Selmy to address him in a manner becoming a (decrepit, fatuous, thinned) Ghiscari monarch (*Dance* 1,028). This man saw true magnificence and radiance in Daznak's Pit. His response, in Sandnerian terms, is to possess it, and his order to that effect – "Kill it! *Kill the beast!*" (812) – squanders whatever jot of reader sympathy he may have enjoyed. At best, these knights are figures of pathos; Quentyn Martell is out of his depth from the moment he stepped into the narrative and suffers a horrible death through his attempt at Sandnerian domestication. At worst they are villains; Tolkien's Saruman is another example and, significantly, another domesticator.

The theme here is that characters in tales of healing must "engage deeply with the transformative potentials of fantasy" (Clute 338). This is to say that the characters in a tale of healing have to appreciate that things will not be the same after the Sandnerian sublime moment. Sam Tarly and Jon Snow know things have changed after the rout on the Fist. They have a serious, game-breaking problem in relation to which the Watch cannot continue to exist in the thinned, venal state in which it currently abides; there must be a fundamental change in the way they operate. Mance Rayder and Tormund Giantsbane are on their side. Wick Whittlestick and Bowen Marsh, Jon's assassins, cannot lift their eyes above the enmity with the wildlings, and are thus Knights of Doleful Countenance themselves. Note how Jon goes down protecting a manifestation of the magical world – Wun Weg Wun Dar Wun – against such figures, exactly the same paradigm that leads to Daenerys's fateful flight on Drogon. The heroes of a tale of healing cannot domesticate the supernatural, making it work for them; they must accept that the current path they are treading is no longer a valid course of action. Instead, they must work towards it or up to it. They must give up attempts to fully control or understand their world and simply engage with it. Compare Xaro Xhoan Daxos's cynical, finite reckoning that a dragon is worth thirty ships (*Clash* 789) to Roone's innocent yearning to simply see one. Or observe Tyrion Lannister's childhood pastimes:

> When he was still a lonely child in the depths of Casterly Rock, he oft rode dragons through the nights, pretending he was some lost Targaryen princeling, or a Valyrian dragonlord soaring high o'er fields and mountains. Once, when his uncles asked him what gift he wanted for his name day, he begged them for a dragon. "It wouldn't need to be a big one. It could be little, like I am." His uncle Gerion thought that was the funniest thing he had ever heard, but his uncle Tygett said "The last dragon died a century ago, lad." That had seemed so monstrously unfair that the boy had cried himself to sleep that night. (*Dance* 86)

Note the poetic "o'er," indicating Tyrion's adolescent instinct to romanticise these creatures. The child is father to the man. Exploring the cellars of the Red Keep for dragon skulls, the adult Tyrion "expected to find them impressive, perhaps even frightening. He had not thought to find them beautiful. Yet they were" (*Game* 116). They leave this garrulous cynic "wordless and awed" (117). The Imp is not an *alazon*; he fares well in the game of beds; now he appears to be on the right side of cosmic history. Compare Tyrion's dumbstruck reverence to the attitude of the blustering ass who stuck Balerion's skull in the cellar.

Or compare it with that of the people who caused the extinction of the dragons Tyrion lamented as a boy. "Who do you think killed all the dragons the last time around?" spits Archmaester Marwyn. "Gallant dragonslayers armed with swords? The world the Citadel is building has no place in it for sorcery or prophecy or glass candles, much less for dragons" (*Feast* 774–775). The notion that the maesters somehow reasoned the dragons out of existence seems implausible until one recalls that they were advising the Targaryens. Maesters, experts in the intellectual analysis of natural history, engineering, risk management and dynastics, almost certainly had a hand in the Dragonpit, the mechanism by which Daenerys's ancestors sought to domesticate the great beasts. Marwyn's statement could be taken as an accusation of a deliberate, longitudinal conspiracy of Sandnerian possession against the magical weapons of invading foreigners. He may have the truth of it. The mob that storm the Dragonpit in Martin's prequel volume *Fire and Blood* (518–523) certainly demonstrate possession. The Targaryens themselves attempted their own sort of Sandnerian closure at around the same time. The Dragonpit was a method of controlling dragons, and the results of that approach quickly become apparent. "It was noted," says Barristan the Bold, emblematic of past glories and moral authority, "that none of the pit dragons ever reached the size of their ancestors. The maesters say it was because of the walls around them, and the great dome over their heads." (*Storm* 1.109) Even the mighty Balerion, the Black Dread, is an indefatigable symbol of grandness and authority until the Dragonpit is completed, at which point he promptly becomes weak and weary, his passing mourned as an explicit example of Clutean thinning (*Fire and Blood* 334–335). The various neurotic stocktakes of draconic resources by the Targaryens during the section of *Fire and Blood* titled "The Dying of Dragons" (439–440; 450; 453; 463; 490; 557) cannot have helped. A dragon is not a slave.

The pattern extends to the handful of "dragonseeds," non-Targaryen dragonriders who arise during the Dance of the Dragons. Hard Hugh Hammer views Vermithor solely as a coercive instrument. Rather than achieving the dispossessive transcendence of Daenerys, this domesticator dies an unglamorous death, at ground level, before the chapter is out (526–527; 530–531). His dragon dies, its wings shredded, in the confusion of the dance (534). By contrast the odd peasant girl Nettles leaves the war altogether, mounting Sheepstealer and vanishing "in the morning mists, never to be seen again at court or castle" (499). Her wage for this poetic rejection of earthly power is a discrete lifetime of romantic modality, living with Sheepstealer in a cave in the Vale of Arryn, ascending to almost mythic status as the "fire witch" "worshipped" by the Burned Men (678). Martin repeatedly implies that these creatures – "flesh-and-blood beings that are nonetheless magical in their essence" (Kaveney 295) – are not mere weapons. They are dramatic effect – the "dynamic forces" (Sandner 164) of the supernatural – made flesh. Bought under control – closed, in Sandnerian terms – dragons simply do not work.

This point is evident in Daenerys's day. Observe how Admiral Groleo, so enraptured by the sight of the flying dragons that he renamed his ship

Balerion in their honour, grumpily remembers it by its former Pentoshi name when Daenerys cages Viserion and Rhaegal (*Dance* 461). Tyrion's boyhood dreams of flying o'er fields and mountains demonstrate the correct method of considering dragons. These creatures are not facts to be analysed; they are truths to be valued at an emotional level, for the majesty and mystique they impart to the world around them. To do otherwise is to disengage with the true nature of the written world, to become a Knight of Doleful Countenance. A character's attitudes towards the Clutean healing of their world is a key yardstick of who and what they really are – another demonstration of Tolkienian Recovery in action.

This is not to say that Daenerys should or will win the game of thrones. Such is speculation. Nor does it mean that the Targaryen restoration that Varys, Illyrio Mopatis and Jon Connington have been plotting is necessarily the best thing for Westeros. What Martin's authorial attitude towards dragons proves that he is writing high fantasy, which Clute defines as concerning itself with matters affecting the destiny of worlds. (466) Though his work dwells on sour young men scrubbing skid-marks off the underwear of dribbling invalids (*Feast* 15), it does so, per Johnston, to create scope for redemptive healing, based around a reverent, engaged, ennobling estimation of humanity's relationship with that process. That is to say that this story has all the makings of an effective example of the neo-Romantic "high argument" that William Gray observes in certain mythopoeic fantasists, inspiring meditation on "the imaginative intuition of reality" (157). Gray takes the term *high argument* from M.H. Abrams, who in turn borrows it from William Wordsworth to label the poet's effort to provide a substitute for religion by showing "the power of the mind as itself adequate, by consummating a holy marriage with the external universe" (28). The Romantics met the challenge to Christian faith presented by the rationalism of the eighteenth century – an incidence of thinning in the primary world – by proposing as a substitute Abrams's "natural supernaturalism," the secular sanctification of the observable universe and the celebration of the human capacity to observe it. Awe – that is, dispossession of the self in the face of something beyond one's understanding – is a central tenet of Romanticism. That requires something awesome, in the strict sense of the term, something arresting and powerful that overflows rational analysis. This is what the rebirth of dragons in Martin's written world accomplishes. It is why Jhogo puts aside his misogyny to follow Daenerys, Barristan Selmy seeks her out, Jorah Mormont doggedly seeks her forgiveness, why Missendei loves her and Mollander clings to stories of her. Whether Daenerys ends up on the Iron Throne or not, she has kickstarted a process of healing, given people something to believe in a world where no such quantity seemed to be left. It is also why this story is so popular. Readers partake in something of the character's experience, a "reconciliation of humanity with itself and with nature in which experience re-appropriates the lost vision of innocence" (Gray 4).

If this sounds like a rather lofty claim for a series of airport novels about dragons, it should be noted that this is exactly what popular tales of dragons are for. The modern fantasy tradition is at heart a descendant of Romanticism, though more of the German variety than the English branch championed by Wordsworth. German Romantics like Novalis were consciously embarked upon an attempt to create "a new mythology that would express, and perhaps initiate, a social and even a cosmic revolution" (Gray 14), one based on dispossessive innocent faith inspired by the aestheticised supernatural. Such tales were seized upon by nineteenth-century British writers, principally George MacDonald, who became a formative influence on twentieth-century fantasists ranging from the harrowingly reductive David Lindsay to the Christian apologist C.S. Lewis. Not all fantasists since have consciously utilised the mythopoeic potential of their art. All offer echoes of the Romantic program, however, for a reason observed by Mendlesohn's schema, demonstrated in Todorov's, and analysed in Sandner's. The core business of the modern fantasy text is the rhetorical confrontation of the reader with something they have never seen before, something they must accept with the "vision of innocence" Gray observes in the Romantic experience, and contrast it with those components of the narrative – principally humanity – that they do recognise. Tyrion Lannister cried himself to sleep after being denied this.

In other words – and once again – the story launches the Recovery Tolkien propounded. Flying is only valuable insofar as it provides a fresh perspective on the world. Tyrion may occasionally fantasise about roasting his father with dragonfire (*Game* 119). But those thoughts came after his father's treatment of Tysha, and after his instinctive childhood fantasies of "flying o'er fields and mountains," the longed-for experience of a disabled person to see and travel his world free of encumberments. A world containing reborn dragons suddenly offers the possibility of this, and with it a fresh look at the world that one might see from the back of such a beast. The world is bigger, broader, deeper, richer and restored to a state that the adolescent Tyrion imagined. It prompts a re-establishment of childlike faith, however coloured it may be by political concerns as to what Daenerys may actually be planning (*Dance* 86). This fresh look at the fundamental nature of the world and the human relationship with it is the essence of Tolkienian Recovery. This is exactly what Roone wants, what Jorah Mormont has received and, crucially, what an engaged reader experiences. The purpose of tales of fantasy, Tolkien states, is to refresh and re-emphasise the natural, to recapture the "humility and innocence" of the child; "in that sense only a taste for them may make us, or keep us, childish" ("On Fairy-Stories" 136; 146). Recalling his own introduction to fantasy, Tolkien famously observes

"I desired dragons with a profound desire. Of course, in my timid body I did not wish to have them in the neighbourhood, [...] but the world that contained even the imagination of Fáfnir was richer and more beautiful, at whatever cost of peril" (135). That is what is happening to readers of *A Song of Ice and Fire*. The appeal of this story lies not in its sex and violence but in that it allows the engaged reader to close *A Dance with Dragons*, put it on their nightstand, and go to sleep just as Tyrion does in Illyrio's litter, with "[their] heart listening for the beat of leathern wings" (*Dance* 87). The world that contains the imagination of Drogon is richer and more beautiful as a result. The aestheticised experience of the world that might be, says Tolkien, prompts the reader to re-engage with the world that is.

A Song of Ice and Fire is a story of the rebirth of a world and the refreshment of humanity's relationship to it, as directed and emphasised by the discovery that their world contains more than those humans thought it did. Martin offers an almost encyclopaedic survey of the possible reactions to that discovery. Samwell Tarly rises to the occasion, stamping down on the supernatural. In doing so he reveals in spite of himself that, like the heroes of Stoker's *Dracula*, the watchers on the Wall do have – on a fundamental, human level – what it takes to meet the icy challenge coming to them. Martin's schemers, his cosmic *alazons* plotting to kill their brothers, Cain-like, despite the fact that winter is coming – Stannis, Cersei, Victarion – seek by contrast to mechanise the magic, to get it working for them. This crystalises Martin's depiction of their hubris; as in Tolkien's legendarium, Sandnerian domestication is the act of the abject fool. Ser Davos Seaworth is an innocent victim of magic, condemned by the insidious misdeeds of others to have his entire identity infected and fragmented by something he never wanted and cannot effectively avoid. Finally, Daenerys Targaryen gives herself openly and willingly to her encounter with the supernatural, holding nothing back. The courage to dispossess herself in this way is rewarded by the transcendent state of having her identity irrecoverably merge with and be redefined by an ineffaceable sign of the richness and power of the universe. Daenerys's response is the most interesting and far-reaching because it restores something that was lacking, something whose absence is emblematic of the thinning of Martin's world. In doing so she establishes Clute's great movement from thinning to healing. By making the reader privy to a hypothesised human interaction with a deepened and enriched world, *A Song of Ice and Fire* demonstrates modern fantasy's Romanticist capacity as the post-Enlightenment delivery system for aestheticised religious experience.

This explains the impact of its televisual extrapolation. The most important line in *Game of Thrones* is not any of the dynastic mottos or aphorisms used as episode titles. The line that typifies, exemplifies and encapsulates the series is spoken by Tyrion Lannister in the episode

"Home" as he meets Viserion and Rhaegal under the Pyramid of Meereen – "But here you are." The "*but*" indicates the sudden joyous turn. Tyrion never expected the Consolation of seeing his world healed. Perhaps those who reflect upon *Game of Thrones* with sentences beginning "I normally hate fantasy but..." did not expect that experience either. But Martin's contact with the key Romantic aspects of the fantasy form – aspects often overlooked by sceptics – have carried over into television. On both page and screen this story provides the emotional solace of a fresh perspective on the world and humanity's place within it.

Conclusions

While writing this monograph, I was approached to review another book for a journal. In my review, I speculated that the purpose of literary criticism was to account for the impact the subject texts have on their culture. With that thought in mind, it is worth acknowledging one of the less interesting, but also less arguable, reasons for the popularity of *A Song of Ice and Fire* – it got on TV. For all that the internet has changed and will continue to change the media landscape, television remains a pervasive and influential medium, and the preferred method by which many people consume fiction. Martin's tale made the jump to television at a particularly opportune time. His work attracted attention during the "golden age of television," when the medium has at least momentarily overtaken cinema as the dominant method by which writers use audio-visual means to portray psychologically and morally engaging narratives. With this comes an increase in funding, a seriousness of purpose, and an indulgence of talent. *Game of Thrones* is therefore a deftly funded (not "lavishly," as the producer's ability to effectively manage resources is the real story there) level-headed, long-format drama. It is in a very different league from the threadbare 2004 television treatment of Ursula le Guin's *Earthsea* novels, the tepid monster-of-the-week pantomime of *Hercules: The Legendary Journeys* (1995–1999) or the BBC's serious and well-intentioned but – responsibly – short-running 2000 adaptation of Mervyn Peake's Titus novels. The show will be remembered as a major watershed in the history of television fantasy, and possibly television itself. The espousal of Martin's work by television producers and viewers is crucial to his profile – and thus to my ability to place a monograph about a non-canonical writer with a reputable academic publisher.

The influence of the show can be overestimated, however. Praise of *Game of Thrones* is frequently inflected by an abiding bemusement that a tale of fantasy would interest the general public. "Be careful," admonished television reviewer Fiona Rae of *The New Zealand Listener* in 2012, "This might turn you into a nerd" (67). As the fourth season began in 2014, she conceded it had "finally made nerds of us all" (67). Internet comedy troupe Screen Junkies have accused the show of "using violence and boobs to trick non-nerds into liking fantasy." That joke works on the assumption that such trickery is necessary, that the most objectionable thing about this famously confrontational series is its use of the supernatural and that most people would rather watch a child being burned alive (as happens to the screen iteration of Princess Shireen) than a teenager riding a dragon. This line of thinking is evident among the show's ardent supporters, such as journalist Ben Machell:

> The show's popularity has meant that millions of otherwise normal people have become fantasy nerds. For a fantasy nerd like me, this has been amazing; for the first time in my life I've been able to talk to strangers about dragons without them reaching for their personal alarm. But with the final season possibly coming as soon as July 2018, a doubt has taken hold; what happens when it's all over and everybody moves on? I'll be back where I started. Just another nerd, exposed and alone. (7)

Machell makes a valid observation about the cultural prominence of *Game of Thrones*. Television dates. One of the few predictions I care to place on record about Martin's tale is that comedy writers will eventually use caricatures of his fans to demonstrate their skits are set in the 2010s just as references to *Dynasty* and *Seinfeld* are used to place comedies in the 1980s or 1990s. Nevertheless, Machell once again demonstrates the assumption that fantasy is of no interest to "normal people," but is rather the preserve of exposed, lonely "nerds." The term *nerd* first appears in print as the name of an imaginary animal in Dr. Seuss's 1950 book *If I Ran the Zoo*. Seized upon at random as a derisory label for intellectuals, it was subsequently applied, via a second leap of logic, to fantasy readers. *Geek* is slightly older, originally referring to less-esteemed American carnival acts in the early twentieth century, but ended up with a similar meaning in the 1980s. It also rhymes with *Reek*. To name something is to control it, as Ramsay Bolton demonstrates. Having invented a class of people for the pleasure of using appealing nonsense words dreamed up by their grandparent's generation, society has become haunted, it seems, by the fear of becoming subject to this control. *Game of Thrones* has not changed this. For all the talk about "fantasy for people who hate fantasy," many still vehemently dislike the show precisely, it seems, *because* it is fantasy. While writing this book I have encountered numerous fans of *Breaking Bad*, *The Sopranos* and *Peaky Blinders* – shows evincing the sexposition, violence and confrontational moral landscapes for which Benioff and Weiss's story has been criticised – who scorn *Game of Thrones* sight-unseen, defensively dismissing the notion that a show "about dragons" could possibly be of any interest to them. "I never watch any show like that," boasted a *Breaking Bad* fan of my acquaintance, "and I never will." The parallel with Sandnerian possession is remarkable. Possession is one of Sandner's negative responses, one born of fear, whereby Machell's "normal people" reiterate their normality and thus guard against inherently objectionable transgressive elements. "I'd be interested in hearing about that," opined a neighbour upon learning the subject of this book, "if you were writing about literally any other type of literature." The flip side of the *Game of Thrones* phenomenon has been an entrenchment of attitudes among those for whom the fear of being taken for a nerd is clearly very real.

And so, a long-term reader of fantasy might respond, here we go again. Whatever the long-term cultural status of *Game of Thrones*, its success has placed Martin alongside H.P. Lovecraft, George Lucas and J.K. Rowling as an architect of millennial folklore. Yet fantasy remains firmly cemented in many imaginations as the literary equivalent of a communicable disease, avoidable via scrupulous application of the prophylactic of correct and sober taste, its followers to be scorned for their self-inflicted cultural injuries like soldiers with gonorrhea. When a fantasy breaks this quarantine, explanations must be found. Shippey relates how when *The Lord of the Rings* won a bookseller's poll as the greatest novel of the twentieth century, sceptics accused the Tolkien Society of having conspired to skew the results of this wholly unofficial snapshot of public opinion by voting as a block (2002 xxii). In the 2010s, criticism of *Game of Thrones* has similarly departed from the assumption that its ratings somehow contravene an organic state of affairs; only nerds like fantasy. Quite where the critics who voice such opinions were looking when the *Harry Potter* and *Lord of the Rings* films demonstrated the popularity of fantasy remains unclear. There is something of Clute's Knight of Doleful Countenance about this, a refusal to acknowledge a central point and a concern instead with "contriving solutions to the problems of getting through the day" (544). Commentators have pondered Martin's violence, lampooned his sex and overstated the innovation of his sophisticated moral landscape, seemingly reluctant to explore the possibility that this tale may be popular precisely *because* it employs fantasy's long-established capacity for accentuating human concerns in literature. Critics may very well question exactly how, or how effectively, Martin does this. This book is my attempt to address those points. I have no place questioning the decision of observers such as Machell to self-identify as nerds. But spec-fic – fantasy, science fiction and supernatural horror – is well-established as probably the dominant popular literary form of the late twentieth and early twenty-first centuries. (Shippey 2002 xvii) Far from being an aberration, *Game of Thrones* has simply demonstrated this point in a way that lends itself to pictorial representation, saliently via the highly visual, video-friendly medium of the internet. As a practitioner of this pervasive and hugely resonant cultural form, Martin absolutely deserves discussion. Again, this is why I wrote this book. But the question is not how he "tricked" "normal people" into reading fantasy. To ask this reveals more about the critic than the subject – a hallmark of poor criticism. Normal people do read fantasy. Fantasy is, invariably, about normal people, about putting human beings in fresh and revealing lights. The question is how Martin's use of fantasy sells his experiments in depicting human emotion, ambition and morality.

Martin's work has been called an "epic fantasy" (Garcia and Antonsson x). Epic is a poetic form as well as an adjective, and length is one of its more incidental features (standard modern editions of Homer's two epics evince smaller page counts than any of Martin's volumes to date). More characteristic is its encyclopaedic nature, the sense that a given example of the form ranges across the imagination of its subject culture, depicting or gesturing towards all that the culture considers noteworthy or valuable in a single narrative. In this sense, Martin's work could certainly be described as an epic fantasy or, rather, an epic *of* fantasy, an inventory-in-action of the various approaches to the requirements of the genre and the effects they can achieve.

Martin's moral ambiguity is impressive but by no means groundbreaking. Fantasy serves primarily as a method of providing experimental conditions in which to weigh the human soul, as practitioners such as Mervyn Peake, J.K. Rowling and J.R.R. Tolkien demonstrate. What makes Martin's practice of the same technique seem fresh, particularly to those who take Tolkien as typical of the tradition, is his dismissal of Frye's higher modes, and his use of the ironic mode to interrogate claims of nobility. Although Martin does this exceedingly well, this technique has precedent in twentieth-century fantasy. It is precisely what Terry Pratchett built a career by doing. While Martin's bleak narrative may seem a long way from Pratchett's comedic ones, the two authors employ very similar techniques to call the presumption of the characters into question. Deprived of the inherent dignity of Frye's higher modes, characters must think through their positions and statements and act accordingly. In a further parallel with Pratchett, characters who go to that effort are in fact granted the sort of modal dignity their less astute colleagues are denied. Syrio Forel and Qhorin Halfhand die as heroes; the tragedy of Catelyn Stark carries its full weight of drama. Rather than being innovative, Martin's interrogation of the moral literacy of his characters is so evident because it is imputed into the very levels of literary being on which those characters exist.

The same goes Martin's sexual discourse. Martin's characters are theatrically, ostentatiously human, and he is engaged on an investigation into how that capacity influences their use of the public authority with which their medievalist milieu attributes them. To engage the emotions those characters must be calibrated, however subtly, on a moral scale, which the reader must construct themselves, independently of the putative subject matter of the tale. Emerging naturally through Martin's dedication to low mimesis, his frank discussion of the sexual mores of Westeros creates that scale. This activates Iser's phenomenological model of reading, delegating aspects of his characterisation to the reader while at the same time encouraging them to build the characters in roughly the stature Martin hoped for them to have. The creative stake the reader has in the characters explains why so many readers find Martin's people so resonant. Once this strategy becomes apparent, furthermore, a pattern quickly emerges. Martin uses the device to encourage the reader themselves to separate those who are genuinely a part of the subject medievalist regime and those who are merely coping with it. This shows that Martin is using much the same technique that the classic Gothic novelists use; the iniquities of an imagined past are highlighted by being visited upon those not wholly belonging to that milieu. With this thought in mind, the sexual self-determination of some of Martin's women becomes conspicuous as an act of rebellion against an emblematic patriarchy.

Martin's strategies for drawing the reader into his narrative extend to his fantasy world-building. Fantasies must be explained, their deviations from the primary world communicated somehow to the reader. Martin's use of Mendlesohnian immersive rhetoric for the preponderant bulk of his world-building has a number of powerful effects. The practice of building a world from ironic pointers is, on a broad level, phenomenological. Martin has not created a world so much as upended a world-building kit on the reader's nightstand and stepped back to watch them assemble the resulting mess into a reasoned picture of a world. As with his sexual discourse, this imposes upon the readers a creative stake in the story. They must think this world through in a manner very different from that demanded by portal-quest exposition. Immersion also pushes the reader to see things very much through the eyes of the focaliser. By seeing what is strange about Westeros accounted for by rational argument, they can appreciate the thought processes and emotional states of the characters with an immediacy that other expository techniques rarely achieve. Arya Stark's time as a scullion in Harrenhal is the obvious example. Most importantly of all, however, Mendlesohnian immersion is, in its pure state, an uncompromisingly rationalistic technique that functions by exploding assumption and revealing an absence of inherent meaning. Rather than any truth, the reader must construct a world from a chaos of rationalistic contingencies. Something means something because of something else, which is also dependent on something further, which can be proved via further observation, and so on. This creates Clute's thinning effect, the notion that the world is less magical, less robust than it once was, simply because the interrogative reading process will not allow the mystique of magic or ideology to abide intact. Martin's indictment of a medievalist society not living up to the standards it sets for itself prospers in such a thinned environment. This is particularly the case in chapters focalised by Sansa Stark, who retains her idealism, not as a demonstration of personal naivete, but as a point of reference in a penetrating indictment of an absence. This makes the thinning of Westeros her core subject. This is why Martin's world feels so bleak; much of the focalisation is dedicated to demonstrating that something that should be there is missing.

Martin emphasises this impression further by using different Mendlesohnian techniques to tell the stories of the two half-brothers who venture north of the Wall, Bran Stark and Jon Snow. Bran's tale is a portal-quest, his journey laid out for him by the instructions of those – Osha, Jojen Reed, Coldhands, Leaf – whose explanations must be taken as fundamentally sound for the story to retain any narrative motility. Only that which is known can be acted upon. Jon Snow, by contrast, suffers a Mendlesohnian intrusion, a tale motivated by that which is intuited, suspected and feared rather than what is known. Isolated and held back from a complete grasp of the situation, Jon Snow *cannot* know anything, because the species of fantasy he focalises is predicated on the marooning the focaliser in a status of awareness that there is something wrong, but inability to grasp or correct the problem. Though very different, these two tales share a crucial point of similarity. Where the bulk of Martin's focalisation emphasises an absence of essential meaning, these two subplots emphasise a presence of some sort of truth in the world – accepted and acted upon in Bran's tale, gratingly suspected in Jon's. Rather than running contra to the sense of thinning Martin builds in the immersive mainstream of his narrative, these presences help deepen that impression by way of contrast. The moral illiteracy of Westeros is made all the more apparent in light of the urgent need for Martin's characters to pull themselves together and unite against a common enemy. The contrast places the reader in the same heterodiegetic position that Sansa Stark occupies diegetically, observing the absence of humanity while retaining the need for it in their frame of reference. This is a textbook example of Tolkienian Recovery, the re-establishment of a clear view of the essential position of humanity in the world via its juxtaposition with literary artefacts that exist as points of contrast therewith. Once again, via his use of the conventions of fantasy, Martin stage-manages the reader's engagement with the tale to formidably far-reaching effect.

Outside the tales of Bran and Jon, Martin's presentation of the supernatural is frequently one of superstition and accusation; it is often unclear exactly which claims of thaumaturgy are accurate. If this is unusual among modern genre fantasists, then it is open to analysis via the Todorovian schema of the fantastic as a lack of clarity between what is magical (marvellous) and what is simply unnerving (uncanny). Martin's medievalism, established as following the conventions of Gothicism, is an exercise in establishing the Todorovian uncanny, depicting shocking violence and inhumanity. Martin cannot afford to have any of his characters fundamentally behave differently from the others for fear of lessening the reader's phenomenological involvement in the text. When he wishes to have his readers inveigh upon one of his characters, therefore, he propagates the invective impulse that Tobin Siebers identifies in the Todorovian fantastic, inviting the reader to suspect that characters like Aeron Greyjoy and Qyburn are not only inhumane but actually inhuman. The career arc of Cersei Lannister, from attempting to forestall witchcraft to trying to conduct it herself, closely follows the formulation that Siebers identifies in James's *The Turn of the Screw*. Martin's employment of unambiguous magic, furthermore, demonstrates Todorov's notion of the dissolution of median disequilibria in action. Melisandre's shadow demons resolve the Stormlands campaign without requiring a resolution to the bitter familial dysfunction that the conflict represents. Similarly, the looming catastrophe beyond the Wall provides an overall shape to the game of thrones itself, a large-scale median disequilibrium that the Westerosi cannot get out of the same way they got into it. The story therefore moves forward while the human failings that caused it abide in unalloyed forms. This, again, prompts Tolkienian Recovery, the use of the supernatural to highlight the natural.

Martin's characters gradually become aware of the existence of the supernatural in a world they believe to have thinned out beyond such possibilities. They respond in a variety of ways, covering all four of the responses identified by David Sandner. Samwell Tarly rises to the challenge, revealing who he truly is as he takes possession of moments of horrendous, inhuman danger. Stannis Baratheon seeks to domesticate the supernatural to further his existing human goals. Davos Seaworth fragments under magical pressure, his identity merging with that he passionately sought to avoid. Daenerys Targaryen, meanwhile, voluntarily dispossesses her existing identity and allows her being to merge with that of her dragons to become a true Targaryen. By doing so she enacts the great movement John Clute identifies in the modern fantasy tradition, the transition from thinning to healing, a restoration of lost truth. Daenerys has given back the dragons. This restores to Martin's world a great emblem of its loss. Those who take a cynical attitude to this restoration are knights of doleful countenance persisting in opposition to the direction of their world. Those who, like Daenerys, dispossess themselves of their previous worldview partake of its healing. The same goes for the engaged reader. At heart Martin's tale demonstrates the Romanicist high argument of modern fantasy, its capacity to encourage the reader to take a fresh look at their world and appreciate it anew. Once again, this is Tolkienian Recovery in action.

The assertion that Martin's tale enacts so many of the patterns of modern fantasy should not be taken as an accusation of unoriginality.

Rather it shows an author in command of his chosen literary form. A poetic analogy helps to illustrate the point. Anybody with a droll idea can probably squeeze it into an AABBA rhyme scheme, but the result will not be a good limerick. A skilled writer will use that form to service their joke, proposing a situation in the first two lines, escalating comic tension in the third and fourth, then using the fifth to release that tension with a punchline linked by rhyme to the initial situation. Similarly, writers do not produce timeless sonnets by shoehorning tender sentiment, however sincere, into fourteen lines. They use the form as emotional punctuation, employing its metre, couplets and quatrains to give rhetorical structure and emphasis to feelings. The skilled poet – a skilled *writer* – is one who uses the conventions of form to service, rather than constrain, his or her content. Martin has taken the conventions of fantasy – its expository imperatives, its capacity to establish moments or periods of epistemological uncertainty, its essentially Romantic contrast between the real and unreal – and used them to mould and direct reader attention to his tale.

The effect of all this is apparent in the fact that the last three chapters of this book all come back around to Tolkienian Recovery. However *A Song of Ice and Fire* is remembered, it will not primarily be as a story about dragons, except perhaps among its more facetious detractors. Engaged readers will remember them as stories of well-rounded, vivid characters struggling in situations of urgent public and private conflict. Martin has created that vividness and urgency by deft use of the fantasy form. Modern fantasy provides points of contrast and crisis that reveal the true human nature of the characters in ways Martin has employed to remarkable effect. These characters are realistic in large part because of the unreality that surrounds them. Martin depicts a pageant of intensely human experiences – hate, envy, illness, greed, fraternal duty, parental piety, Oedipal conflict, moral quagmires, vaulting and thwarted ambition, innocence, experience, guilt, repentance, redemption, idealistic women struggling in a man's world, the joy and discovery of adolescent sex, the death of an old man, the innocent, uncomplicated rage of a wronged child. These qualities shine brighter and hotter, and take sharper, clearer shape in the reader's mind, for having been placed under the shadow of dragon's wings. In *A Song of Ice and Fire*, lots of people live.

Bibliography

George R.R. Martin

George R.R. Martin. *A Clash of Kings*. 1998. London: Harper Voyager, 2011.
———. *A Dance with Dragons*. 2011. London: Harper Voyager, 2012.
———. *A Feast for Crows*. 2005. London: Harper Voyager, 2011.
———. *Fire and Blood*. London: Harper Voyager, 2018.
———. *A Game of Thrones*. 1996. London: Harper Voyager, 2011.
———. *A Storm of Swords Part 1: Steel and Snow*. 2000. London: Harper Voyager, 2011.
———. *A Storm of Swords Part 2: Blood and Gold*. 2000. London: Harper Voyager, 2011.

Primary Sources by Other Authors

I: Fiction and Literature

Aeschylus. *The Libation Bearers*. Trans. Richmond Lattimore. *Greek Tragedies*. Eds. Lattimore and David Grene. Vol. 2. Chicago (IL): U of Chicago P, 1960. 1–43.
"Alaeddin, or the Wonderful Lamp." 1884. Trans. Richard Burton. Ed. Bennett A. Cerf. New York: The Modern Library, 1997. 731–837.
Apollodorus. *The Library*. Trans. George James Frazer. Vol. 1. London: William Heinemann, 1954.
Beowulf. Trans. Dick Ringler. Indianapolis (IN): Hackett Publishing Company, 2007.
Clarke, Susanna. *Johnathan Strange and Mister Norrell*. London: Bloomsbury, 2004.
Diodorus Siculus. *Library of History*. Trans. C.H. Oldfather. Vol. 4. London: William Heinmann, 1946.
Eddison, E.R. *The Worm Ouroboros*. 1922. London: Ballantyne, 1972.
Homer. *Iliad*. Trans. A.T. Murray. Vol. 2. London: William Heinemann, 1946.
———. *Odyssey*. Trans A.T. Murray. Vols. 1–2. London: William Heinemann, 1919.
James, Henry. "The Turn of the Screw." 1899. *The Turn of the Screw and Other Stories*. Ed. T.J. Lustig. Oxford: Oxford UP, 1998. 113–236.
Lewis, Matthew. *The Monk*. 1796. London: Penguin, 1998.
Lovecraft, H.P. "The Call of Cthulhu." 1925. *Lovecraft: Tales*. Ed. Peter Straub. New York: Library Classics of the United States, 2005. 167–196.

———. "Notes to 'The Shadow Over Innsmouth'." 1949. *Collected Essays Vol. V: Autobiography and Miscellany*. Ed. S.T. Joshi. New York: Hippocampus Press, 2006. 249–253.
———. "The Shadow Over Innsmouth." 1931. *Lovecraft: Tales*. Ed. Peter Straub. New York: Library Classics of the United States, 2005. 587–653.
MacDonald, George. "The Light Princess." 1864. *The Complete Fairy Tales*. Ed. U.C. Knoepflmacher. New York: Penguin, 1999. 10–36.
———. "The Truth." 1889. *Unspoken Sermons: Third Series*. Grand Rapids (MI): Christian Classics Ethereal Library, 2005. 23–32.
Orwell, George. *Nineteen Eighty-Four*. 1949. London: Penguin, 1977.
Peake, Mervyn. *Gormenghast*. 1949. London: Vintage Books, 1992. 369–752.
———. *Titus Groan*. 1946. London: Vintage Books, 1992. 7–367.
Plato. *The Republic*. Trans. Paul Shorey. Vol. 1. London: William Heinemann, 1935.
Pratchett, Terry. *Carpe Jugulum*. London: Doubleday, 1998.
———. *Guards! Guards!* London: Corgi, 1989.
———. *Hogfather*. London: Corgi, 1997.
———. *Maskerade*. London: Corgi, 1996.
———. *Mort*. London: Corgi, 1987.
———. *Reaper Man*. London: Gollancz, 1991.
———. *Sourcery*. London: Gollancz, 1988.
———. *Witches Abroad*. London: Corgi, 1992.
Pullman, Philip. *Northern Lights*. 1995. London, Scholastic, 1998.
Rowling, J.K. *Harry Potter and the Chamber of Secrets*. London: Scholastic, 1999.
———. *Harry Potter and the Deathly Hallows*. London: Bloomsbury, 2007.
———. *Harry Potter and the Half-Blood Prince*. London: Bloomsbury, 2005.
———. *Harry Potter and the Philosopher's Stone*. London: Bloomsbury, 1997.
Stoker, Bram. *Dracula*. 1897. *Dracula*. Ed. John Paul Riquelme. Boston and New York: Bedford and St. Matins, 2002. 23–369.
Sturluson, Snorri. *Egil's Saga*. Trans. Gwyn Jones. New York: Twayne Publishers and the American-Scandinavian Foundation, 1960.
Tolkien, J.R.R. *The Fellowship of the Ring, Being the First Part of The Lord of the Rings*. 1954. 2nd edition. London: Unwin, 2004.
———. *The Hobbit, or There and Back Again*. 1937. London: Harper Collins, 1991.
———. *The Return of the King, Being the Third Part of The Lord of the Rings*. 1955. 2nd edition. London: Unwin, 2004.
———. *The Silmarillion*. Ed. Christopher Tolkien. London: Unwin, 1977.
———. *The Two Towers, Being the Second Part of The Lord of the Rings*. 1954. 2nd edition. London: Unwin, 2004.
Vance, Jack. *The Dying Earth*. 1950. *Tales of the Dying Earth*. New York: Gollancz, 2002. 1–130.
———. *Lyonesse*. 1983. London: Gollancz, 2008.
———. *Rhialto the Marvellous*. 1984. *Tales of the Dying Earth*. New York: Gollancz, 2002. 577–741.
Vergil. *Aeneid*. Trans. C. Day Lewis. Oxford: Oxford UP, 1986.
Volsungasaga. The Saga of the Volsungs. Trans. George K. Anderson. East Brunswick (NJ): Associated UP, 1982. 21–156.

Völundarkvitha. Trans. Henry Adams Bellows. *The Poetic Edda*. Ed. Bellows. Princeton (NJ): Princeton UP and New York: American Scandinavian Foundation, 1936. 252–268.

II: Journalism, Interviews and Contemporary Reviews

Bausells, Martha. "George R.R. Martin in Quotes: 'I Love Writing about Bastards.'" *The Guardian* 11th August 2014. Accessed 18th August 2015. Web.
Gross, David. "Bookwyrms." *Dragon Magazine* #235 (November 1996). 59–61.
Grossman, Lev. "The American Tolkien." *Time* 166.21 (2005). Accessed 30th March 2015. Web.
———. "George R.R. Martin: An American Tolkien for a Jaded Age." Time.com. Accessed 13th May 2018. Web.
Hibberd, James "The Fantasy King." *Entertainment Weekly* 22nd July 2011. Accessed 18th August 2015. Web.
Machell, Ben. "Twenty Things about the New Year We Should Start Worrying about Now." *The Times Magazine*. 9th December 2017. 5–7.
Martin, George R.R. "From Game to Book or, the Birth of a Shared World." Tor.com 6th June 2011. Accessed 18th November 2018. Web.
McNutt, Myles. "*Game of Thrones*: You Win or You Die." *Cultural Learnings* 29th May 2011. Accessed 11th May 2018. Web.
Rae, Fiona. "Television." *New Zealand Listener* 235.3,773 (1st September 2012). 67.
———. "Television." *New Zealand Listener* 243.3,856 (27th April 2014). 66–67.
Wilson, Edmund. "Ooh, Those Awful Orcs!" *The Nation* 182.15 (14th April 1956). 312–314.

Film and Television

I: Game of Thrones

NOTE – all entries in this section are television broadcasts produced by Home Box Office of New York.
"Beyond the Wall." Dir. Alan Taylor. 20th August 2017.
"Book of the Stranger." Dir. Daniel Sackheim. 15th May 2016.
"Breaker of Chains." Dir. Alex Graves. 20th April 2014.
"The Climb." Dir. Alik Sakharov. 5th May 2013.
"The Dragon and the Wolf." Dir. Jeremy Podeswa. 27th August 2017.
"Eastwatch." Dir. Matt Shackman. 13th August 2017.
"The Ghost of Harrenhal." Dir. David Petrarca. 29th April 2012.
"The Gift." Dir. Miguel Sapochnik. 24th May 2015.
"Hardhome." Dir. Miguel Sapochnik. 31st May 2015.
"Home." Dir. Jeremy Podeswa. 1st May 2016.
"The Laws of Gods and Men." Dir. Alik Sakharov. 11th May 2014.
"Mhysa". Dir. David Nutter. 9th June 2013.
"Mother's Mercy." Dir. David Nutter. 14th June 2015.
"Oathbreaker." Dir. Daniel Sackheim. 8th May 2016.
"The Red Woman." Dir. Jeremy Podeswa. 24th April 2016.

"Unbent, Unbowed, Unbroken." Dir. Jeremy Podeswa. 17th May 2015.
"Walk of Punishment." Dirs. David Benioff and D.B. Weiss. 14th April 2013.
"The Watchers on the Wall." Dir. Neil Marshall. 8th June 2014.
"The Wolf and the Lion." Dir. Brian Kirk. 15th May 2011.
"You Win or You Die." Dir. Daniel Minahan. 29th May 2011.

II: Other

"The Black Seal." *The Black Adder.* Dir. Martin Shardlow. British Broadcasting Corporation, London, 20th July 1983. Television.

"*Game of Thrones* for Women." *Funny Girls* Youtube account. Accessed 11th May 2018. Web.

"*Game of Thrones*: Gwendoline Christie, Maisie Williams & More Make Up Theme Tunes." *Entertainment Weekly* Youtube account. 30th April 2016. Accessed 11th May 2018. Web.

Hogfather. Dir. Vadim Jean. Sky One, 2006. Perf. Michelle Dockery, David Jason, Ian Richardson, Marc Warren. Film.

"Honest Trailers: *Game of Thrones* Vol. 2." *Screen Junkies* Youtube account. Accessed 12th May 2018. Web.

"How the Gang Got Together." *Maid Marian and Her Merry Men.* Dir. David Bell. British Broadcasting Corporation. London, 16th November 1989. Television.

Independence Day. Dir. Roland Emmerich. Twentieth-Century Fox, 1996. Perf. Jeff Goldblum, Bill Pullman, Will Smith. Film.

"Milfay." *Carnivalé.* Dir. Rodrigo Garcia. Home Box Office, Los Angeles, 14th September 2003. Television.

Monty Python and the Holy Grail. Dirs. Terry Gilliam and Terry Jones. Python Pictures, 1975. Perf. Graham Chapman, John Cleese, Gilliam, Eric Idle, Jones, Michael Palin. Film.

"The Queen of Spain's Beard." *The Black Adder.* Dir. Martin Shardlow. British Broadcasting Corporation, London, 6th July 1983. Television.

Star Wars Episode IV: A New Hope. Dir. George Lucas. Lucasfilm, 1977. Perf. Carrie Fisher, Harrison Ford, Alec Guiness, Mark Hamil. Film.

"Whacking Day." *The Simpsons.* Dir. John Lynch. Gracie Films. Los Angeles, 29th April 1993. Television.

"Witchsmeller Pursuivant." *The Black Adder.* Dir. Martin Shardlow. British Broadcasting Corporation, London, 13th July 1983. Television.

Critical Works

Abrams, M.H. *Natural Supernaturalism: Tradition and Revolution in Romantic Literature.* New York: W.W. Norton and Company, 1971.

———, and Geoffrey Galt Harpham. *A Glossary of Literary Terms.* 9th edition. Boston (MA): Wadsworth Cengage Learning, 2009.

Alesi, Danielle. "The Power of Sansa Stark: A Representation of Female Agency in Late Medieval England." *Game of Thrones versus History: Written in Blood.* Ed. Brian Pavlac. Hoboken (NJ): Wiley & Sons, 2017. 161–170.

Antonsson, Linda, and Emilio M. Garcia. Foreword. *Game of Thrones and Philosophy: Logic Cuts Deeper Than Swords.* Ed. Henry Jacoby. Hoboken (NJ): Wiley & Sons, 2012. ix–xii.

Armitt, Lucie. *Theorising the Fantastic*. London: Arnold, 1996.

Ashley, Mike. "Succubus." *The Encyclopaedia of Fantasy*. Eds. John Clute and John Grant. 2nd edition. London: Orbit, 1999. 904.

Attebery, Brian. *The Fantasy Tradition in American Literature from Irving to Le Guin*. Bloomington and Indianapolis: Indiana UP, 1980.

———*Strategies of Fantasy*. Bloomington and Indianapolis: Indiana UP, 1992.

———. "Structuralism." *The Cambridge Companion to Fantasy Literature*. Eds. Edward James and Farah Mendlesohn. Cambridge: Cambridge UP, 2012. 81–90.

Bayless, Martha. "Disney's Castles and the Work of the Medieval in the Magic Kingdom." *The Disney Middle Ages: A Fairy-Tale and Fantasy Past*. Eds. Susan Aronstein and Tison Pugh. New York: Palgrave MacMillan, 2012. 39–56.

Bell, Christopher. "Riddle Me This: The Moral Disengagement of Lord Voldemort." Legilimens! *Perspectives in Harry Potter Studies*. Ed. Bell. Cambridge: Cambridge Scholars, 2013. 43–66.

Booth, Wayne C. *A Rhetoric of Irony*. Chicago (IL): U of Chicago P, 1974.

Botting, Fred. "In Gothic Darkly: Heterotopia, History, Culture." *A Companion to the Gothic*. Ed. David Punter. Oxford: Blackwell, 2000. 3–14.

Bould, Mark, and Sherryl Vint. "Political Readings." *The Cambridge Companion to Fantasy Literature*. Eds. Edward James and Farah Mendlesohn. Cambridge: Cambridge UP, 2012. 102–112.

Brooke-Rose, Christine. *A Rhetoric of the Unreal: Studies in Narrative and Structure, Especially of the Fantastic*. Cambridge: Cambridge UP, 1981.

Byron, Glennis, and David Punter. *The Gothic*. Oxford: Blackwell Publishing, 2004.

Carpenter, Humphrey. *J.R.R. Tolkien: A Biography*. London: Allen and Unwin, 1977.

Carroll, Shiloh. *Medievalism in A Song of Ice and Fire and Game of Thrones*. Cambridge: D. S. Brewer, 2018.

Clute, John. "Fantasy." *The Encyclopaedia of Fantasy*. Eds. John Clute and John Grant. 2nd edition. London: Orbit, 1999. 337–339.

———, and John Grant. "Fantasyland." *The Encyclopaedia of Fantasy*. Eds. John Clute and John Grant. 2nd edition. London: Orbit, 1999. 341.

———. "Healing." *The Encyclopaedia of Fantasy*. Eds. John Clute and John Grant. 2nd edition. London: Orbit, 1999. 458.

———. "High Fantasy." *The Encyclopaedia of Fantasy*. Eds. John Clute and John Grant. 2nd edition. London: Orbit, 1999. 466.

———. "Knight of Doleful Countenance." *The Encyclopaedia of Fantasy*. Eds. John Clute and John Grant. 2nd edition. London: Orbit, 1999. 544–545.

———. "Recognition." *The Encyclopaedia of Fantasy*. Eds. John Clute and John Grant. 2nd edition. London: Orbit, 1999. 804–805.

———. "Seven Samurai." *The Encyclopaedia of Fantasy*. Eds. John Clute and John Grant. 2nd edition. London: Orbit, 1999. 853.

———. "Thinning" *The Encyclopaedia of Fantasy*. Eds. John Clute and John Grant. 2nd edition. London: Orbit, 1999. 942–943.

———. "Wrongness." *The Encyclopaedia of Fantasy*. Eds. John Clute and John Grant. 2nd edition. London: Orbit, 1999. 1,038–1,039.

Cornwell, Neil. *The Literary Fantastic from Gothic to Postmodernism*. London: Harvester Wheatsheaf, 1990.

Corrigan, Richard H. "The War in Westeros and Just War Theory." *Game of Thrones and Philosophy: Logic Cuts Deeper than Swords*. Ed. Henry Jacoby. Hoboken (NJ): Wiley & Sons, 2012. 49–60.

Cowlishaw, Brian. "What Maesters Knew: Narrating Knowing." *Mastering the Game of Thrones: Essays on George R.R. Martin's A Song of Ice and Fire*. Eds. Jes Battis and Susan Johnston. Jefferson (NC): MacFarland, 2015. 57–70.

Craft, Christopher. "'Kiss Me with Those Red Lips': Gender and Inversion in Bram Stoker's *Dracula*." *Dracula: Contemporary Critical Essays*. Ed. Glennis Byron. New York: St. Martin's Press, 1999. 93–118.

Croft, Janet Brennan. *War in the Works of J.R.R. Tolkien*. Westport (CT): Praeger, 2004.

Day, William Patrick. *In the Circles of Fear and Desire: A Study of Gothic Fantasy*. Chicago (IL): U of Chicago P, 1985.

De Camp, L. Sprague. *Literary Swordsmen and Sorcerers: The Creators of Modern Fantasy*. Sauk City (WI): Arkham House, 1976.

DeCoste, D. Marcel. "Beyond the Pale? Craster and the Pathological Reproduction of Houses in Westeros." *Mastering the Game of Thrones: Essays on George R.R. Martin's A Song of Ice and Fire*. Eds. Jes Battis and Susan Johnston. Jefferson (NC): MacFarland, 2015. 225–242.

Fallis, Don. "It is a Great Crime to Lie to a King." *Game of Thrones and Philosophy: Logic Cuts Deeper than Swords*. Ed. Henry Jacoby. Hoboken (NJ): Wiley & Sons, 2012. 19–32.

Finke, Laurie A., and Martin B. Schichtman. *Cinematic Illuminations: The Middle Ages on Film*. Baltimore (MD): Johns Hopkins UP, 2010.

Flieger, Verlyn. "A Postmodern Medievalist?" *Tolkien's Modern Middle Ages*. Eds. Jane Chance and Alfred K. Siewers. New York: Palgrave MacMillan, 2005. 17–28.

———. *Splintered Light: Logos and Language in Tolkien's World*. 1983. 2nd edition. Kent (OH): Kent State UP, 2002.

Frankel, Valerie Estelle. *Mythology in Game of Thrones*. Brooklyn (NY): Thought Catalogue Books, 2015.

———. *Winter is Coming: Symbols and Hidden Meanings in A Game of Thrones*. Brooklyn (NY): Thought Catalogue Books, 2013.

———. *Women in Game of Thrones: Power, Conformity and Resistance*. Jefferson (NC): MacFarland, 2014.

Frye, Northrop. *Anatomy of Criticism: Four Essays*. Princeton (NJ): Princeton UP, 1957.

Glover, David. *Vampires, Mummies and Liberals: Bram Stoker and the Politics of Popular Fiction*. Durham (NC) and London: Duke UP, 1996.

Grant, John. "Genre Fantasy." *The Encyclopaedia of Fantasy*. Eds. John Clute and John Grant. 2nd edition. London: Orbit, 1999. 396.

Gray, William. *Fantasy, Myth and the Measure of Truth: Tales of Pullman, Lewis, Tolkien, MacDonald and Hoffman*. Basingstoke: Palgrave MacMillan, 2009.

Gresham, Karin. "Cursed Womb, Bulging Thighs and Bald Scalp: George R.R. Martin's Grotesque Queen." *Mastering the Game of Thrones: Essays on*

George R.R. Martin's A Song of Ice and Fire. Eds. Jes Battis and Susan Johnston. Jefferson (NC): MacFarland, 2015. 151–169.

Hackney, Charles H. "Silk Ribbons Tied Around a Sword: Knighthood and the Chivalric Values in Westeros." *Mastering the Game of Thrones: Essays on George R.R. Martin's A Song of Ice and Fire.* Eds. Jes Battis and Susan Johnston. Jefferson (NC): MacFarland, 2015. 132–150.

Hahn, David. "The Death of Lord Stark: The Perils of Idealism." *Game of Thrones and Philosophy: Logic Cuts Deeper than Swords.* Ed. Henry Jacoby. Hoboken (NJ): Wiley & Sons, 2012. 75–86.

Hogan, Patrick Cohn. *Affective Narratology: The Emotional Structure of Stories.* Lincoln (NB): U of Nebraska P, 2011.

Hume, Kathryn. *Fantasy and Mimesis: Responses to Reality in Western Literature.* New York: Methuen, 1984.

Iser, Wolfgang. *The Implied Reader: Patterns of Communication in Prose Fiction from Bunyan to Beckett.* Baltimore (MD): Johns Hopkins UP, 1974.

Jackson, Rosemary. *Fantasy: The Literature of Subversion.* New York: Methuen, 1981.

James, Edward. "Tolkien, Lewis and the Explosion of Genre Fantasy." *The Cambridge Companion to Modern Fantasy Literature.* Eds. James and Farah Mendlesohn. Cambridge: Cambridge UP, 2012. 62–78.

Jensen, Halle Strandgaard, and Magnus Qvistgard. "Oh, My Sweet Summer Child: Children and Childhood in *Game of Thrones.*" *Game of Thrones versus History: Written in Blood.* Ed. Brian A. Pavlac. Hoboken (NJ): Wiley & Sons, 2017. 137–146.

Johnston, Susan. "Grief Poignant as Joy: Dyscatastrophe and Eucatastrophe in *A Song of Ice and Fire.*" *Mythlore* 119/120 (Fall/Winter 2012). 133–154.

Johnstone, Ian. "Despite His Evil Actions." *Peake Studies* 7.2 (Summer 2001). 9–12.

Jones, Andrew Zimmerman. "Of Direwolves and Gods." *Beyond the Wall: Exploring George R.R. Martin's A Song of Ice and Fire.* Ed. James Lowder. Dallas (TX): Benbella Books, 2012. 107–122.

Kaveney, Roz. "Dragons." *The Encyclopaedia of Fantasy.* Eds. John Clute and John Grant. 2nd edition. London: Orbit, 1999. 295–296.

Killeen, Jarlath. *Gothic Literature 1825–1914.* Cardiff: U of Wales P, 2009.

Langford, David. "Low Fantasy." *The Encyclopaedia of Fantasy.* Eds. John Clute and John Grant. 2nd edition. London: Orbit, 1999. 597.

Langford, Jonathan. "Why the Academy is Afraid of Dragons: The Suppression of the Marvellous in Theories of the Fantastic." *Science Fiction, Canonization, Marginalisation and the Academy.* Eds. George Slusser and Gary Westfahl. Westport (CT): Greenwood Press, 2002. 51–64.

Larrington, Carolyne. *Winter is Coming: The Medieval World of Game of Thrones.* London and New York: I.B. Tauris, 2016.

Little, Edmund. *The Fantasts.* Amersham: Avebury Publishing, 1982.

Lowder, James. "Introduction: In Praise of Living History." *Beyond the Wall: Exploring George R.R. Martin's A Song of Ice and Fire.* Ed. Lowder. Dallas (TX): Benbella Books, 2012. xiii–xviii.

MacDonald, George. "The Fantastic Imagination." *A Dish of Orts.* 1893. London: Tutis Digital Publishing, 2008. 195–200.

Makdisi, Saree. "Romantic Cultural Imperialism." *The Cambridge History of English Romantic Literature.* Ed. James Chandler. Cambridge: Cambridge UP, 2009. 601–620.

Manlove, Colin. *The Fantasy Literature of England.* London: Palgrave, 1999.

———. *Modern Fantasy: Five Studies.* Cambridge: Cambridge UP, 1975.

McGillis, Roderick. "Fantasy as Miracle: George MacDonald's *Miracles of the Lord.*" *George MacDonald: Literary Heritage and Heirs.* Ed. McGillis. Wayne (PA): Zossima Press, 2008. 201–215.

Mendlesohn, Farah. *Rhetorics of Fantasy.* Middletown (CT): Wesleyan UP, 2008.

———, and Edward James. *A Short History of Fantasy.* 2009. 2nd edition. Faringdon (Oxfordshire): Libri Publishing, 2012.

Mighall, Robert. *The Geography of Victorian Gothic Fiction: Mapping History's Nightmares.* Oxford: Oxford UP, 1999.

Napolitano, Marc. "Sing for Your Little Life: Story, Discourse and Character." *Mastering the Game of Thrones: Essays on George R.R. Martin's A Song of Ice and Fire.* Eds. Jes Battis and Susan Johnston. Jefferson (NC): MacFarland, 2015. 35–56.

Neuhaus, Jessamyn. "Marge Simpson, Blue-Haired Housewife: Defining Domesticity in *The Simpsons.*" *The Journal of Popular Culture.* 43.4 (July 2010). 761–781.

Pavlac, Brian. "Introduction: The Winter of Our Discontent." *Game of Thrones versus History: Written in Blood.* Ed. Pavlac. Hoboken (NJ): Wiley & Sons, 2017. 1–15.

Pratchett, Terry. "Notes from a Successful Fantasy Author: Keep It Real." 2006. *A Slip of the Keyboard: Reflections on Life, Death and Hats.* London: Doubleday, 2014. 83–86.

Punter, David. *The Literature of Terror: A History of Gothic Fictions from 1765 to the Present Day.* New York: Longman, 1980.

Riggs, Don. "Continuity and Transformation in the Religions of Westeros and Western Europe." *Game of Thrones versus History: Written in Blood.* Hoboken (NJ): Wiley & Sons, 2017. 173–184.

Rosenberg, Alyssa. "Men and Monsters: Rape, Myth-Making, and the Rise and Fall of Nations in *A Song of Ice and Fire.*" *Beyond the Wall: Exploring George R.R. Martin's A Song of Ice and Fire.*" Ed. James Lowder. Dallas (TX): Benbella Books, 2012. 15–28.

Roth, Phyllis A. "Suddenly Sexual Women in Bram Stoker's *Dracula.*" *Dracula: Contemporary Critical Essays.* Ed. Glennis Byron. New York: St. Martin's Press, 1999. 30–42.

Saham, Inbar. "Brienne of Tarth and Jaime Lannister: A Romantic Comedy within HBO's *Game of Thrones.*" *Mythlore* 126 (Spring/Summer 2015). 49–71.

Sandner, David. *Critical Discourses of the Fantastic, 1712–1831.* Farnham: Ashgate, 2011.

Schultz, David. E. "From Microcosm to Macrocosm: The Growth of Lovecraft's Cosmic Vision." *An Epicure in the Terrible: A Centennial Anthology of Essays in Honour of H.P. Lovecraft.* Eds. Schultz and S.T. Joshi. London and Toronto (ON): Associated UP, 1991. 199–219.

Scoble, Jesse. "A Sword without a Hilt: The Dangers of Magic in (and to) Westeros." *Beyond the Wall: Exploring George R.R. Martin's A Song of Ice and Fire.* Ed. James Lowder. Dallas (TX): Benbella Books, 2012. 123–140.

Shippey, Tom. "Orcs, Wraiths and Wights: Tolkien's Images of Evil." *J.R.R. Tolkien and His Literary Resonances: Views of Middle-Earth.* Eds. George Clark and Daniel Timmons. Westport (CT) and London: Greenwood Press, 2000. 183–196.

———. *J.R.R. Tolkien: Author of the Century.* New York: Houghton Mifflin, 2002.

Siebers, Tobin. *The Romantic Fantastic.* Ithaca (NY) and London: Cornell UP, 1984.

Spector, Caroline. "Power and Feminism in Westeros." *Beyond the Wall: Exploring George R.R. Martin's A Song of Ice and Fire.* Ed. James Lowder. Dallas (TX): Benbella Books, 2012. 169–188.

Spurr, David. *The Rhetoric of Empire: Colonial Discourse in Journalism, Travel Writing, and Imperial Administration.* Durham (NC) and London: Duke UP, 1993.

Stableford, Brian. "Dying Earth." *The Encyclopaedia of Fantasy.* Eds. John Clute and John Grant. 2nd edition. London: Orbit, 1999. 305.

Staggs, Matt. "Petyr Baelish and the Mask of Sanity." *Beyond the Wall: Exploring George R.R. Martin's A Song of Ice and Fire.* Ed. James Lowder. Dallas (TX): Benbella Books, 2012. 141–152.

Todorov, Tzvetan. *The Fantastic: A Structural Approach to a Literary Genre.* 1970. Trans. Richard Howard. 2nd edition. Ithaca (NY): Cornell UP, 1975.

———. "The Typology of Detective Fiction." 1966. *The Poetics of Prose.* Ed. Todorov. Ithaca (NY): Cornell UP, 1977. 42–52.

Tolkien, J.R.R. "*Beowulf*: The Monsters and the Critics." 1936. *The Monsters and the Critics and Other Essays.* Ed. Christopher Tolkien. London: George Allen & Unwin, 1983. 5–48.

———. "On Fairy-Stories." 1939. *The Monsters and the Critics and Other Essays.* Ed. Christopher Tolkien. London: George Allen & Unwin, 1983. 109–161.

Trębecki, Grezgorz. *Worlds so Strange and Diverse: Towards a Genealogical Taxonomy of Non-Mimetic Literature.* Cambridge, Cambridge Scholars, 2015.

Vaught, Susan. "The Brutal Cost of Redemption in Westeros, or, *What* Moral Ambiguity?" *Beyond the Wall: Exploring George R.R. Martin's A Song of Ice and Fire.* Ed. James Lowder. Dallas (TX): Benbella Books, 2012. 89–106.

Walker, Jessica. "Just Songs in the End: Historical Discourses in Shakespeare and Martin." *Mastering the Game of Thrones: Essays on George R.R. Martin's A Song of Ice and Fire.* Eds. Jes Battis and Susan Johnston. Jefferson (NC): MacFarland, 2015. 71–91.

Weiskel, Thomas. *The Romantic Sublime.* Baltimore (MD) and London: The Johns Hopkins UP, 1986.

Williamson, Jamie. *The Evolution of Modern Fantasy from Antiquarianism to the Ballantine Adult Fantasy Series.* New York: Palgrave MacMillan, 2015.

Wittingslow, Ryan Michell. "All Men Must Serve: Religion and Free Will from the Seven to the Faceless Men." *Mastering the Game of Thrones: Essays of George R.R. Martin's A Song of Ice and Fire*. Eds. Jes Battis and Susan Johnston. Jefferson (NC): MacFarland, 2015. 113–131.

Young, Helen. *Race and Popular Fantasy Fiction: Habits of Whiteness*. New York: Routledge, 2016.

Index

For Product Safety Concerns and Information please contact our EU representative GPSR@taylorandfrancis.com
Taylor & Francis Verlag GmbH, Kaufingerstraße 24, 80331 München, Germany

www.ingramcontent.com/pod-product-compliance
Lightning Source LLC
Chambersburg PA
CBHW071528110726
47908CB00003B/980

* 9 7 8 1 0 3 2 0 9 3 4 8 2 *